POSTCARD HISTORY SERIES

Evansville

On the Front Cover: The cover shows a busy scene in front of the old post office on Second Street sometime around 1900. Just up the way was the old Acme Hotel at the corner of Sycamore Street. Vickery Brothers wholesale grocers and the Business Men's Association Building were across the street, behind the trees. The post office building, which now serves as an event center, is about the only thing left from this view. (Courtesy of the Engler family.)

On the Back Cover: A crowd gathers in the beer garden at the old Cook's Park. Located just east of Pigeon Creek, the park provided an array of activities for visitors. It survived into the 1930s, but by the time the Columbia/Delaware Bridge was built in 1956, hardly a trace of the park remained. A new display along the Pigeon Creek Greenway Passage highlights the old park. See page 108 for more about Cook's Park. (Courtesy of the Engler family.)

POSTCARD HISTORY SERIES

Evansville

Joseph Engler

ARCADIA PUBLISHING

ISBN 978-0-7385-9436-1

Published by Arcadia Publishing
Charleston, South Carolina

Printed in the United States of America

Library of Congress Control Number: 2012939426

For all general information contact Arcadia Publishing at:
Telephone 843-853-2070
Fax 843-853-0044
E-mail sales@arcadiapublishing.com
For customer service and orders:
Toll-Free 1-888-313-2665

Visit us on the Internet at www.arcadiapublishing.com

Happy 200th birthday, Evansville!

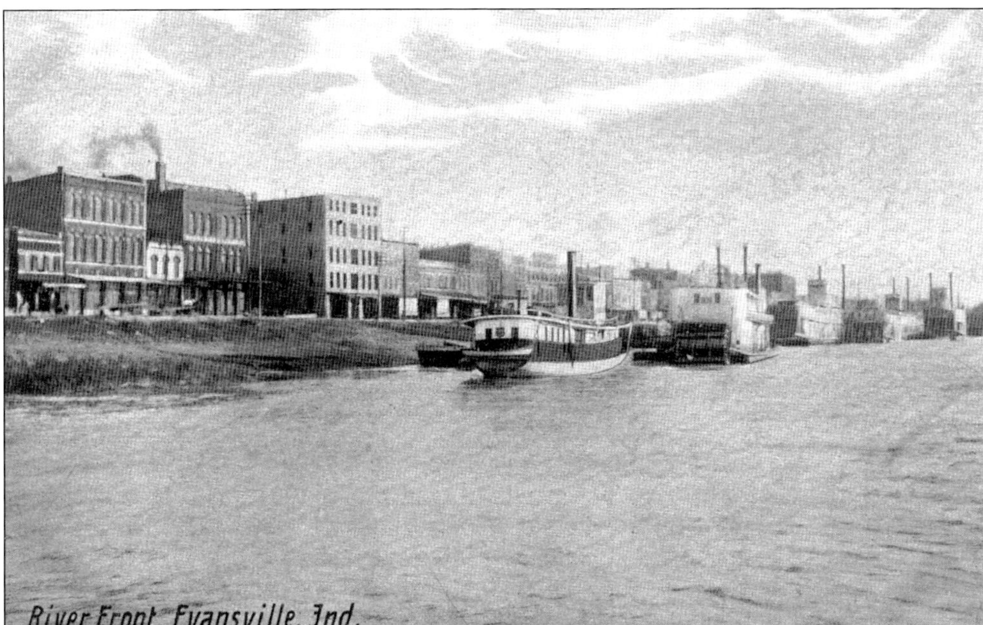

In this c. 1910 postcard, boats line up along Evansville's riverfront to deliver goods to the stores on Riverside Drive—this view illustrates why the street was originally called Water Street. The tall buildings in the foreground are centered around Vine Street, including the (white) five-story Anchor Supply. The company expanded this building in the 1930s but relocated to US Highway 41, near the airport, in 1969. Many of these buildings were razed around 1970 during urban renewal efforts. (Courtesy of the Engler family.)

Contents

Acknowledgments 6

Introduction 7

1. We Built This City 9
2. Gotta Have Faith 15
3. Did You Know . . . 37
4. Business As Usual 51
5. Is There a Doctor in the House? 79
6. From Point A to Point B 87
7. No Place Like Home 95
8. Leisure Time 107

Acknowledgments

Special thanks go to each of the three local libraries—Willard Library, the Evansville Vanderburgh Public Library (EVPL), and the David L. Rice Library at the University of Southern Indiana. I began my research at Willard Library, looking through old pictures, and became fascinated with discovering where buildings were located and when they existed. Several hours were also spent at the EVPL Central Library looking through old newspaper articles on microfilm and browsing historic books in the Indiana Room. I want to explicitly thank the EVPL for allowing the use of several postcards from its digital collection, one of the best online resources for researching Evansville history.

I am a proud member of and would like to thank the Preservation Alliance of Evansville (PAE), which was founded in 1979 to support and encourage the preservation of historic buildings and structures in and around Evansville, Indiana. Through education and activism, PAE works at its mission of saving historically and architecturally significant buildings, structures, and districts to maintain and improve life in our shared community. PAE holds meetings, conducts lectures, develops press releases, and assists the public in obtaining information on preservation issues including education, historic buildings for sale, funding, and laws.

Additional thanks go to my grandmother Mary Rose Engler. Beyond loaning me her postcard collection for use in this book, her passion for the history of Evansville has made for some interesting stories.

Finally, a big thank you goes to my wife, Jennifer, who has put up with countless "did you know?" comments from a husband too interested in history. She would help me spot houses being razed and articles and events related to local history, so I know I'm not the only one obsessed with old Evansville.

Thanks to everyone who helped in the making of this book. It has truly been a fun experience!

For more information on any of the buildings, clubs, or locations in this book, check out HistoricEvansville.com. The website also contains additional postcards not selected for the book, as well as "then and now" images.

INTRODUCTION

Evansville was the vision of Hugh McGary Jr. In 1812, his purchase of land set in motion the events that would make the city what it is today. Evansville's location along the Ohio River, compounded by the fact that it was situated in the middle of the newly formed Vanderburgh County, helped the city get started.

Just to the northwest, the town of Lamasco was founded in 1836. It was laid out using cardinal directions, whereas Evansville was oriented parallel to the river. The two cities grew into each other and their citizens shared similar interests, so Lamasco and Evansville were merged in 1857. Few traces remain of the old Lamasco, though its original layout does explain the odd angles at some downtown intersections.

When it was announced that the Wabash and Erie Canal would terminate in Evansville, the city's future looked prosperous. The canal tanked, however, though the buzz influenced several railroad companies that went on to build routes connected to Evansville. With the rise of the railroads, the city's connection with the larger world helped it to receive goods from and ship goods to the rest of the country.

Because of the town's accessibility to the railroad and to nearby natural resources, Evansville established several manufacturing companies by the early 1900s. These large-scale facilities and a strong workforce helped the city to find a niche during the World War II era. The Evansville Shipyard built tank landing ships (LSTs), and other plants produced war materials, such as plane wings and ammunition. Some of the manufacturing companies later left town, but Evansville is still home to several businesses, some of which are headquartered here.

Nowadays, the city finds a balance between its accessibility to larger metropolises and being an independent city that is the heart of the Illinois-Indiana-Kentucky Tri-State area. Midwestern charm and friendly people continue to make Evansville a desirable place to live.

Finally, I would be remiss if I wrote a postcard book and did not mention their importance in history. Postcards were the equivalent of text messages for older generations. While scanning the images for this book, I was engrossed by the backs of the postcards. The messages were short—sometimes saying little more than to write back—and were surprisingly full of spelling and grammatical errors. Before the age of online reservations and forwarded itineraries, postcards often relayed when someone had arrived or when they would be arriving. One read, "Be at the depot and don't forget us," making me wonder if the postcard arrived in time. Occasionally, postcards were more intimate, such as one that relayed news of losing a baby. Although communication may be much faster today, postcards captured a moment in time that will never be forgotten.

One

We Built This City

Evansville's significance as a city and a power player in the region was reflected in how the town was laid out and how it continued to grow. The river town was founded on a crescent in the Ohio River, and it quickly became the commercial hub of the area. In 1856, Evansville was made a port of entry, and a customhouse was established, signifying the importance of the city as a shipping point. A large city hall and a new courthouse were constructed in the late 1800s, reflecting Evansville's growing size. The addition of fire and police departments helped to keep the city running smoothly. Because of its size and location, government and military bodies established regional offices in town. Over the years, Evansville has come to hold big sway—politically and economically—throughout the Tri-State area.

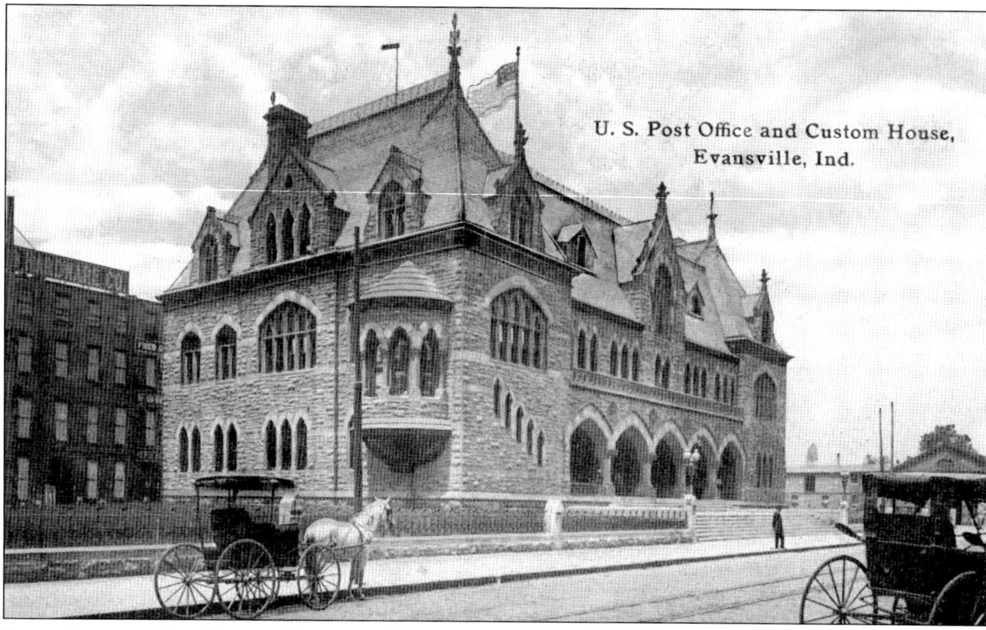

Several years after Evansville was selected as a port of entry into the United States because of the volume of shipping activity on the Ohio River, Congress approved the building of a customhouse. Construction began in 1873, but an economic depression delayed completion until 1879. The combined customhouse and post office, located on Second Street between Sycamore and Vine Streets, cost $200,000 to build. (EVPL.)

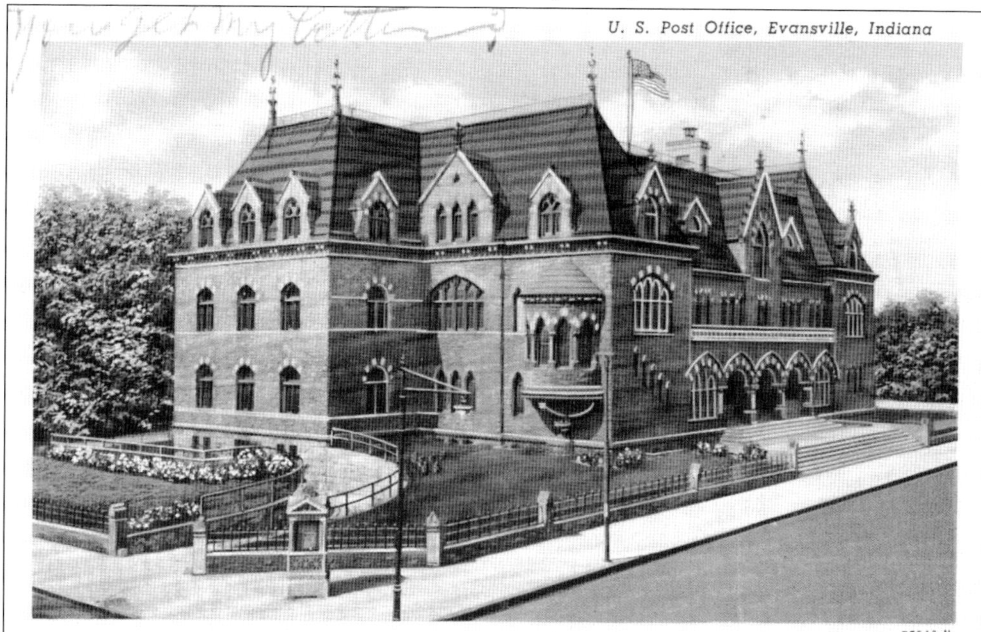

As the city continued to grow, the post office needed additional space, and wings were added to each side of the building in 1916. After 90 years of service, the post office moved to the civic center complex in 1969. The vacant building was eventually converted into the Old Post Office Place shops and offices and, more recently, into a banquet hall. (Engler family.)

Evansville's city hall was built in 1887, when the city was experiencing rapid growth. Constructed at the corner of Third and Walnut Streets, the building included a clock tower that dominated the skyline. In the 1920s, an addition was built along Walnut Street, and part of the tower was removed. The building was vacated when the civic center opened in 1969 and torn down in 1971 to make room for parking. (Engler family.)

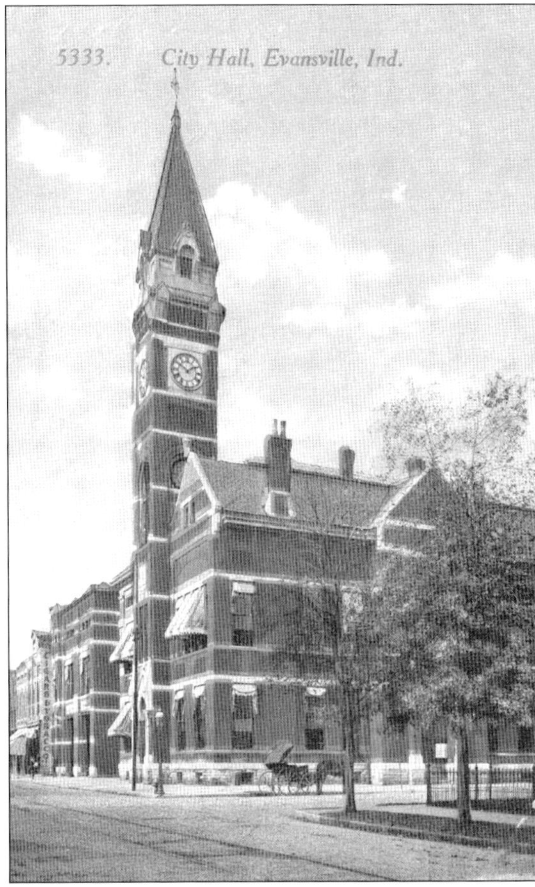

Hose House No. 1, which replaced an old hook and ladder building, was adjacent to the old city hall and built at the same time. It operated as the fire department headquarters for over 80 years. Before the fire station and city hall were demolished in 1971, the fire department combined with Hose House No. 9 (on Olive Street) and relocated to a new Hose House No. 1 on Eighth Street. (Engler family.)

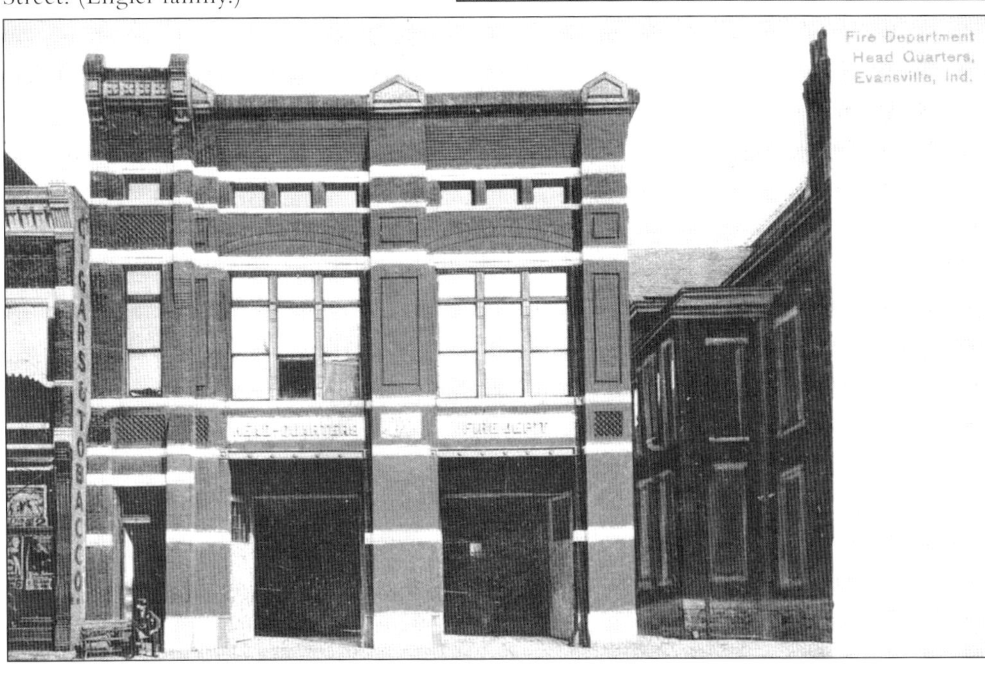

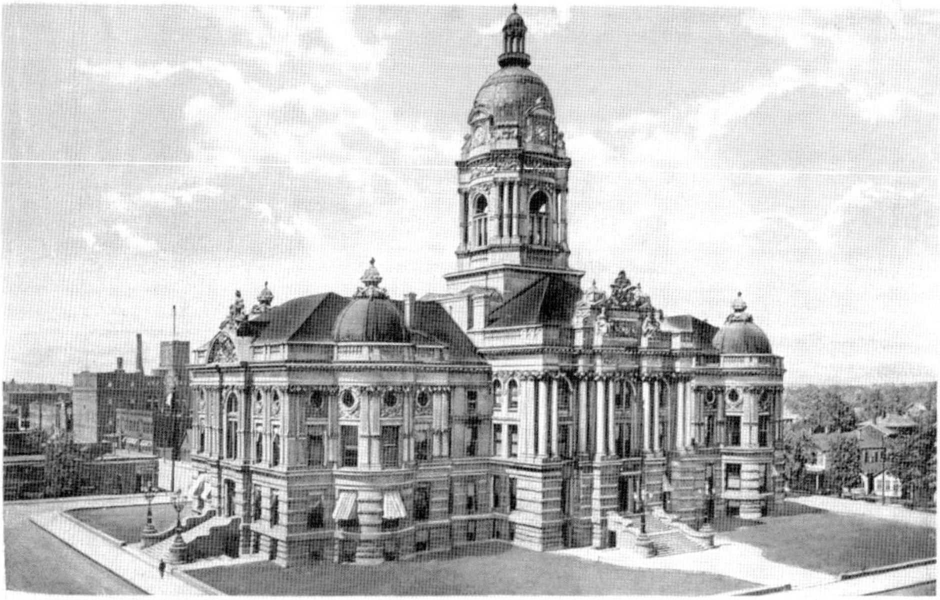

VANDENBURGH COUNTY COURT HOUSE, EVANSVILLE, IND.

The Vanderburgh County Courthouse was erected in 1890 on the block bounded by Fourth, Vine, Fifth, and Court Streets. Following its move to the new civic center in 1969, there was a push to demolish the old structure. The Conrad Baker Foundation became guardian of the historic building, and it now serves as a home for some city and county offices. The old Evansville Brewing Company (now Brucken's, a restaurant supply store) is in the background at left. (EVPL.)

County Jail, Evansville, Ind.

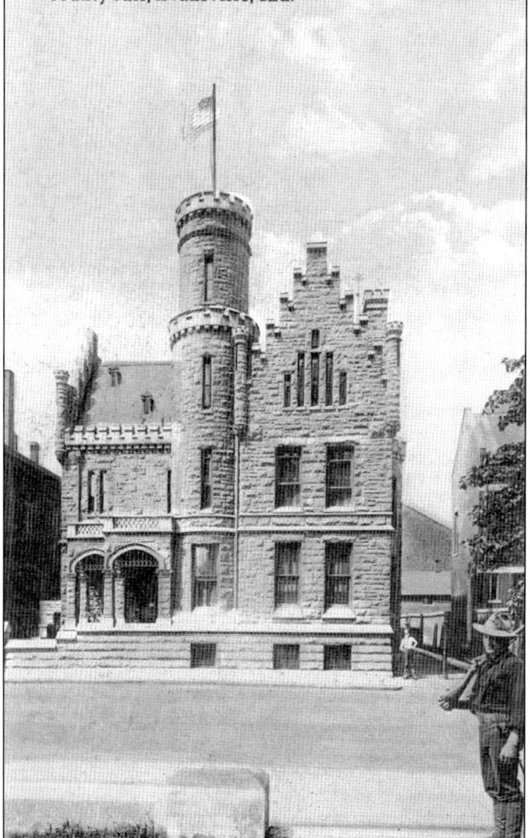

The county jail was built across from the courthouse at about the same time. Completed in 1891, it also served as the sheriff's residence. It, too, was made redundant by the civic center and sat vacant for almost 30 years. The jail was finally converted into office space and is now the home of the law firm Woods and Woods, LLP. (EVPL.)

Hose House No. 5 was built in 1907 along St. Joseph Avenue. The company was previously downtown on Locust Street but moved to this location with the growth of the West Side. This was the last original hose house in operation until the company moved to a new facility on Maryland Street in 1988. The building now houses Brown Family Dentistry. (Estate of Pam and Dennis Beadles.)

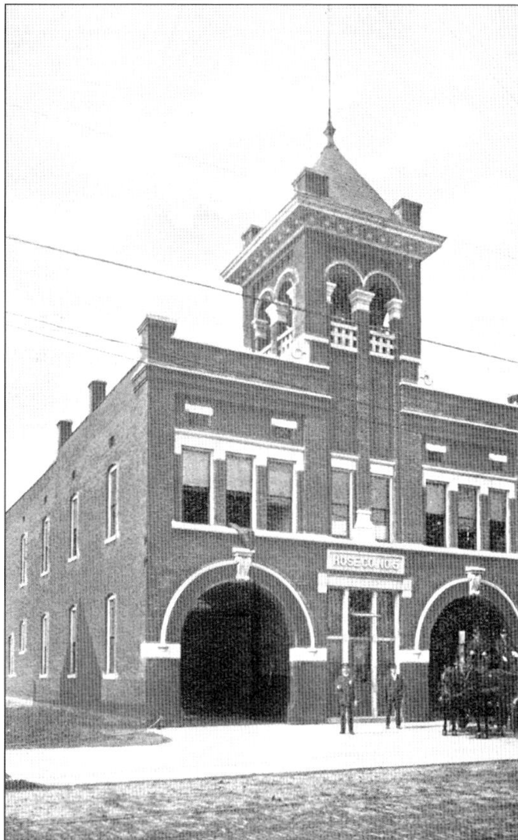

Hose Co. No. 5, West Side, Evansville, Ind.

Famed local architect Clifford Shopbell designed the Soldiers and Sailors Memorial Coliseum. When it was completed in 1917, it was the largest public gathering place in town, surpassing Evans Hall (see page 110). Roberts Municipal Stadium became the venue of choice after it was built in the 1950s, though the coliseum was and still is used for various events, most notably professional wrestling. (Engler family.)

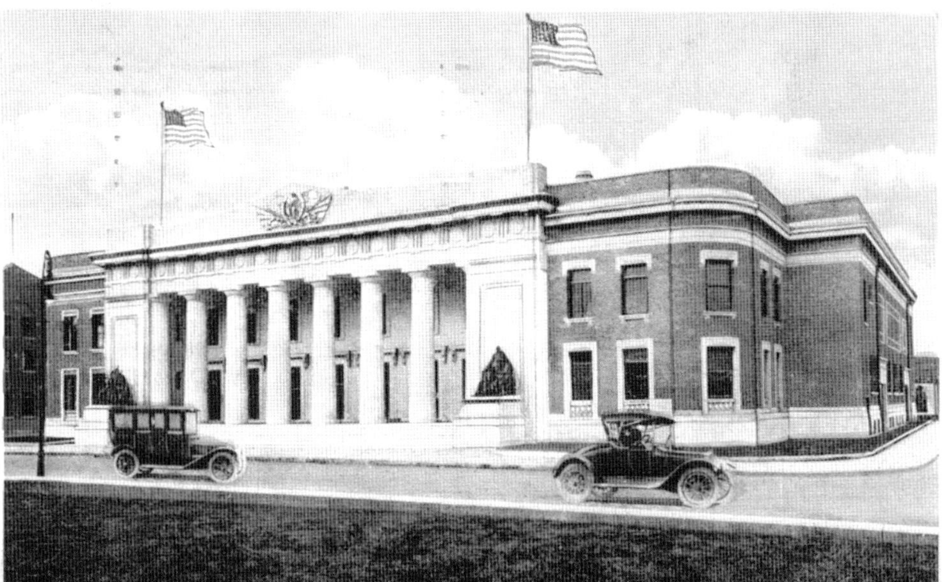

SOLDIERS AND SAILORS MEMORIAL COLISEUM, EVANSVILLE, IND.

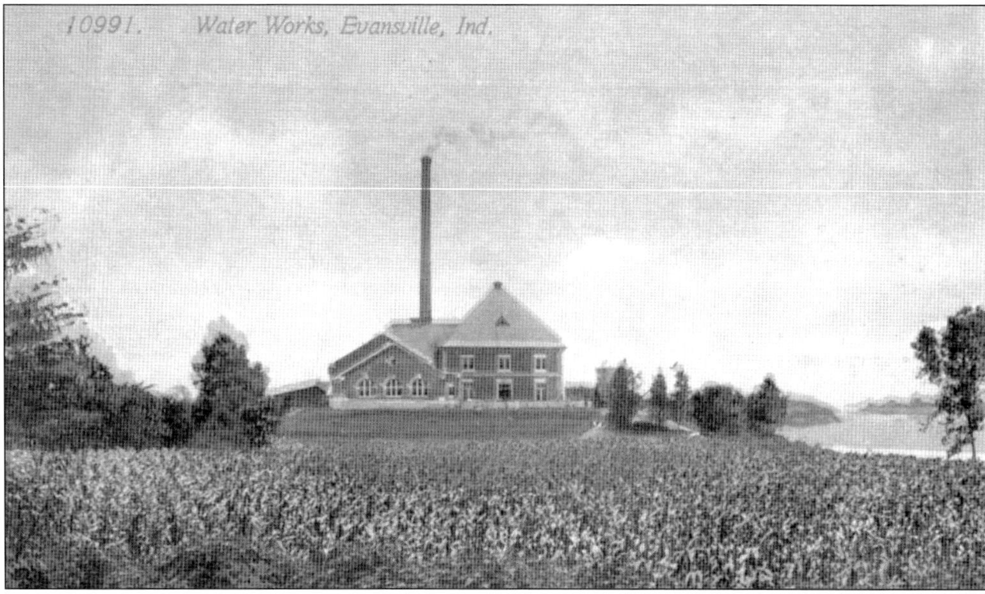

Originally situated closer to downtown, the waterworks facility moved to its current location around the beginning of the 20th century. Despite a filtration plant that was built in 1911 and several subsequent additions, the view shown in this postcard is still easily recognized. Just as it did over a century ago, the water department filters water from the Ohio River and converts it for drinking—though it now serves many more citizens. (EVPL and the Topper family.)

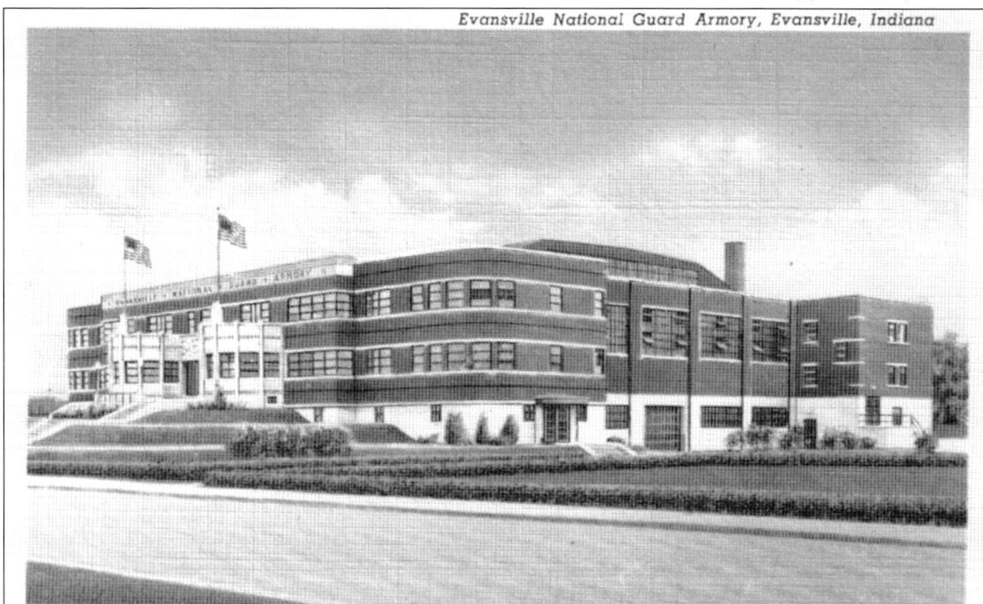

The Evansville National Guard Armory was located on North Main Street until this building on Rotherwood Avenue was completed in 1938. The armory was acquired by the University of Evansville in 1998, after the National Guard moved to a new building. Long before the Ford Center and Roberts Stadium existed, the University of Evansville Purple Aces played basketball games here. (Engler family.)

Two

Gotta Have Faith

One of the vital cogs for a thriving city is religion; it binds people together with a common set of beliefs and helps establish a community. Religious buildings also provide some of the most iconic landmarks, as evidenced by the number of postcards that depict churches and synagogues.

The earliest denominations in Evansville were Baptists and Presbyterians, but the wave of German immigrants accounted for the numerous Catholic, Lutheran, and Evangelical parishes. Today, there are many churches in town, and all work to achieve the same goal—to help shape the faith of Evansville's people.

Other religious organizations—often tied to a specific church—were formed over the years. These were not places of worship, per se, but outreaches that spread a mission or simply helped those in need.

To some, a cemetery was more than just a burial ground. Public cemeteries, as well as those tied to a specific religion, provided a place to spend eternity. Views within the cemeteries have changed little over the years, helping visitors identify their historic elements. Urban crawl caused the city to encroach on some of the early cemeteries, which had to be relocated. Now, in every corner of the city, Evansville's cemeteries provide a quiet place to enjoy the afterlife.

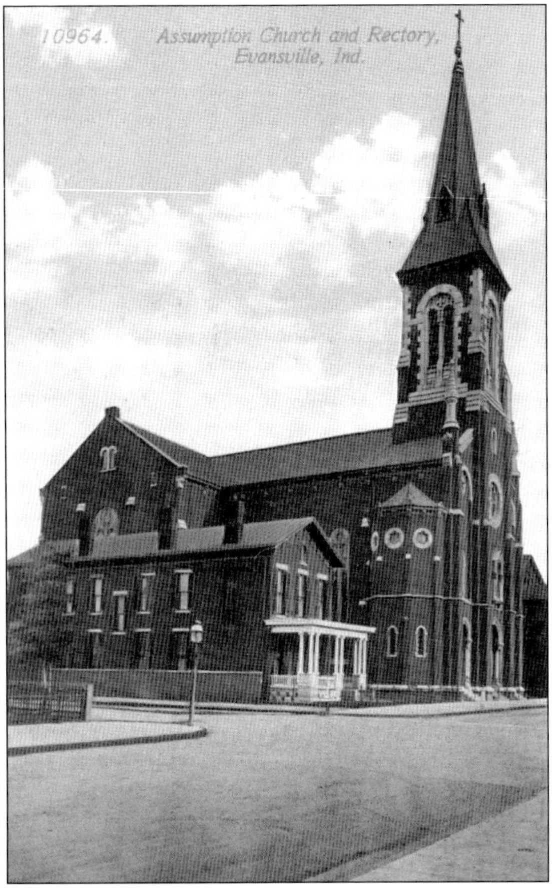

Assumption Church was the first Catholic parish in Evansville, dating back to the 1830s. This building was completed in 1872 at the corner of Vine and Seventh Streets. Described as "one of the most substantial and beautiful edifices in the west," the sanctuary boasted 52-foot-high ceilings. The spire was added in the early 20th century. The beautiful interior (below) contained a fine marble altar from Italy. It and several stained-glass windows were salvaged when the church closed. In 1965, the church was sold to the city—with permission from the Vatican—and was razed to make space for the new civic center buildings. The downtown post office now occupies this site. (Left, EVPL and the Topper family; below, Engler family.)

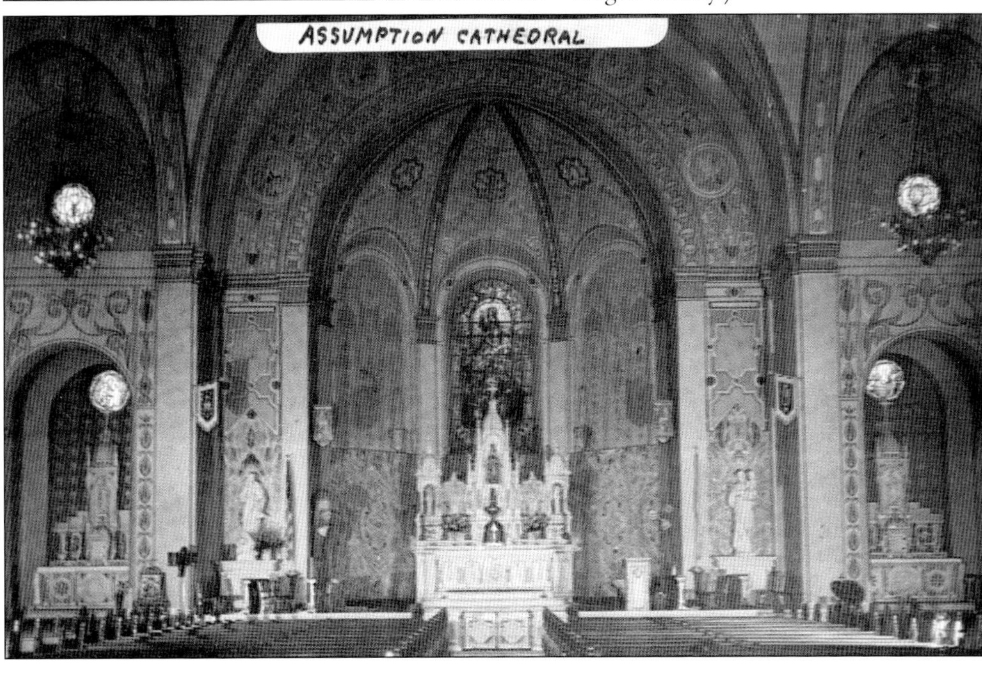

St. Paul's Episcopal Church originated in 1839, when the congregation's first building was constructed on the corner of First and Chestnut Streets. In 1886, renowned architects the Reid Brothers designed this church on the site of the original one. A 1938 fire damaged the church, but it was restored to its original look. (Engler family.)

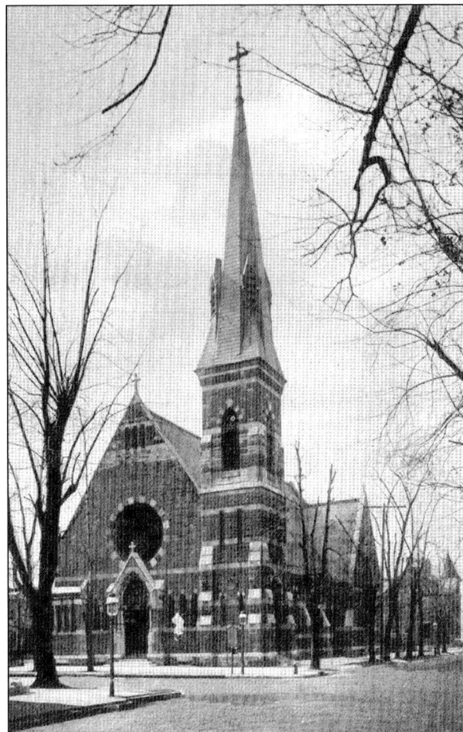

St. Paul's Church, Evansville, Ind.

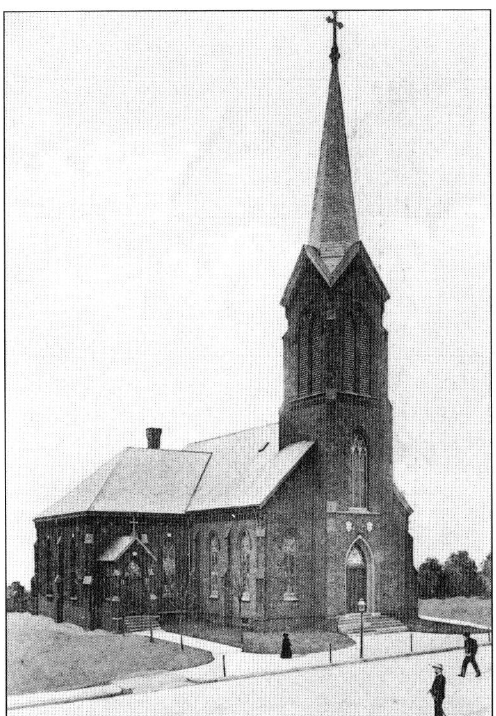

6541 Lutheran Trinity Church, Evansville, Ind.

Trinity Lutheran Church dates back to Lamasco's founding, when land was set aside in 1841 for a church—the parish was founded a few years later. This structure on Illinois Street, between Third and Fourth Avenues, was completed in 1871, though wings were added in the early 1900s. An attached school was built in 1957 and was the initial Evansville Lutheran School. (Engler family.)

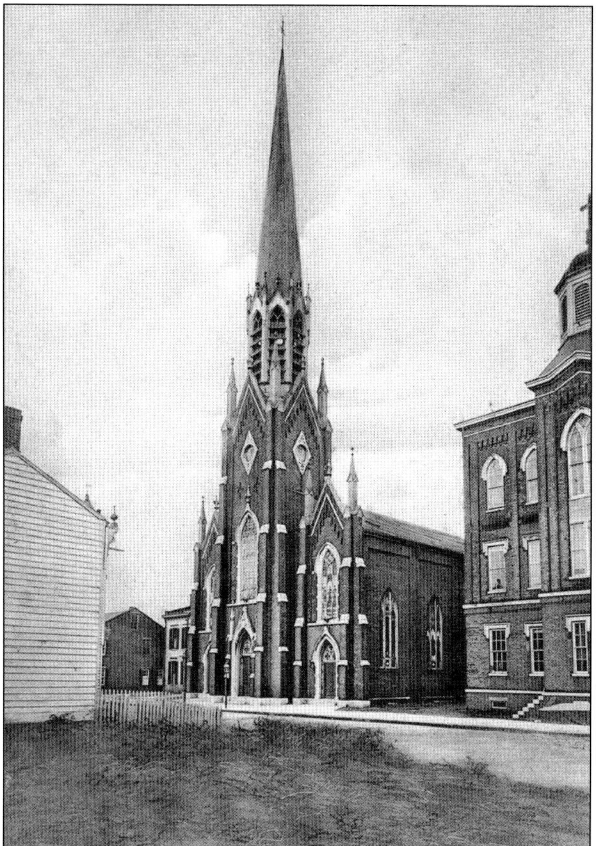

Trinity Catholic Church, Evansville, Ind.

Holy Trinity Church was established as the first German Catholic congregation for the large number of immigrants in Evansville. Built from 1849 to 1851 on Third Street, the church is shown here after its front was altered in the 1870s. A fire on Palm Sunday in 1950 destroyed the beautiful church, and the current, smaller church was built soon after. When Assumption Church closed in the 1960s, Holy Trinity became the city's oldest Catholic parish. (EVPL and the Topper family.)

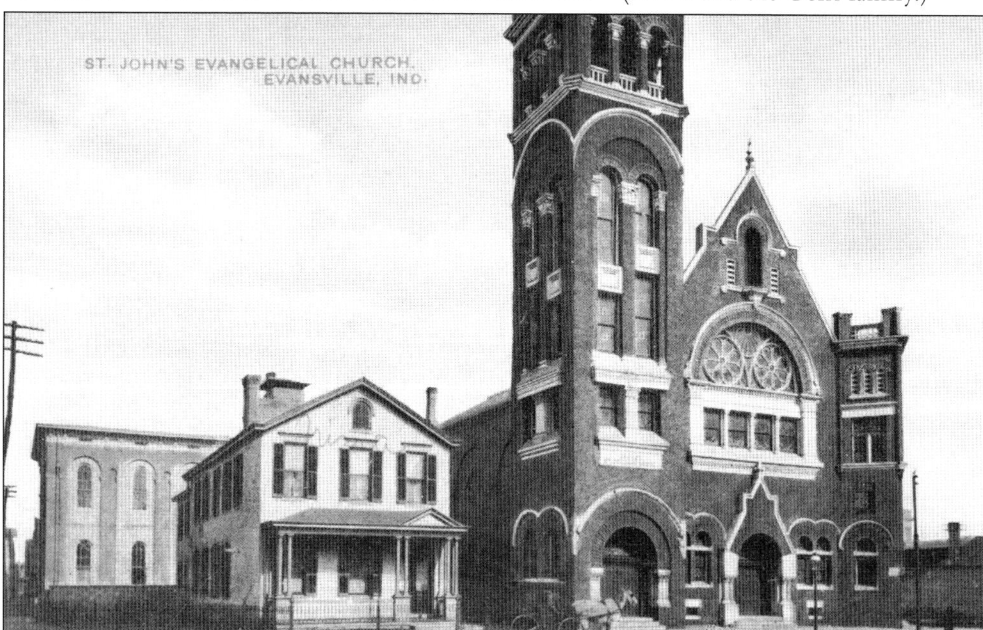

St. John's United Church of Christ was built from 1850 to 1852 on Third Street near Ingle Street. A parish hall was erected adjacent to the church in 1923. The original building was remodeled dramatically in 1950, when a new facade was added. The parish house and school, also visible in this postcard, date back to the 1860s but were later torn down. (EVPL and the Geiss family.)

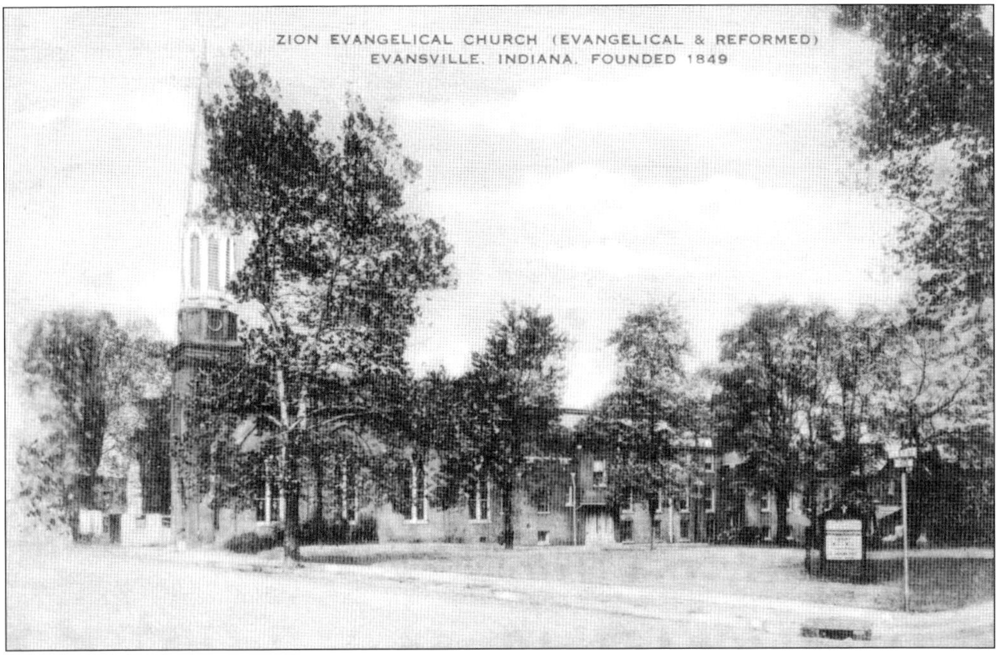

Zion Evangelical Church was built in 1855 on Fifth Street between Ingle and Bond Streets. The church has changed little since it was built, claiming to be "the most historic church building in Evansville," and is listed in the National Register of Historic Places. The attached school behind the church was completed in 1917, replacing an older school building. A parsonage fronting Sixth Street also stands on the back of the lot. (Engler family.)

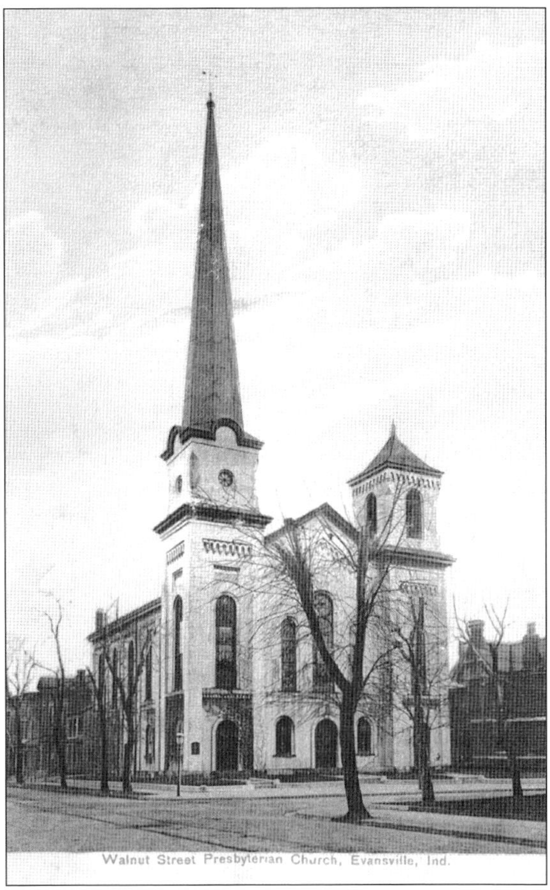

Walnut Street Presbyterian Church was built in 1863 at the corner of Walnut and Second Streets. When the Presbyterian churches joined in 1926, Walnut Street merged with First Presbyterian (then Grace Presbyterian) on Mulberry Street, and this building was sold to the First Christian Church. A fire on December 10, 1944, destroyed the old church, and a new First Christian Church was erected soon after. In 2011, First Christian Church relocated to a new building off of State Highway 57 near McCutchanville. (Engler family.)

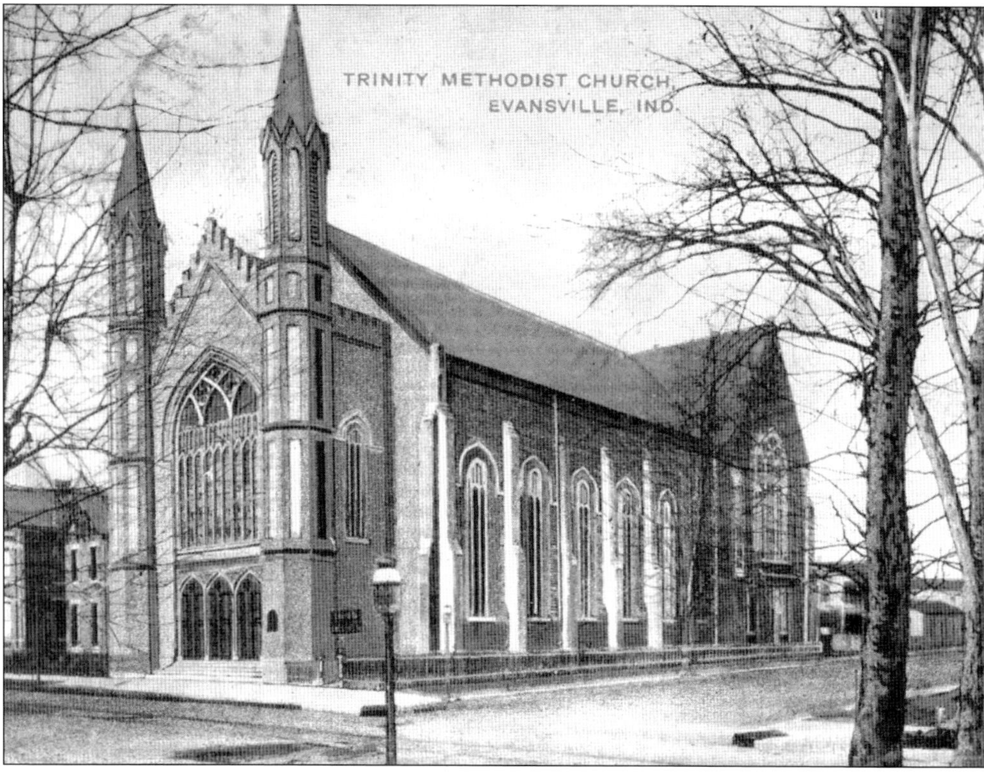

Trinity United Methodist Church, located at Third and Walnut Streets, was the original Methodist church in Evansville, founded as the Locust Street Methodist Episcopal Church. In 1866, the old Methodist Episcopal church moved from Locust Street and was renamed. The church building was designed by architect Henry Mursinna in the Gothic style. In 1925, several houses along Third Street were torn down to create space for an addition to the growing church. The new educational building (visible in the below image) was designed in the Tudor style. Trinity United Methodist, which spawned several other Methodist churches over the years (some still existing and some no longer around), still stands as a downtown landmark. (Above, Engler family; below, EVPL.)

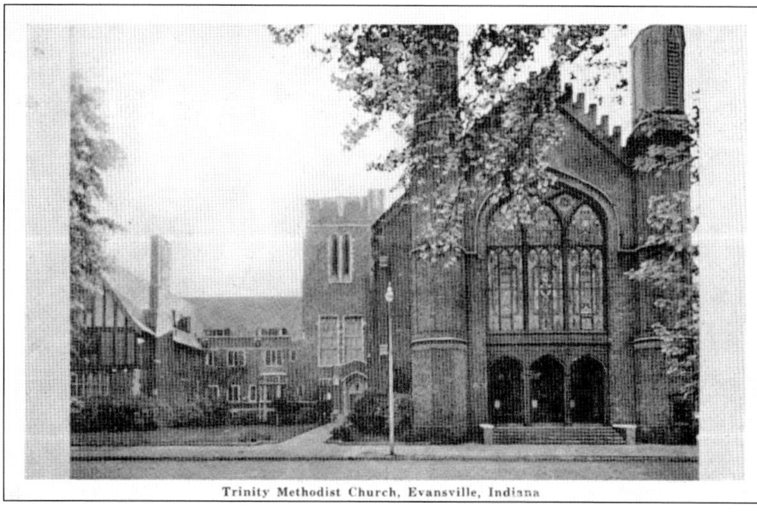

St. Mary Catholic Church was built in 1866 on the 600 block of Cherry Street. In the 1910s, the brick was covered in a stone exterior. The school buildings (one for boys and one for girls) and the parsonage, all of which still stand, date back to the late 1800s. When the original Holy Trinity Church burned down in 1950, St. Mary became the oldest Catholic church building in town. Its school closed in 1973. (Engler family.)

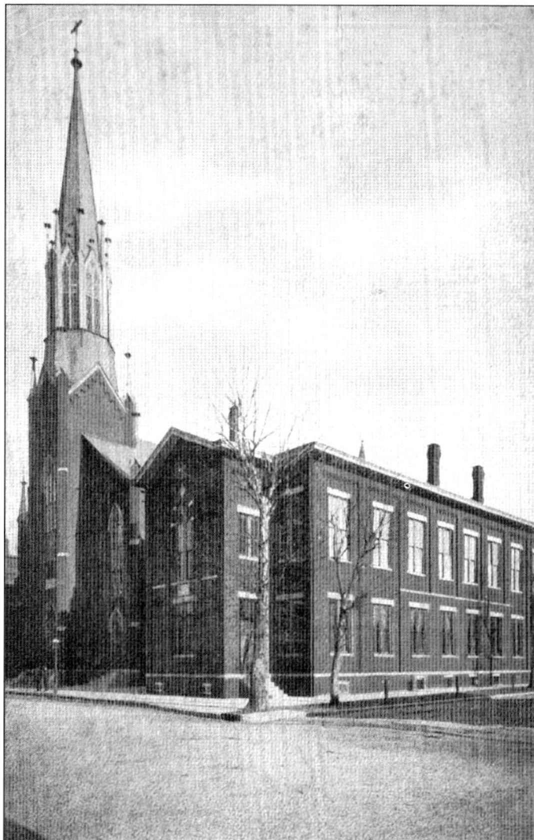

St. Mary's Church, Evansville, Ind.

The German Methodist Episcopal Church (at left in the image below) was built in 1867. As more German-speaking Methodist Episcopal churches were founded, this church adopted the name Fourth Street Methodist Episcopal in 1917. A victim of suburban crawl, the church merged into Bayard Park Methodist Episcopal Church in 1937. The building later became the courthouse annex. After the civic center was built, the old church building's days were numbered, and it was razed in 1973. (Engler family.)

Court House, Catholic Trinity, German M. E. Churches, Sheriff's Residence and Jail, Evansville, Ind.

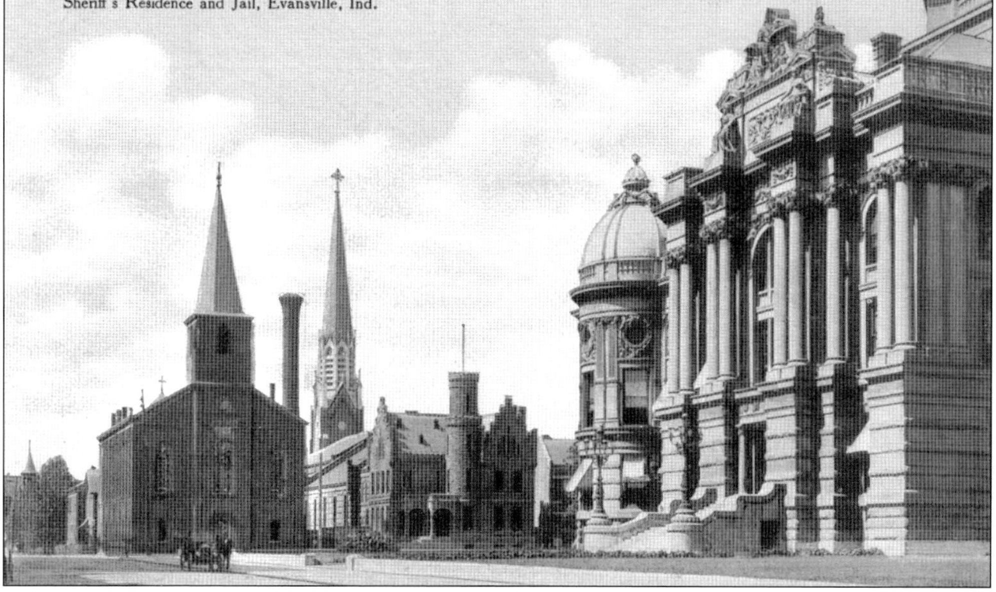

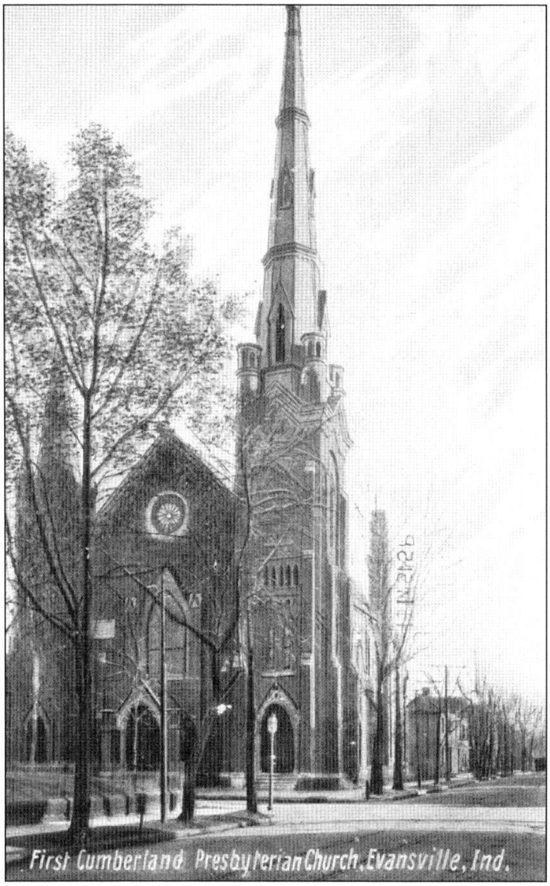

First Cumberland Presbyterian Church was built in 1876 at the corner of Chestnut and Second Streets. When Cumberland Presbyterian rejoined with the Presbyterian churches, the property became surplus, and it was sold to the Scottish Rite Masons in 1909. A new stone front and the removal of its tower in the 1960s altered the scene pictured here, but the present-day view of the side shows that it was once a grand church. (EVPL and the Topper family.)

Simpson Chapel (misspelled "Simson" on the postcard), the predecessor to Simpson United Methodist Church, was built on the West Side in the 1880s after moving from an older site on Pennsylvania Street. A new church was built across Eleventh Avenue in 1912, and the congregation moved into its current building. This chapel was demolished soon after, and a brick home was built on the site, located at 2129 West Illinois Street. (EVPL and the Topper family.)

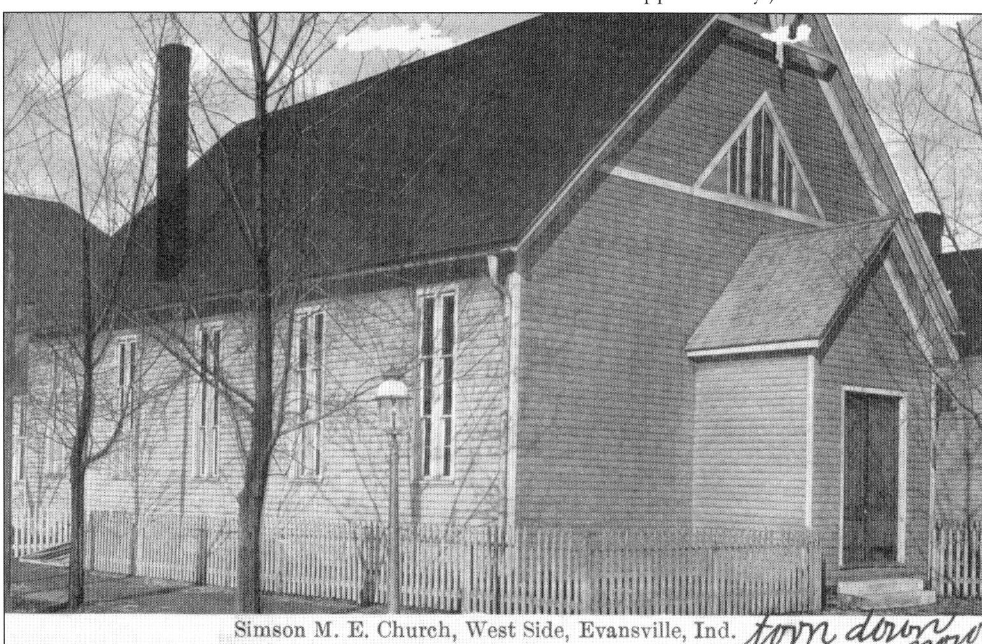

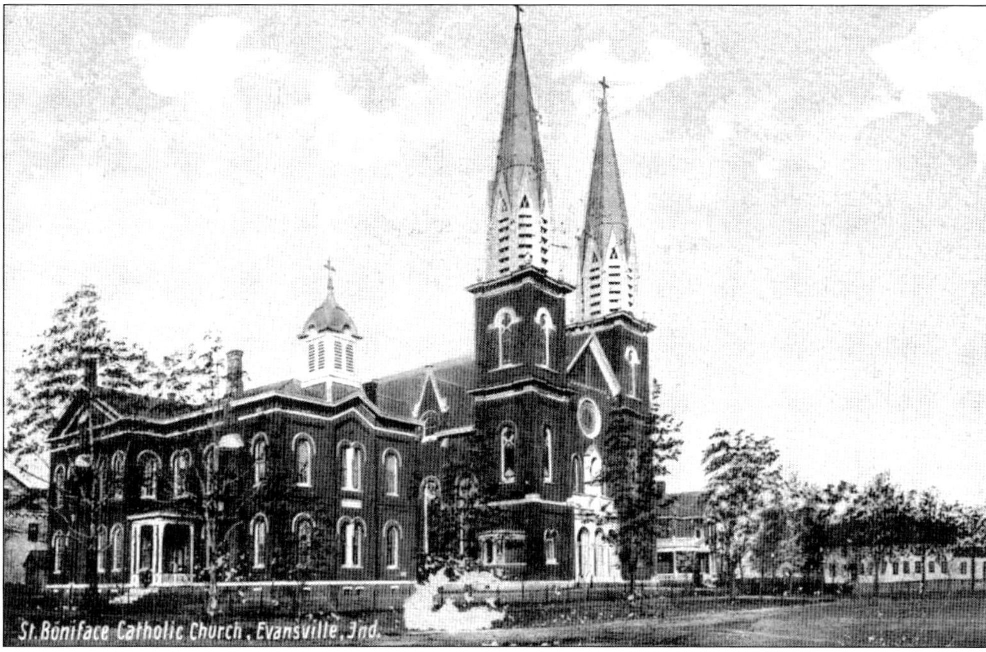

St. Boniface Catholic Church was built in 1881 on Wabash Avenue at the behest of several prominent West Side residents. In 1902, lightning struck the original church, and it burned down. It was promptly rebuilt in the same fashion except for a few small changes. Also shown in the above postcard are, from left to right, the original school (see page 45), the church, the rectory, and the old Wabash Avenue Colored School. The sisters' home (pictured below and only partially visible above) was built in 1907 and was designed by local architects Harris & Shopbell. Originally used as housing for nuns teaching at the school, it now serves the congregation as a multiuse building. St. Boniface is one of a handful of churches in Evansville listed in the National Register of Historic Places. (Above, Engler family; below EVPL and the Topper family.)

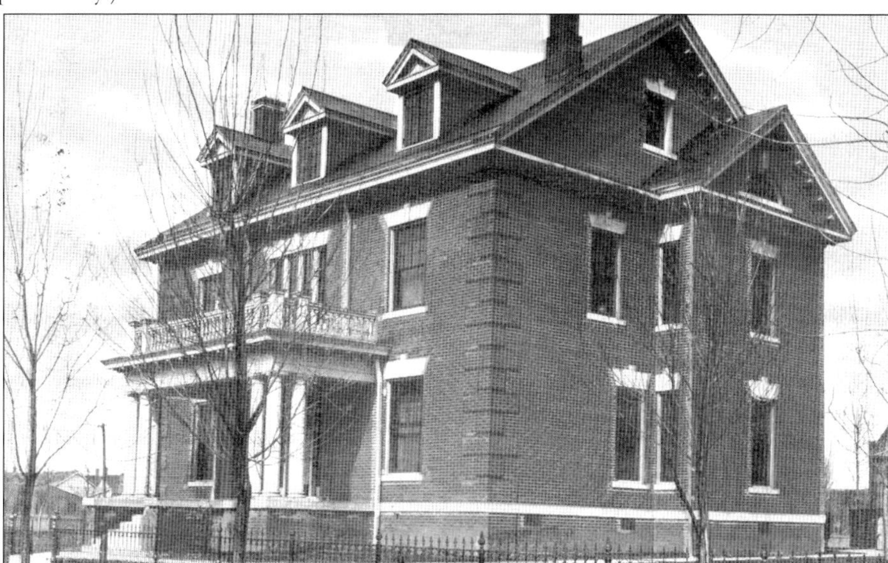

Boniface Sisters Home, West Side, Evansville, Ind.

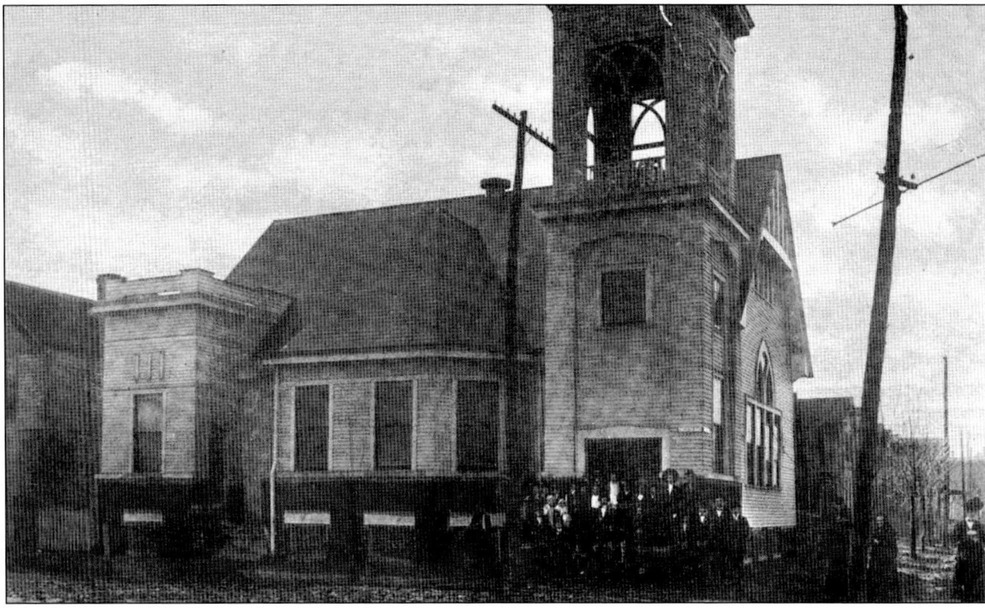

Twelfth Avenue General Baptist Church, originally founded in July 1866 as Independence Church of General Baptists, constructed this building on the corner of Twelfth Avenue and West Indiana Street in 1886 (it is shown here after it expanded around 1900). The church moved to a new building on the other side of Indiana Street in the 1970s; that building is now the Life Choices Maternity and Youth Home. The name was changed to Westwood Church when the congregation moved to Boehne Camp Road in 1996. (EVPL and the Topper family.)

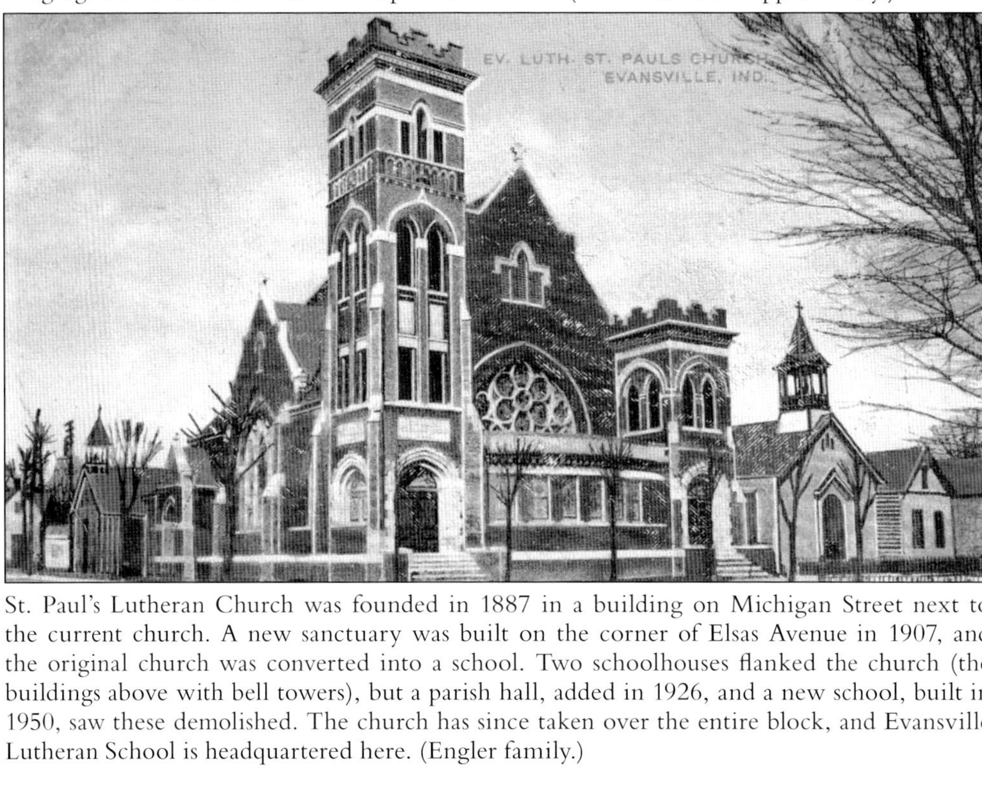

St. Paul's Lutheran Church was founded in 1887 in a building on Michigan Street next to the current church. A new sanctuary was built on the corner of Elsas Avenue in 1907, and the original church was converted into a school. Two schoolhouses flanked the church (the buildings above with bell towers), but a parish hall, added in 1926, and a new school, built in 1950, saw these demolished. The church has since taken over the entire block, and Evansville Lutheran School is headquartered here. (Engler family.)

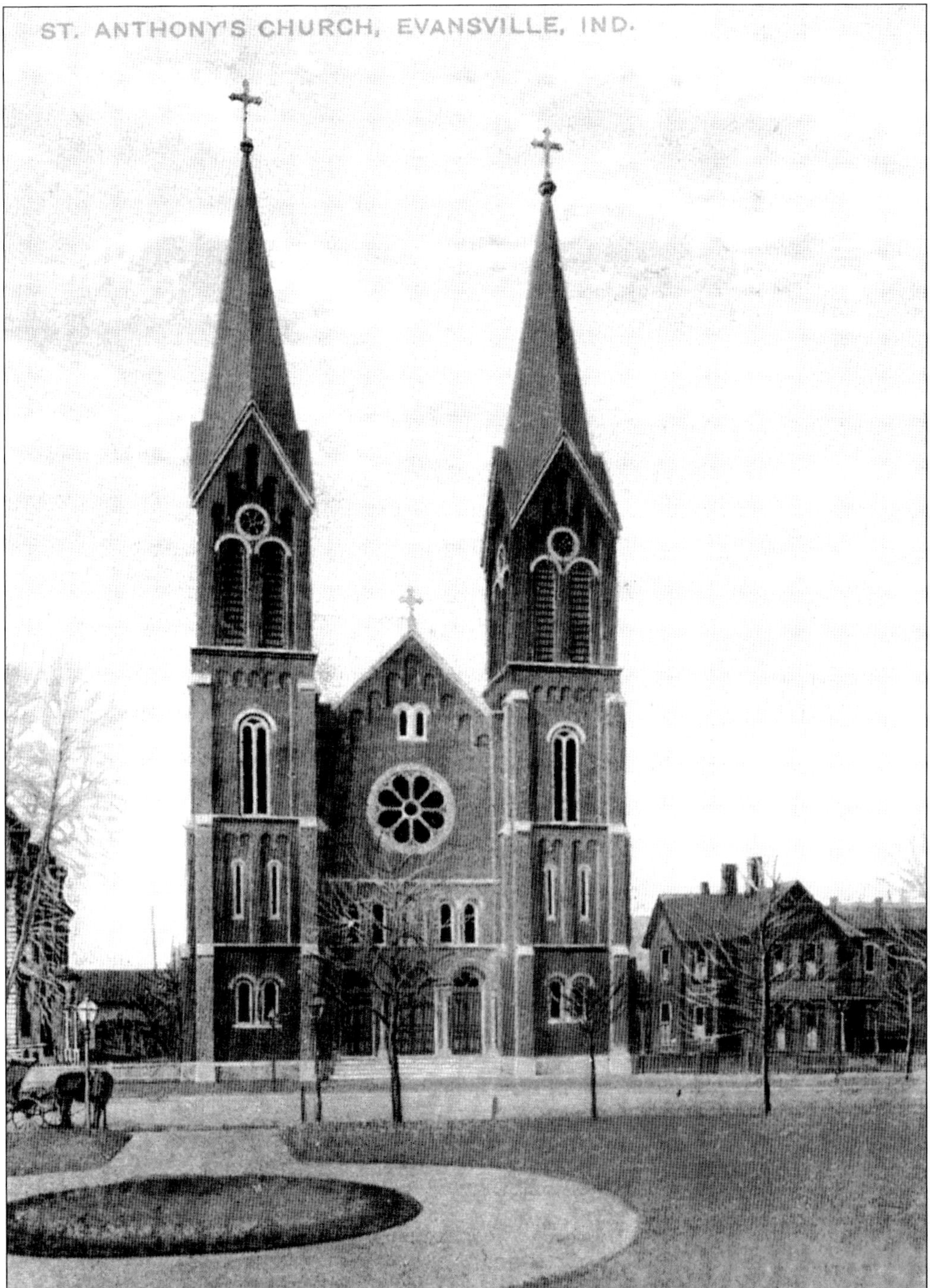

St. Anthony Catholic Church, located at the corner of First Avenue and Columbia Street, was founded in 1888. A church/school building was used temporarily until the current church, shown here, was erected in 1894. The original building was replaced by a new school in June 1932. The old residence, visible at right, was torn down when the convent was built sometime around 1960. (Engler family.)

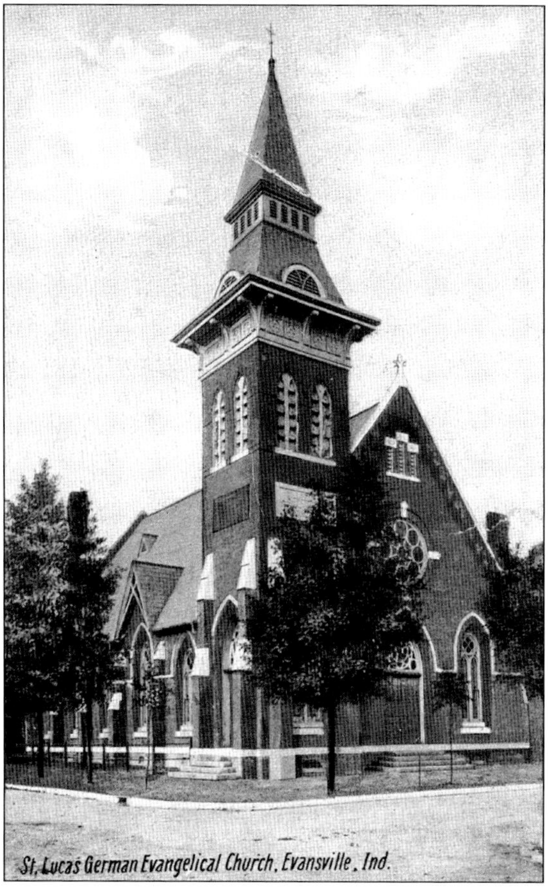

St. Lucas German Evangelical (now St. Lucas United Church of Christ) was built in 1889 to serve the growing North Side. The building on the corner of Virginia Street and Baker Avenue was designed by architect Frank J. Schlotter and dedicated the next year. An addition in the 1920s and another one around 1970 have not much changed the church's appearance. (Engler family.)

Situated catercorner from the church, St. Lucas Hall was built in 1907. The building was designed by Harris & Shopbell as a parish hall and a Sunday school. The c. 1930 addition was dedicated as a parish house. St. Lucas Hall now functions as Lucas Place, which provides transitional housing for those in need. (EVPL and the Geiss family.)

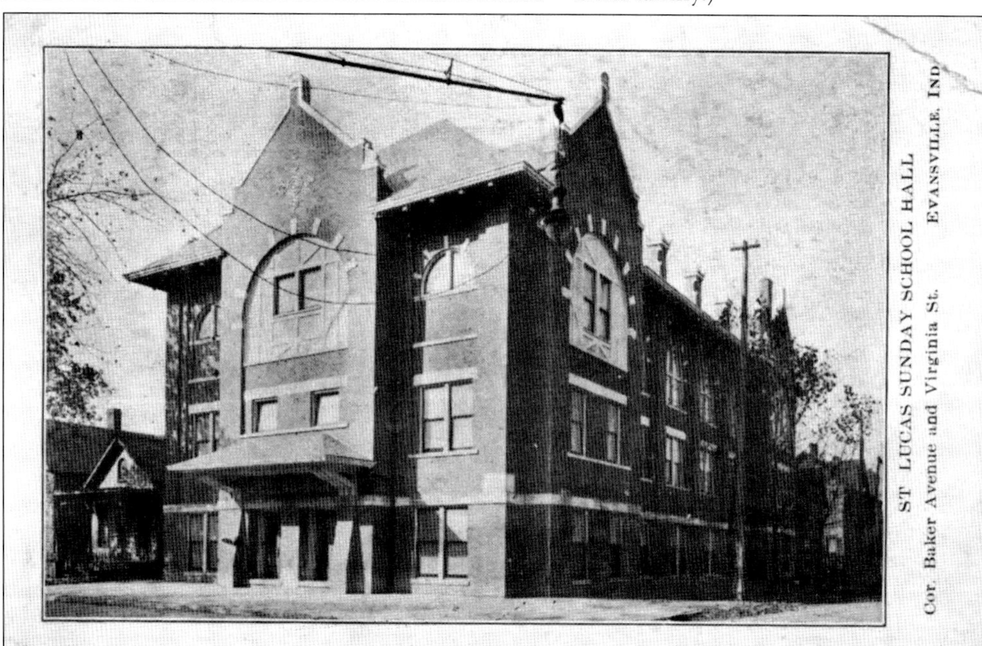

In 1891, St. Paul's United Church of Christ was originally founded as St. Peter's Reformed Church. A few years later, the church at Michigan Street and Twelfth Avenue became St. Paul's Evangelical. A merger in the 1930s joined the Evangelical and Reformed churches, which later became part of the United Church of Christ (UCC). A 1960s addition blended new and old at a time when many congregations were opting to tear down their original church buildings. (Engler family.)

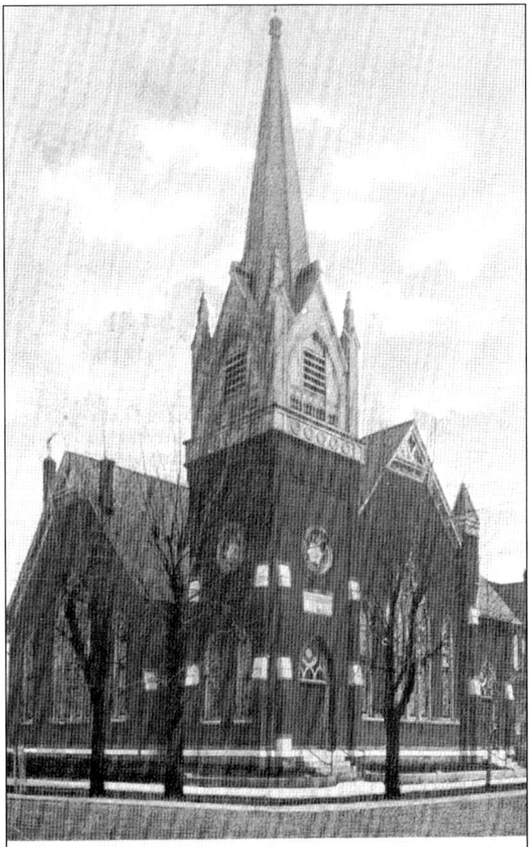

St. Paul's Ev. Church, West Side, Evansville, Ind.

First Christian Church, formerly known as Disciples of Christ, built this church in 1900. The sanctuary contoured the triangle at the intersection of Third Street, Fourth Street, and Blackford Avenue. In 1927, Calvary Baptist Church purchased the building and later built a large educational unit in the rear of the lot. In 1960, this church was torn down for the construction of a modern stone church, which still stands on the site. (Engler family.)

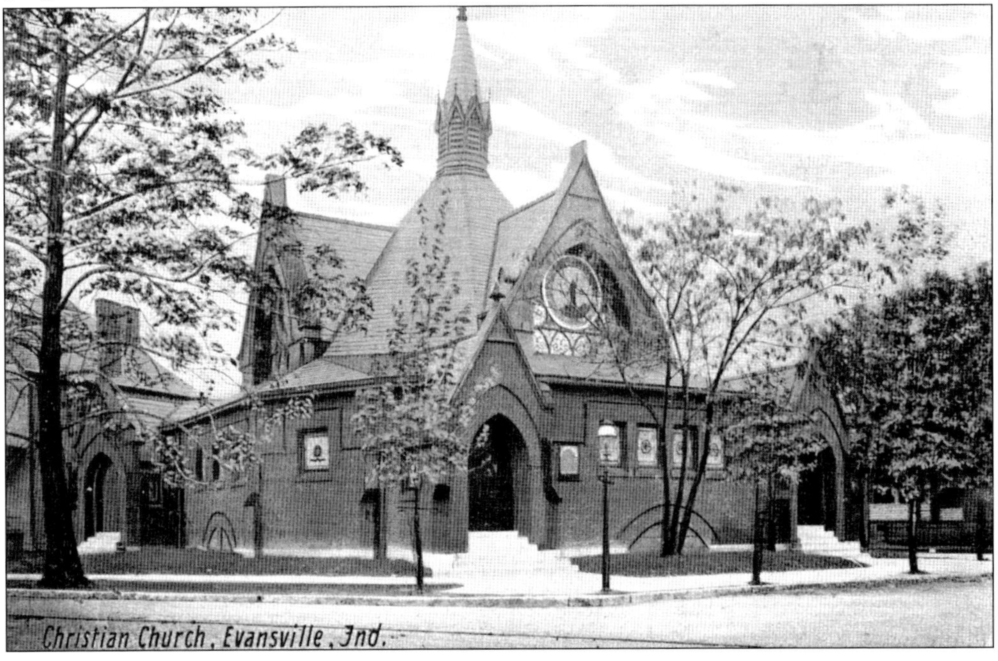

Christian Church, Evansville, Ind.

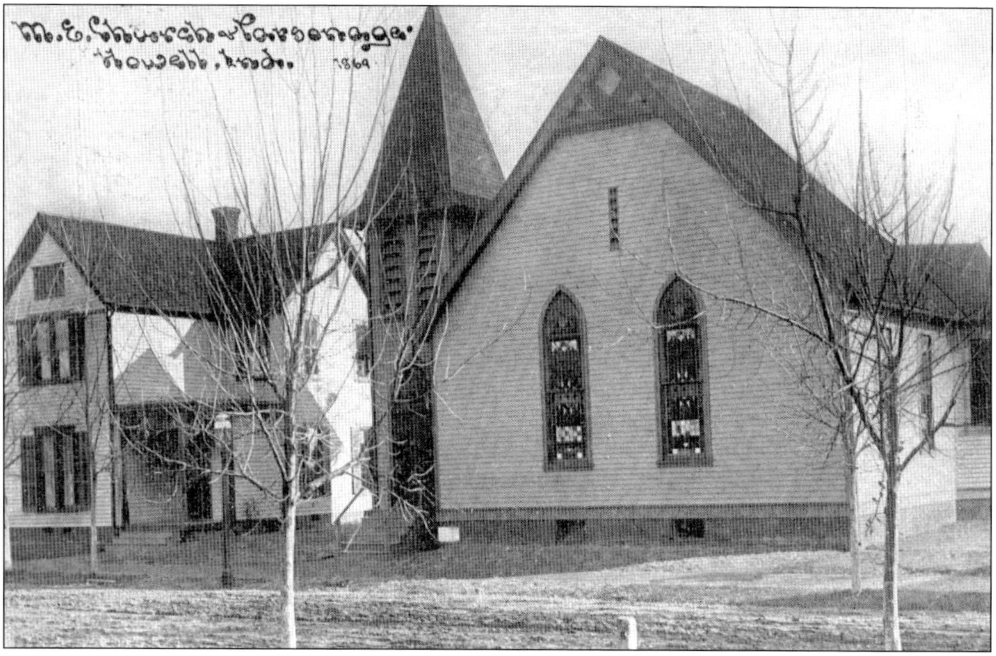

Howell Methodist Episcopal Church served the Howell area (which was then a separate town from Evansville). It was originally located on Daisy Avenue (present-day Cumberland Avenue). After the church moved in the 1920s, the old building was razed and replaced by a bungalow. The parsonage (visible at left) still stands at 1418 Cumberland Avenue. (EVPL and the Topper family.)

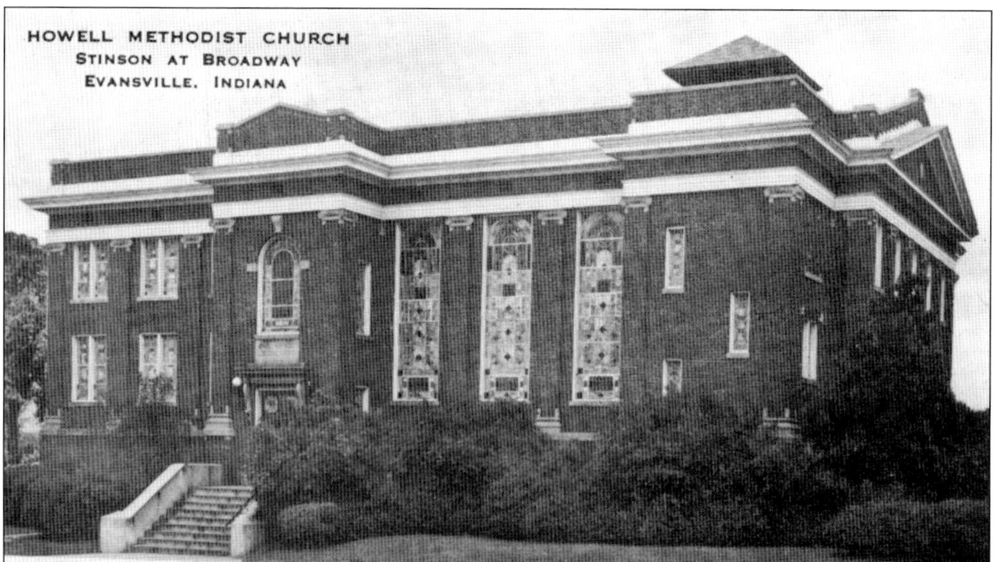

In 1924, a new church was built nearby at the corner of Stinson Avenue and Dearborn Street. The new Howell United Methodist Church was designed by architects Harry E. Boyle & Co. in the Neoclassical style. A large addition was erected in 1956 makes the church easily visible from Broadway Avenue. (EVPL and the Geiss family.)

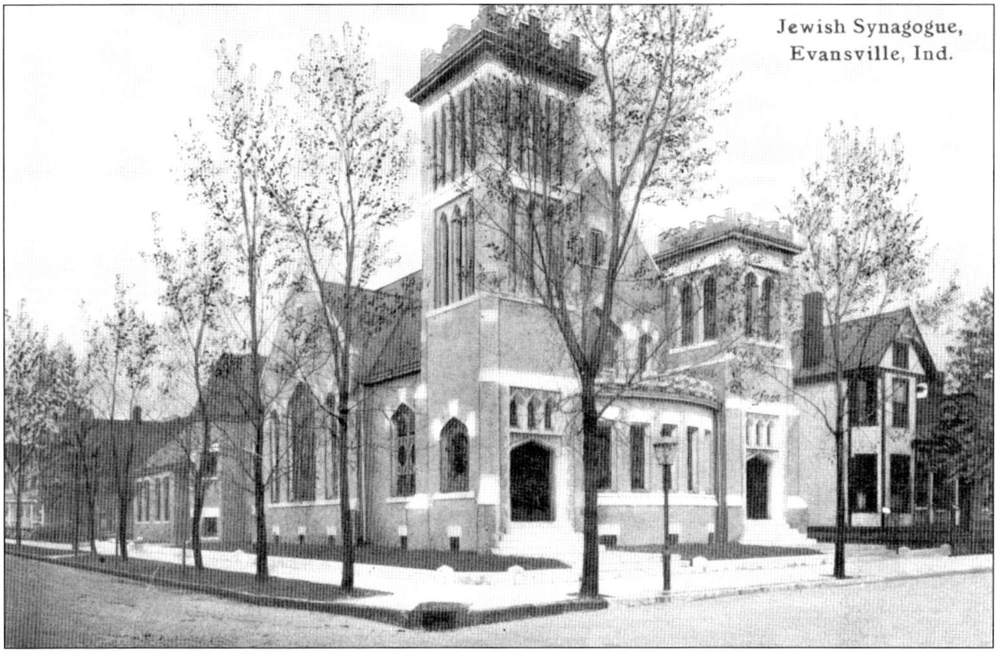

The B'Nai Israel congregation, organized in 1857, moved to the corner of Sixth and Washington Avenue in 1904 and was thereafter known as the Washington Avenue Temple. The congregation remained until 1980, when it merged with Adath Israel and moved into their building farther down Washington Avenue; the old B'Nai Israel building was sold to Patchwork Central. In 1983, it burned in a fire, and although a newer building was completed, the old tower was kept intact and still stands. (EVPL and the Topper family.)

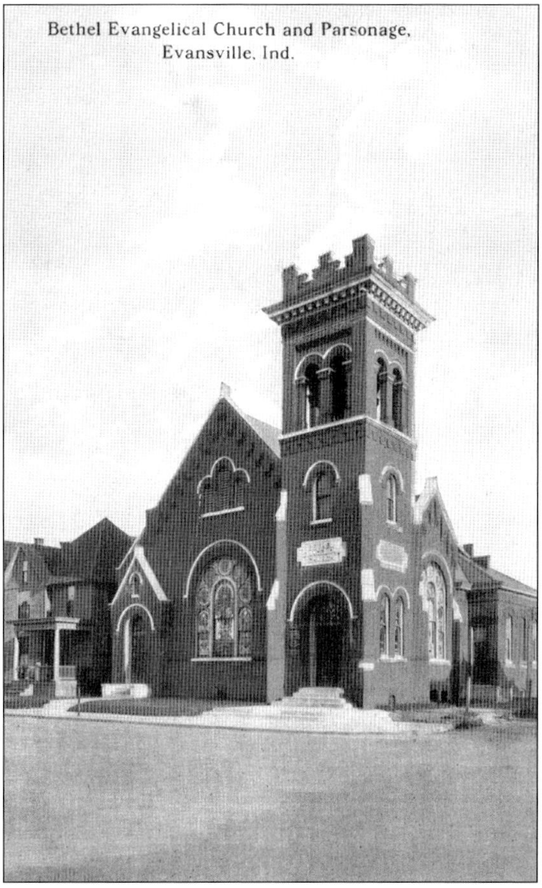

Bethel Evangelical, which split off of St. John's Evangelical, was built in 1904 and 1905. The congregation constructed a church at the corner of Garvin Street and Jefferson Avenue, erected a school around 1912, and built a parish house and auditorium in 1925 connecting it to Madison Avenue. In 1981, the renamed Bethel United Church of Christ congregation relocated to Green River Road. After this building sat vacant for years, it was razed by the city in 1995. (Engler family.)

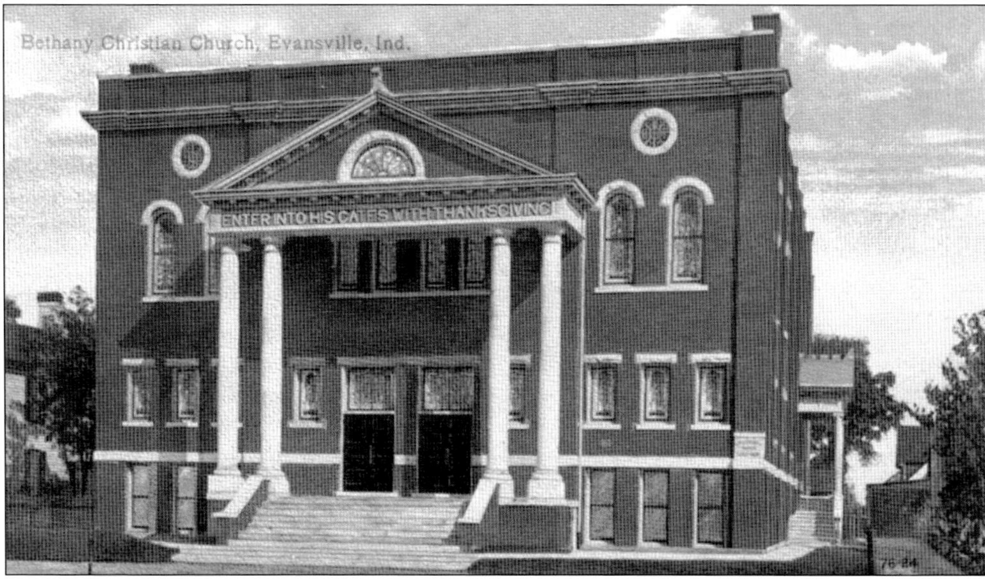

Bethany Christian Church completed this substantial brick building on Columbia Street in 1912. It was founded as a mission of First Christian Church in the late 1890s, located about a block away on Edgar Street. After years of expansion, Bethany finally outgrew the church and moved to Mill Road in 1981. The building was torn down in 1982, and the site—across from Deaconess Hospital—is now home to Orthopaedic Associates. (Engler family.)

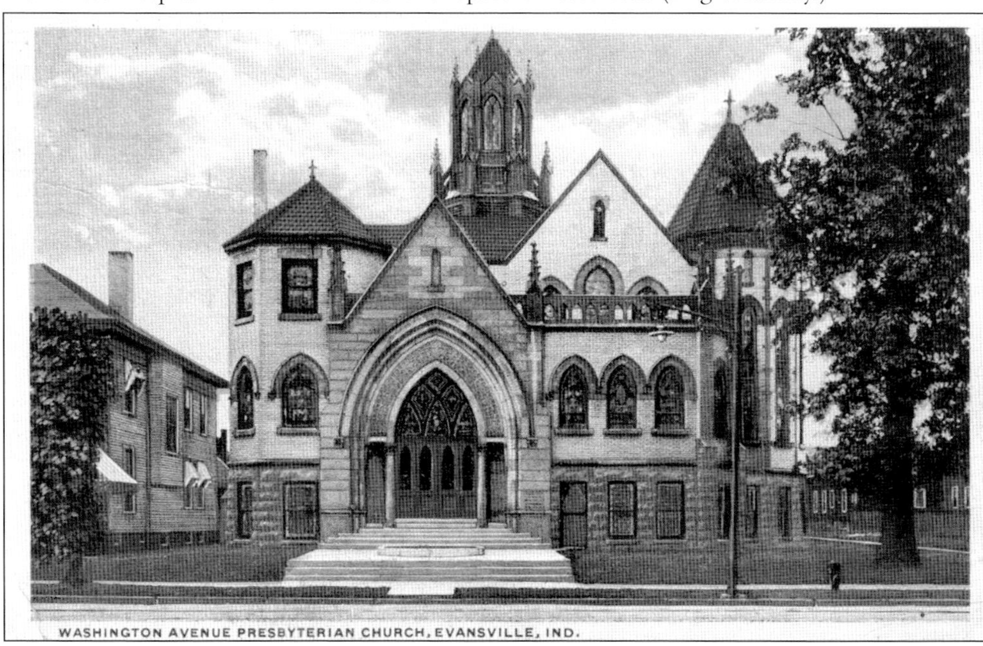

A Presbyterian church was commissioned for the up-and-coming Washington Avenue area after it experienced a boom in the early 1900s. Washington Avenue Presbyterian Church, situated opposite Morton Avenue, was completed in 1914. A Sunday school and an educational unit were added later. In 1999, the church merged with Eastminster Presbyterian and the old building became the Washington Avenue Center outreach mission. This building recently became home to God's Way Church. (Engler family.)

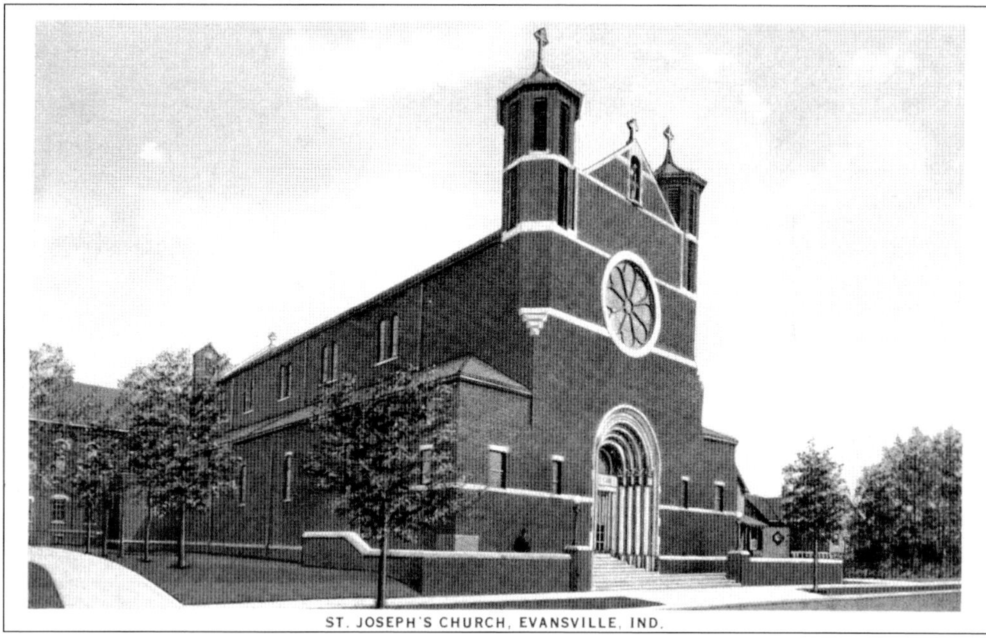

St. Joseph Catholic Church, at the corner of Virginia and Garvin Streets, was established for the growing northeastern suburbs in 1905. It was located on the former site of the old Catholic cemetery, which had moved years earlier to Perry Township and was named St. Joseph Cemetery (see page 36). The present-day church was completed in 1924, and its green roof—now metal instead of tile—stands out even today. (EVPL and the Geiss family.)

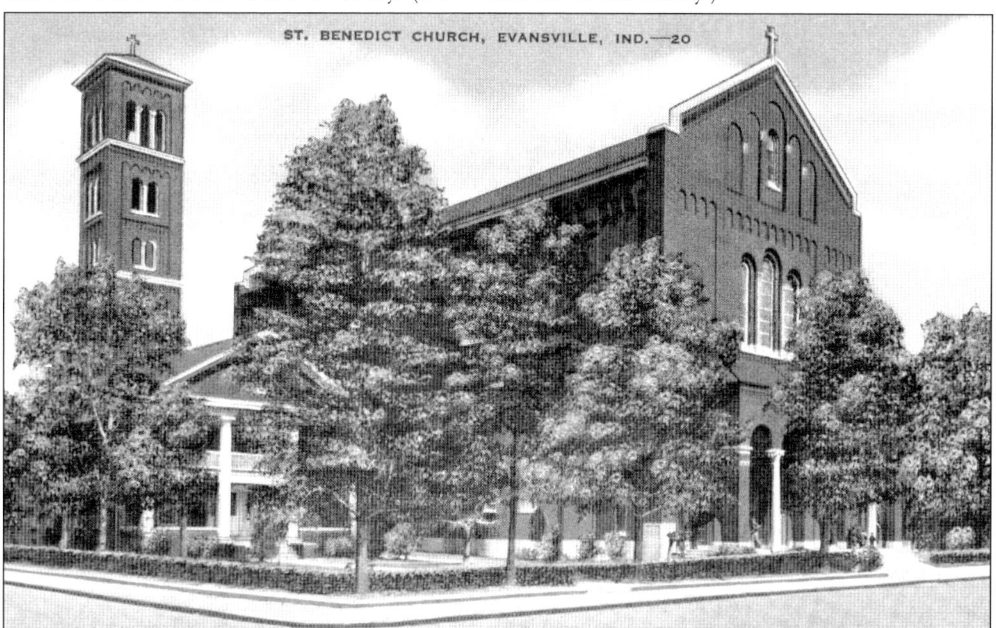

St. Benedict Cathedral on Lincoln Avenue was founded in 1912 and operated for years out of a chapel in the old school. The current church was built in 1927 and 1928 in the Renaissance Revival style and now serves as the cathedral church for the Diocese of Evansville. The rectory is behind the trees at left on the corner of Harlan Avenue. (EVPL and the Topper family.)

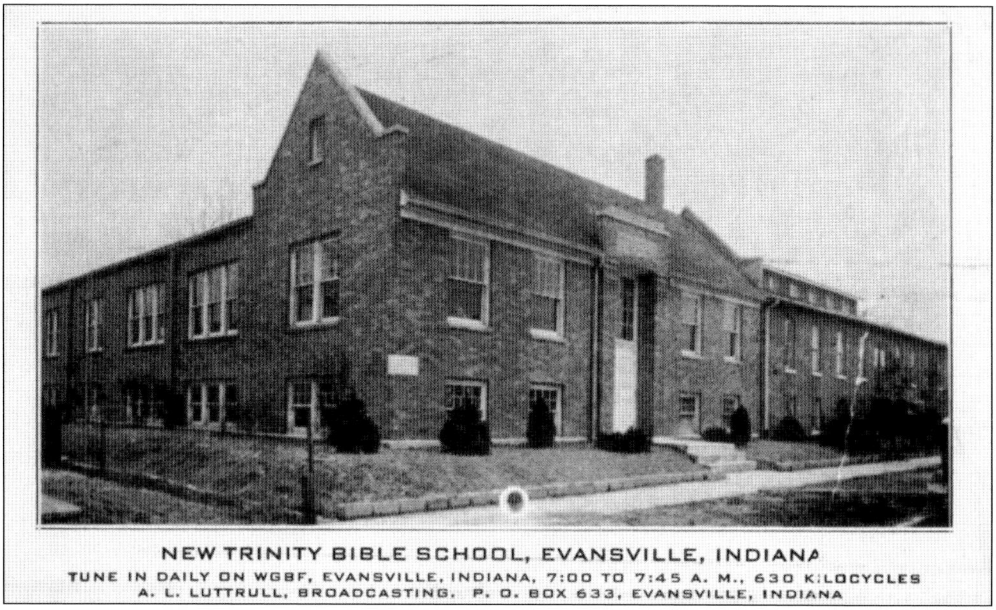

Trinity Wesleyan on Fares Avenue was founded in 1931 as the East Side Trinity Gospel Tabernacle. This postcard advertises its new Bible school, built behind the old church along Indiana Street sometime around 1940. The church became isolated by the cloverleaf at Highway 41 and the Lloyd Expressway, but remained at this site until it relocated to Vogel Road in 2011 and was renamed CrossPointe Trinity Church. (EVPL and the Topper family.)

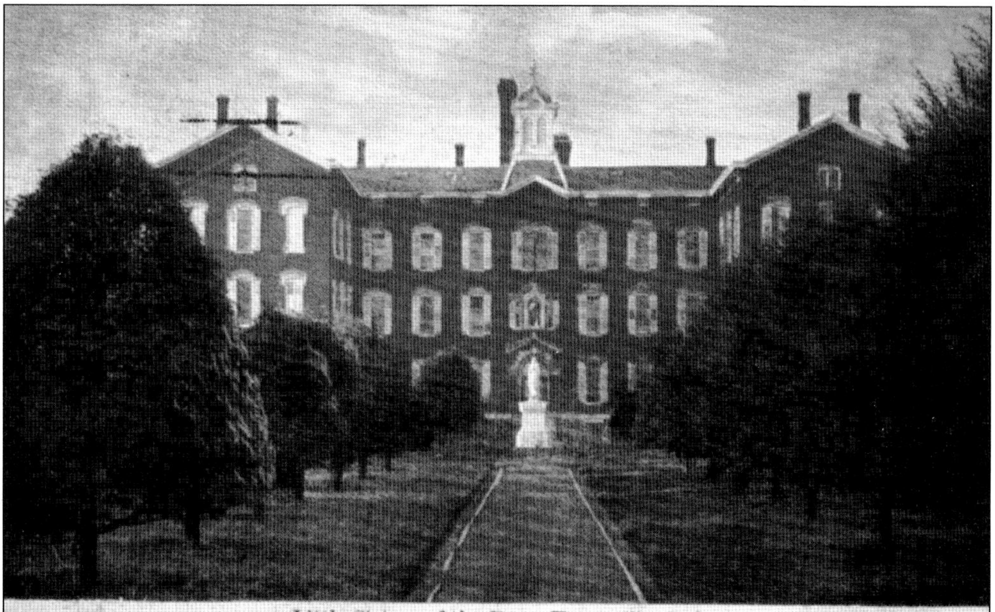

Little Sisters of the Poor on Lincoln Avenue dates back to before St. Benedict was built across the street. The nuns chose a location far removed from the city for a quiet setting and had this brick building erected in 1887. Construction began in 1966 for St. John's Home, which was built in front of the old structure; the old section was razed in 1971, and the completed home was dedicated on July 1, 1973. (Engler family.)

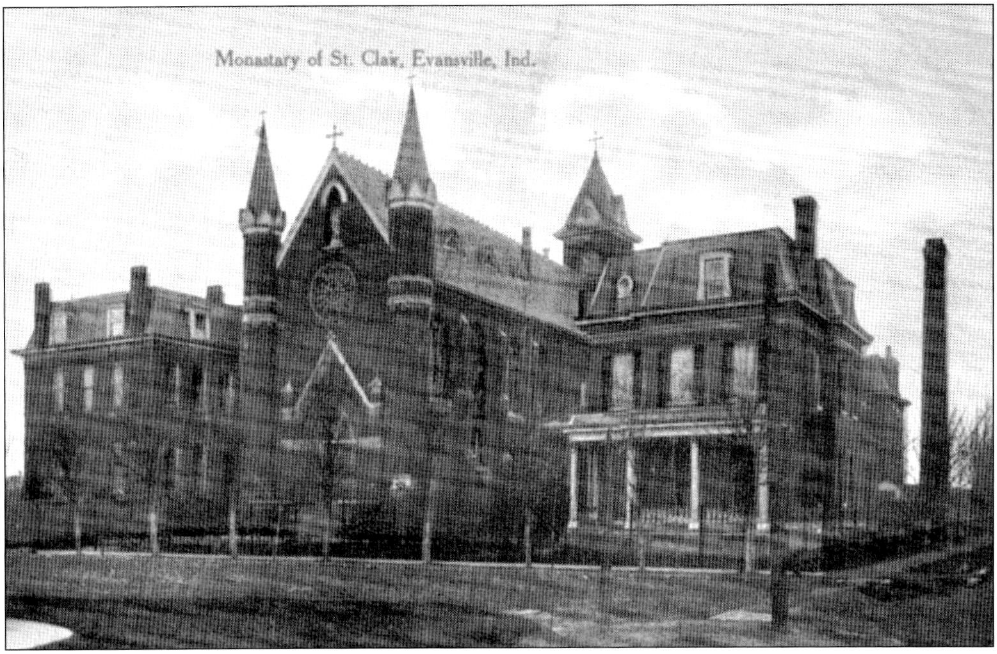

The Monastery of St. Clare (misspelled "Clair" in both postcards) was built in 1897 and was originally in a tranquil location outside the city limits. The postcard below shows the monastery from a distance along Kentucky Avenue, which demonstrates the monastery's isolation from the city. The "Poor Clares," as the nuns were often called, spent their lives within the confines of the monastery serving the needs of the church. After years at this location, the nuns moved in 1984 to a new facility on Nurrenbern Road in Perry Township, returning to a rural setting. The former monastery on Kentucky Avenue is now home to the Evansville Christian Life Center. (Both, Engler family.)

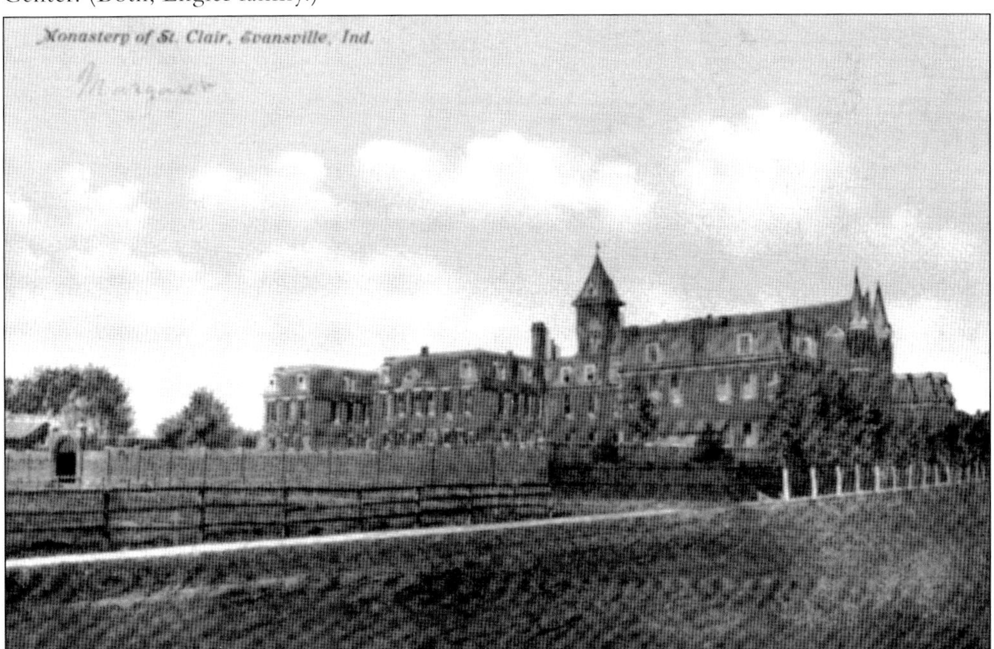

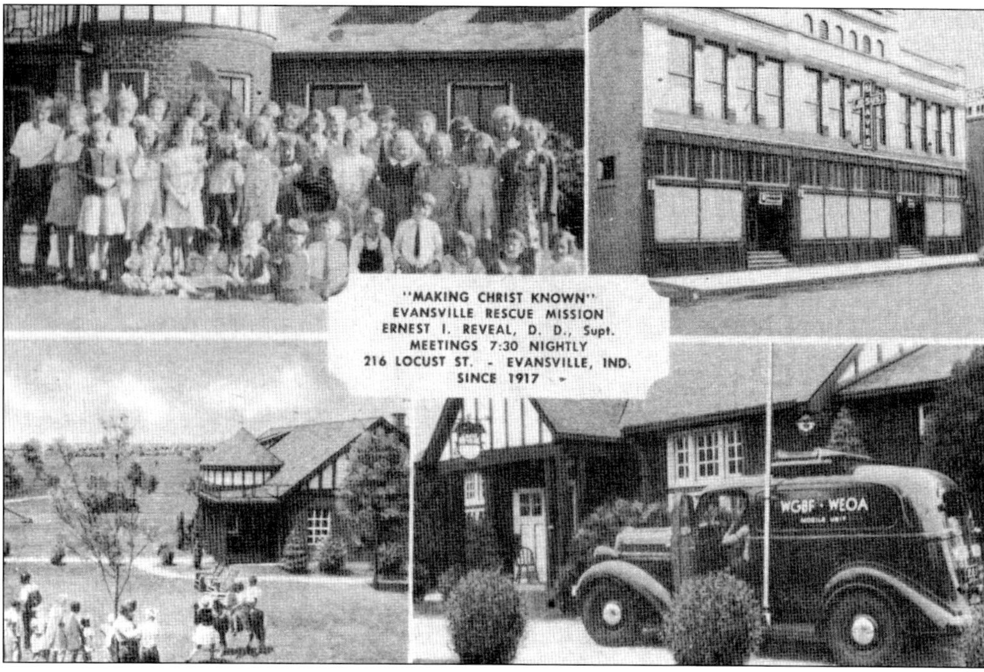

The Evansville Rescue Mission was established in 1917 as an outreach program to help those in need. The upper right corner of this postcard shows the old facility on Locust Street—its home from 1932 until 1972, when it moved to its current location near Central Library. The other images are from Camp Reveal, located on Boonville–New Harmony Road; the Evansville Rescue Mission purchased the 105-acre area in 1927 and set up a camping and retreat facility. (EVPL and the Topper family.)

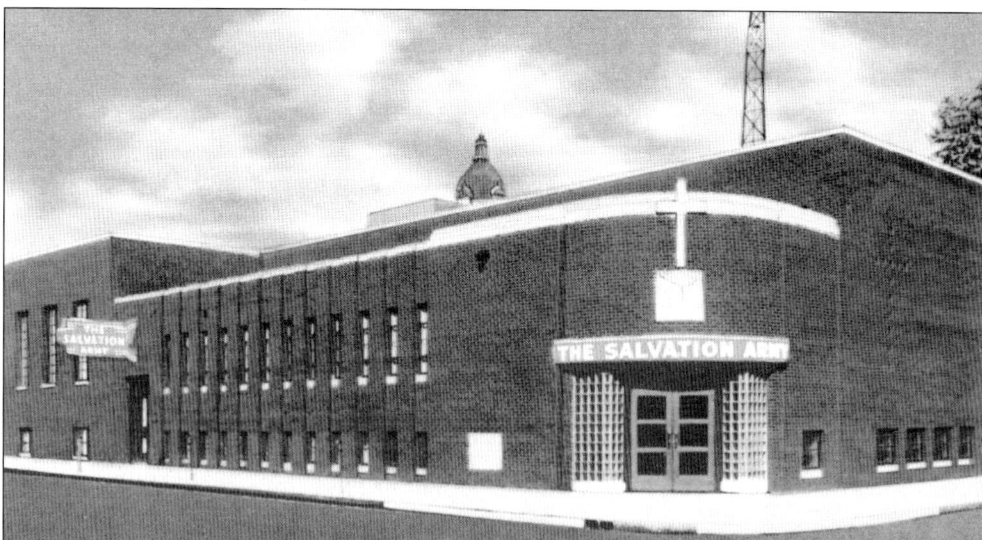

The Salvation Army Citadel was built in 1923 along Sycamore Street. It expanded to Sixth Street when this building was erected on the corner in 1946. The citadel functioned as its headquarters for nearly 70 years, until the Salvation Army moved its offices to the Fulton Avenue facility in 1992. By 2000, the old building had been torn down to make room for the parking garage that now occupies half of the block. (EVPL and the Topper family.)

Oak Hill Cemetery replaced the old city graveyard on Mulberry Street near Fifth Street. The encroaching urban growth forced officials to plan for a new cemetery beyond the city limits. A 56-acre site on Oak Hill Road was chosen in 1852, and burials began the next year. The new Administration Building, completed in 1899, was designed by architects Harris & Shopbell and featured a bell tower, chapel, and office. In 1901, the architects also built the gate (pictured below) at the entrance of the cemetery opposite Willow Road. The red rugby brick wall around the grounds was added in the 1920s after an expansion of the growing cemetery. (Right, EVPL; below, Engler family.)

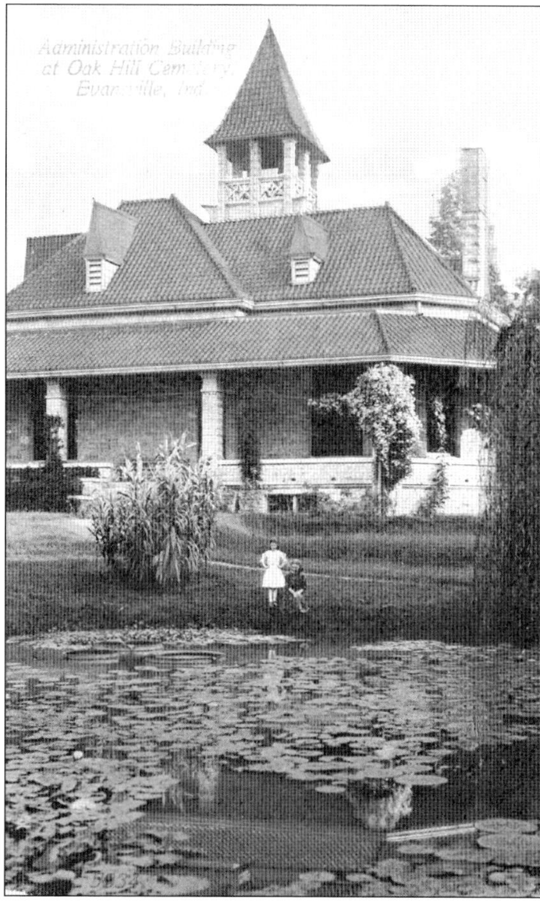

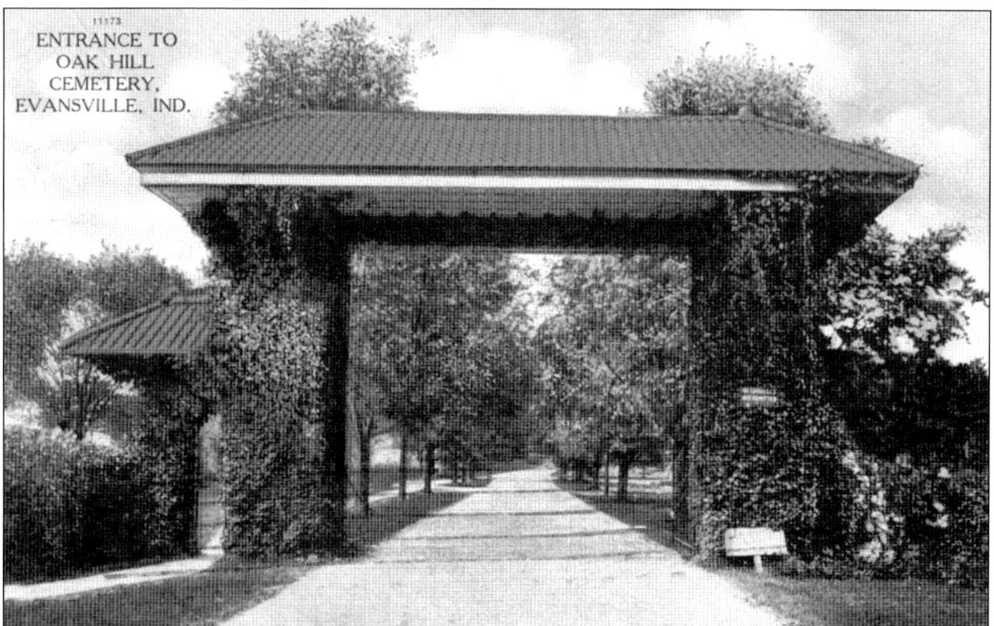

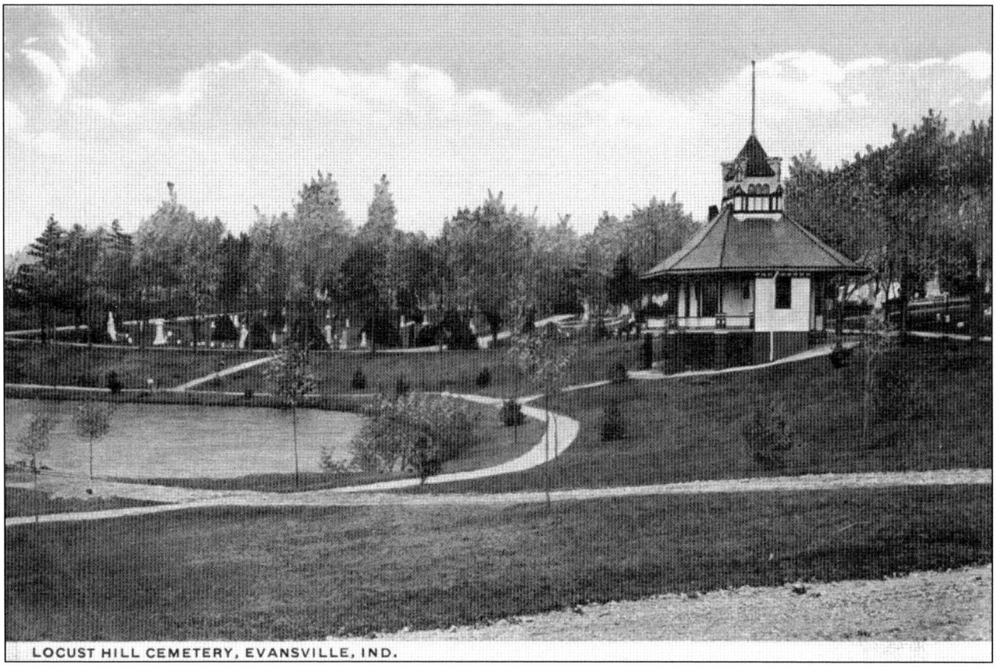

Locust Hill Cemetery was founded around 1870 on Kratzville Road in Center Township. The land was donated from the Kirkpatrick family and was originally set aside as a county cemetery. After much growth, Locust Hill was deeded to the city, which still operates the cemetery today. The lake shown in the postcard has been filled in. (EVPL and the Topper family.)

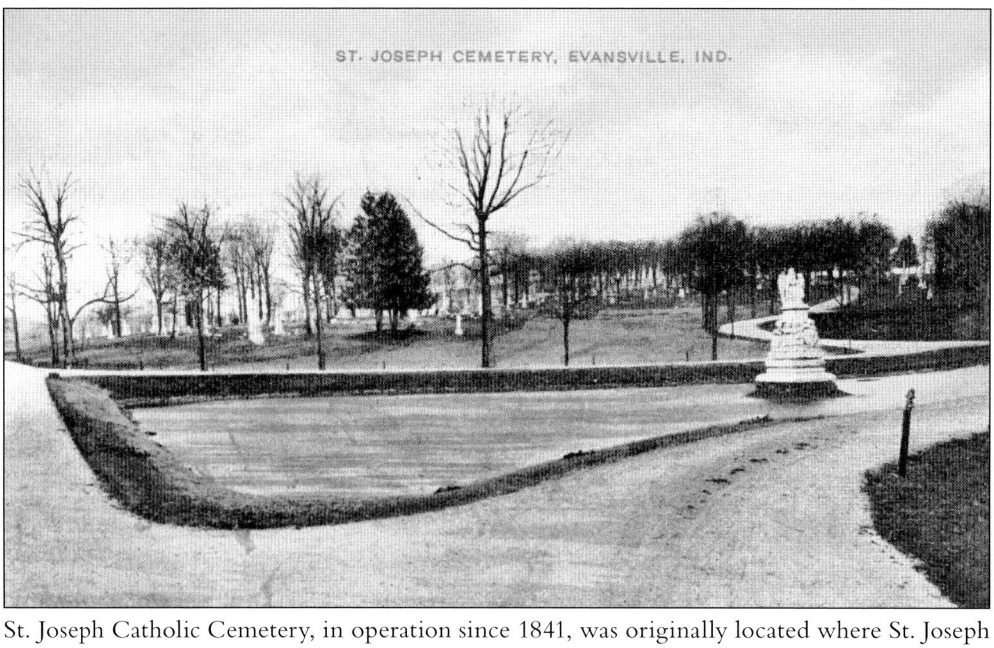

St. Joseph Catholic Cemetery, in operation since 1841, was originally located where St. Joseph Church now stands on Virginia Street. In 1870, the diocese purchased 115 acres of land off Mesker Park Drive in Perry Township, and burials began in the new cemetery in 1872. The office building and front gates were added in 1917. This reflecting pool has been removed, but its statue still rests at the bottom of the main drive. (Estate of Pam and Dennis Beadles.)

Three

Did You Know . . .

A city looking forward must school its young, and from the onset, Evansville was a front-runner in establishing public education. Canal Street School, the first public school building, was completed in 1855 and was later known as Wheeler School; it was razed around 1972. Over the next several years, additional neighborhood schools were built to handle the city's growing population. Evansville Public Schools continued to expand and eventually enveloped the county schools around 1960. Renamed the Evansville Vanderburgh School Corporation (EVSC), it has served the entire county since that time. Parochial schools like Reitz Memorial High School and Evansville Lutheran School have provided an alternative to public schools.

Post-secondary schools and business colleges provide technical training for those seeking an education beyond high school. Evansville procured a college in 1919, when Moore's Hill College relocated, eventually becoming what is now the University of Evansville (UE). Another higher learning institution was established in Evansville when Indiana State University opened an extension school in the 1960s; the university later became independent and was renamed the University of Southern Indiana (USI).

Libraries offer another means of lifelong learning, and Evansville has several. The Evansville Vanderburgh Public Library (EVPL) and Willard Library were instrumental in the research process for this book. The EVPL established several branch libraries in neighborhoods throughout the city.

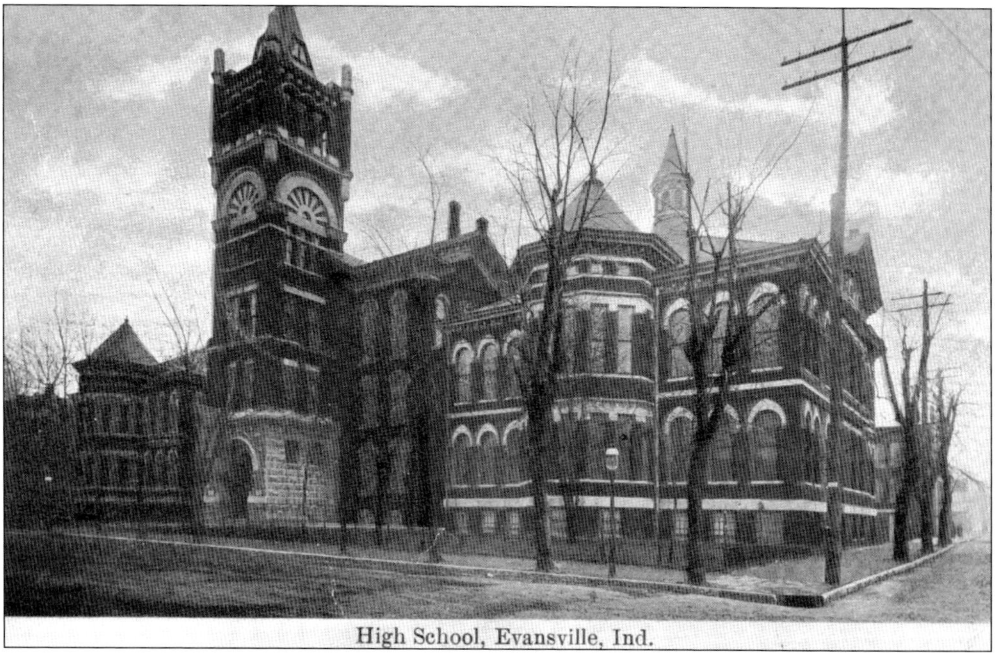

Evansville High School (formally named Central High School after F.J. Reitz High School opened in 1918) was built in 1868 but was significantly altered when the tower and two wings were added in 1898. Above is a view of the enlarged school as seen from the corner of present-day Martin Luther King Jr. Boulevard and Court Street. In 1903, the school acquired the old B'nai Israel synagogue behind it on Sixth Street. It was extensively remodeled and presented as a manual training school, a predecessor of the mechanical arts school. In the c. 1910 image below, a group of schoolchildren stands outside the building at the corner of Court Street. (Above, EVPL and the Geiss family; below, EVPL.)

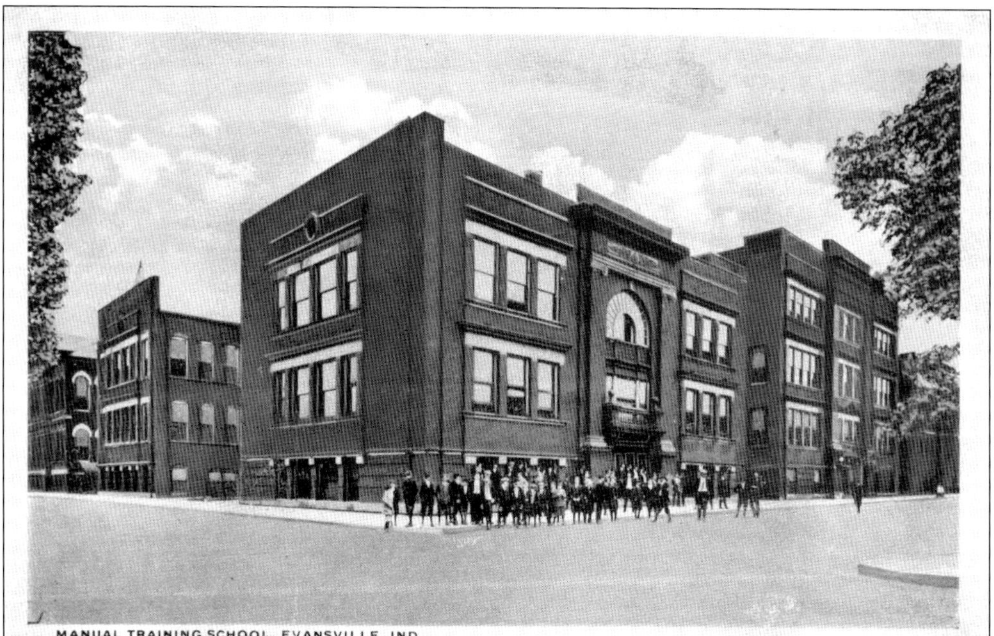

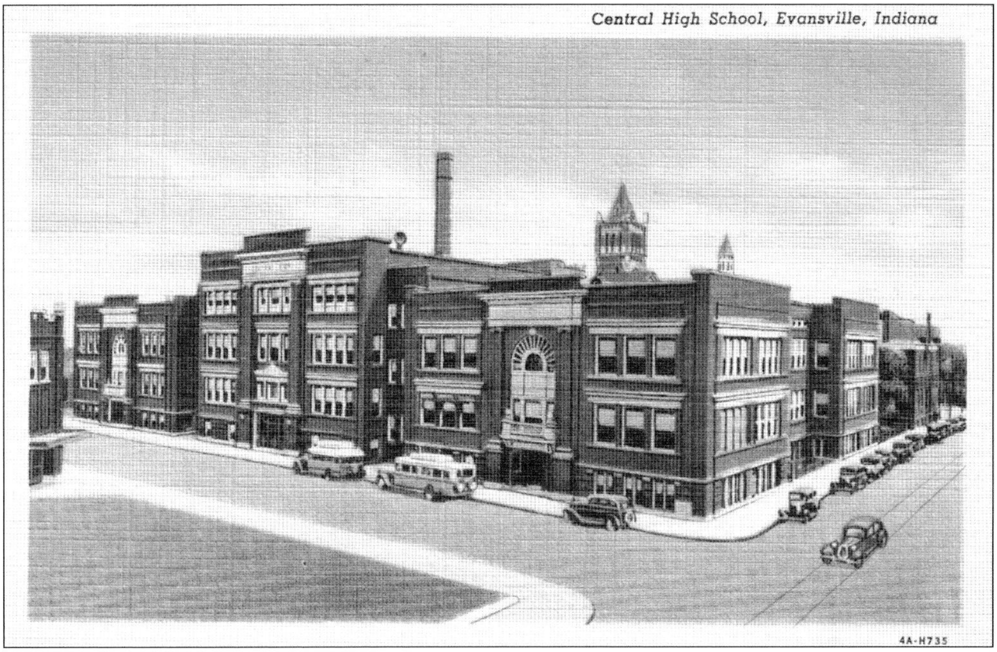

Here is the school after the 1911 junior high building was completed at the corner of Sixth and Vine Streets. Central comprised the entire block after this addition. Below is a view from the same corner during the flood of 1937. Once the school moved to First Avenue, out on the North Side, in 1971, this building earned the moniker "Old Central." However, the whole block was torn down in 1973, and the parking lot now there gives little hint of the school that once graced downtown. Only the 1927 gymnasium, partially visible at far left in the above postcard, remains. It was incorporated into the YMCA facility, but the letters "C.H.S." (for Central High School) are still carved in the stonework. (Above, Engler family; below, EVPL and the Topper family.)

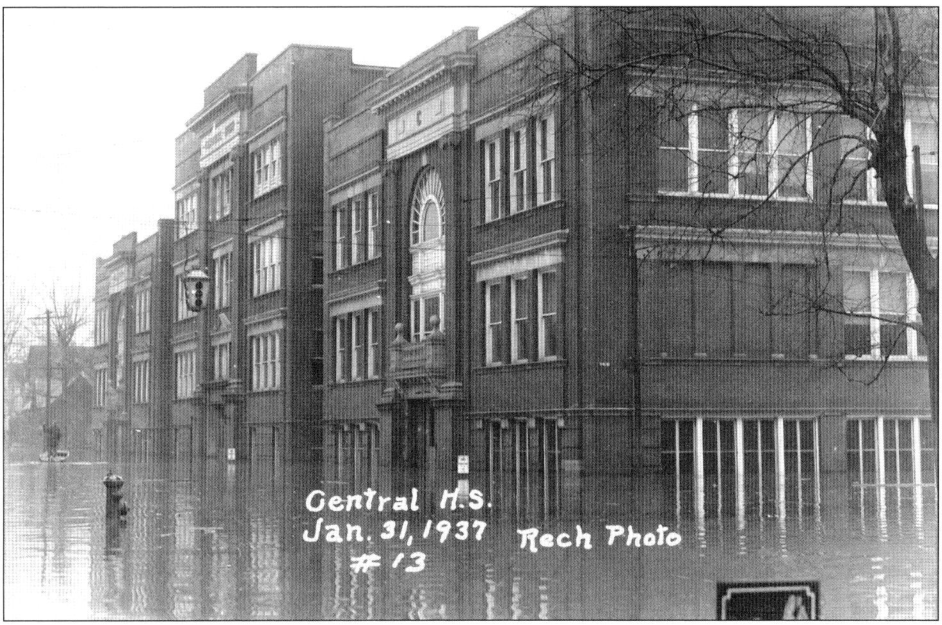

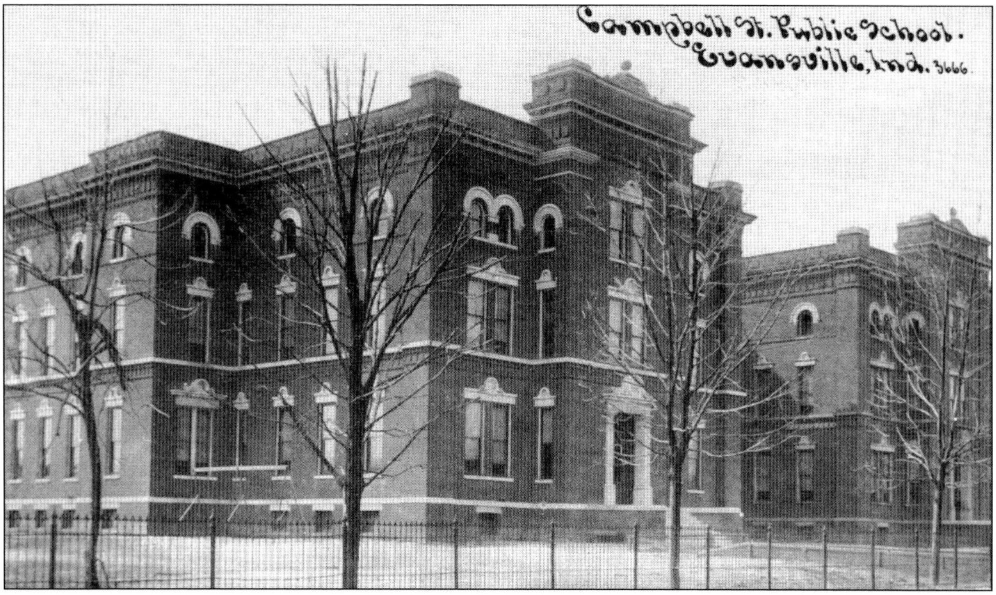

Campbell Street School was built in the Culver neighborhood in 1875. A fire started by a lightning strike burned the school down, and a new building (pictured) was completed in 1905. Campbell was renamed Culver in 1933 after principal John M. Culver. The school was still recognizable after several additions, but after a new building was erected adjacent to the school in 1982, the old city school was razed soon after. (EVPL and the Topper family.)

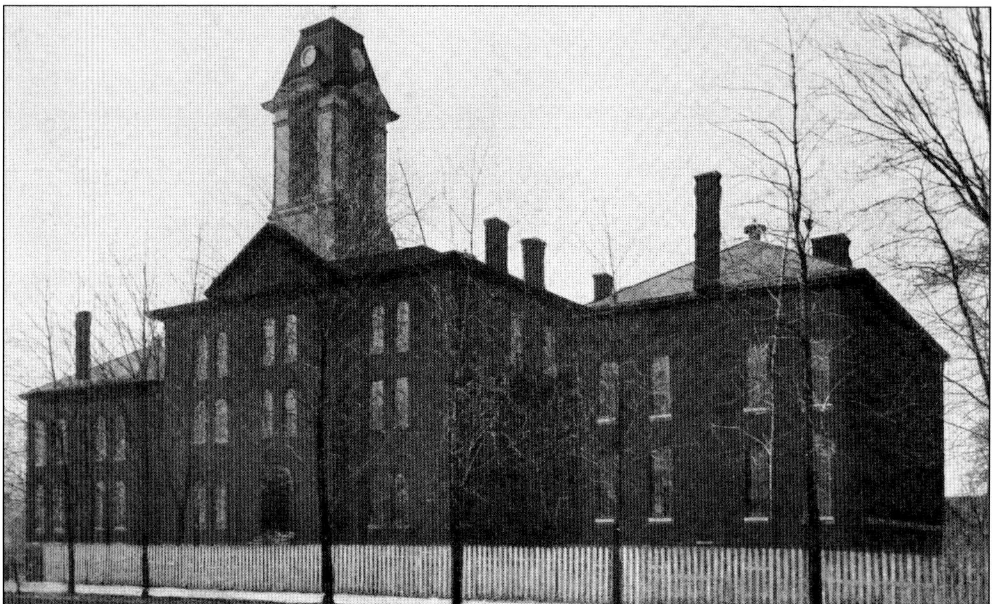

Centennial School was a direct result of Independence (the West Side) being annexed by Evansville. Built in 1876, it was named after the country's centennial and replaced an older school on Wabash Avenue. When Helfrich Park was completed in 1965, the school closed, and, for a while, it served as the original University of Southern Indiana. The main building was razed in 1972, although a 1940s addition along Illinois Street stood until 2003. (EVPL and the Topper family.)

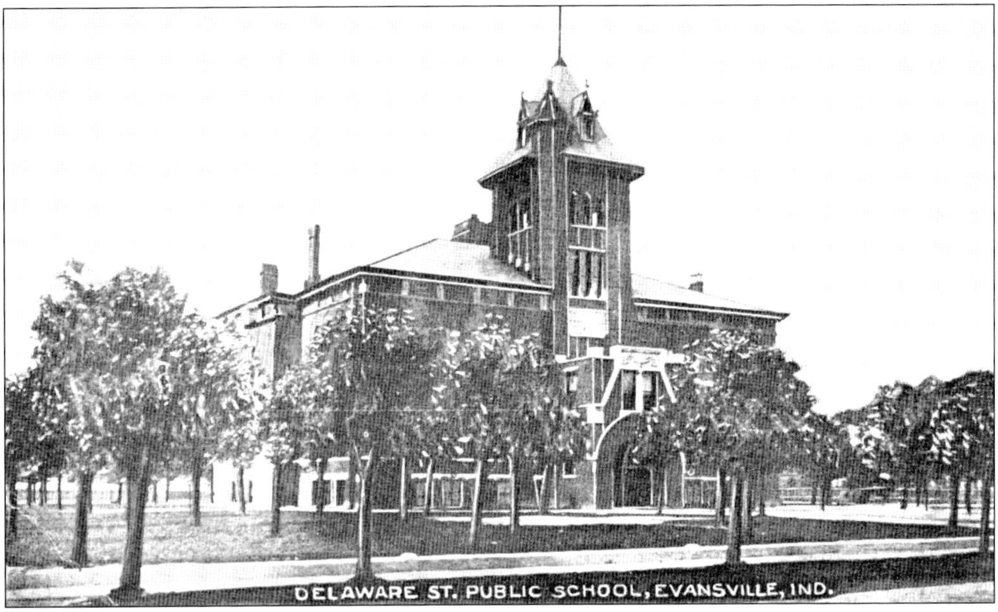

Delaware School dates back to 1896, when a new school was built on Delaware Street at the corner of Garvin Street. By 1915, additions in the rear connected the school all the way to Columbia Street. In 1958, a new school, closer to the street, was built in front of the old one; once it was completed, the original school was torn down. The 1929 gymnasium fronting Columbia Street is now the oldest remaining section. (Estate of Pam and Dennis Beadles.)

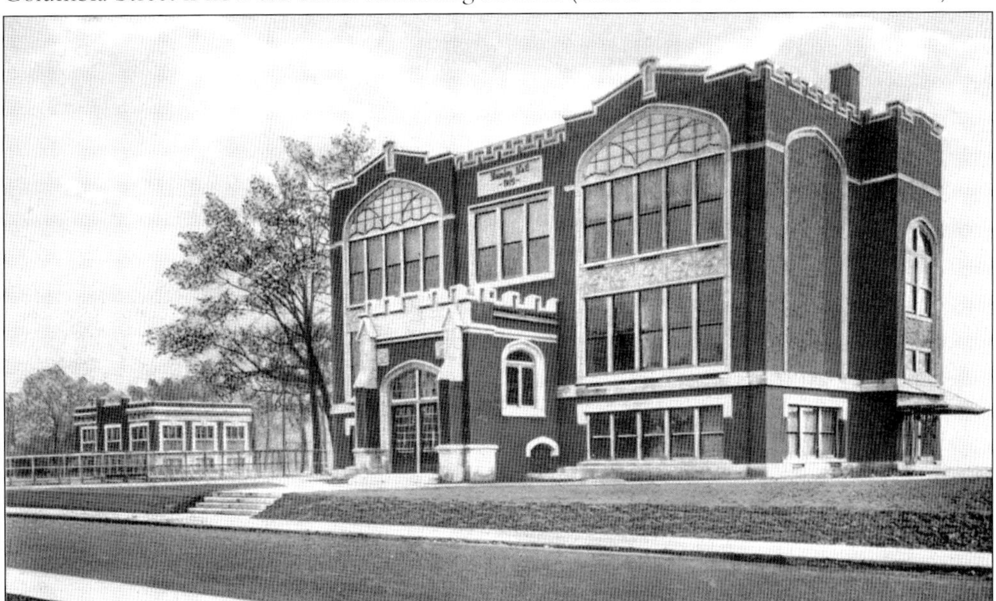

Stanley Hall was originally built in 1900 as Chandler Avenue School. The rapidly expanding East Side, however, promptly necessitated an addition. This 1915 annex was built behind the school, facing Bayard Park Drive. Stanley Hall closed in 1972, and the school—except for the gymnasium and cafeteria—was razed. More recently, the remaining buildings served as an alternative education center until 2006, when the program moved and the building became vacant. (EVPL and the Topper family.)

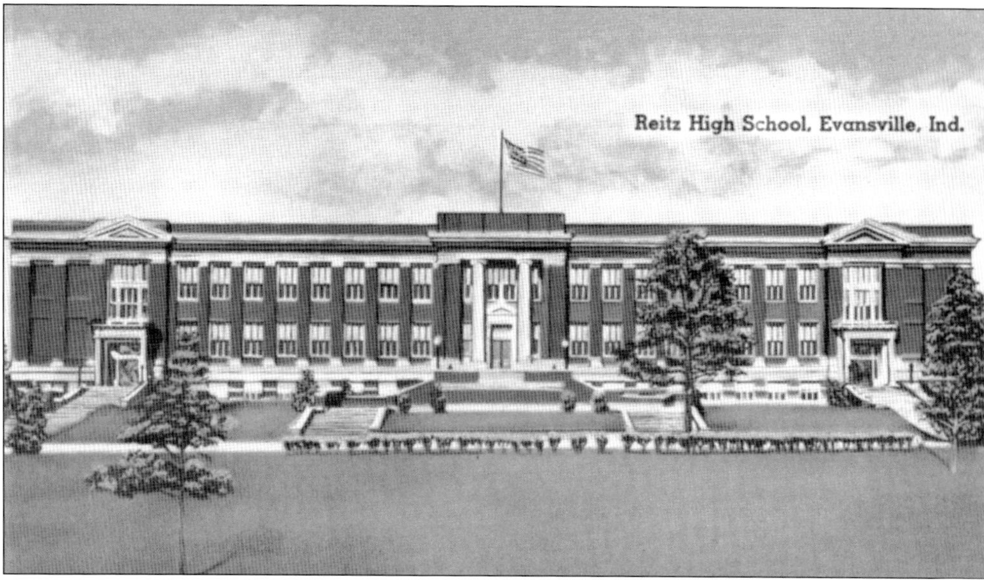

Built in 1918 atop Coal Mine Hill, F.J. Reitz High School was named after philanthropist Francis Joseph Reitz. The area became known as Reitz Hill as the neighborhood grew around the West Side school. Additions after the 1950s significantly altered this view from the corner of Dreier Boulevard and Austin Avenue. The big gym and a wing now jut out from the original front of the school. (EVPL and the Topper family.)

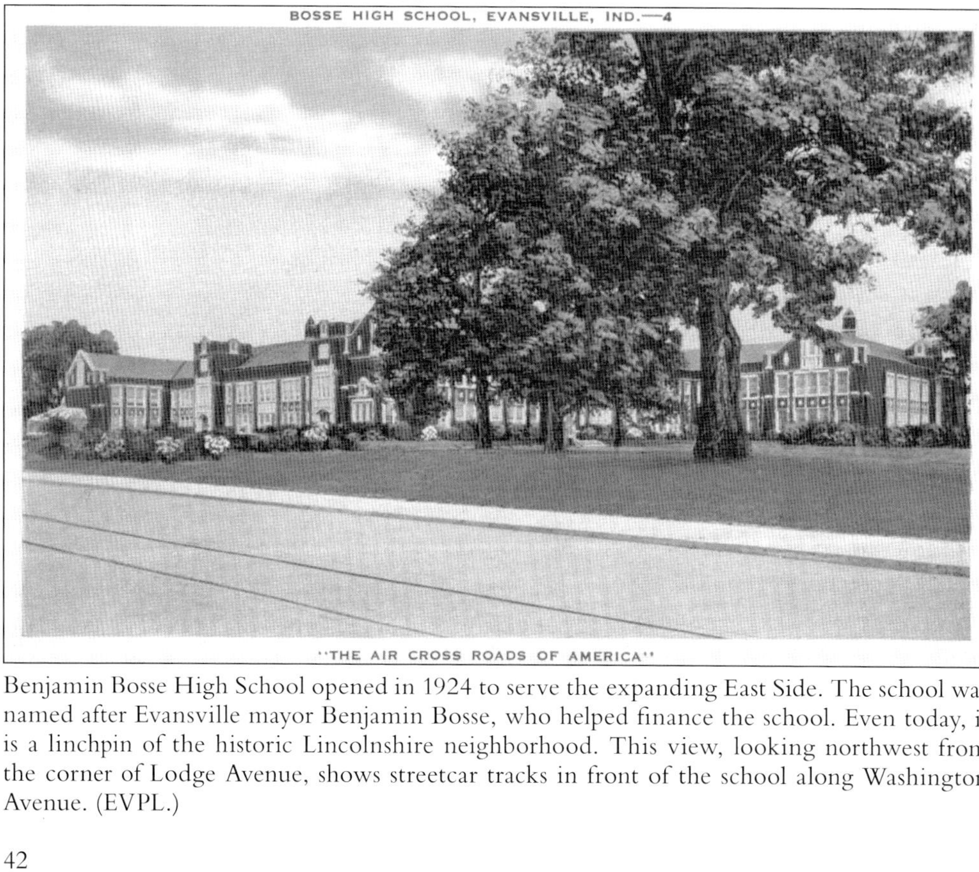

Benjamin Bosse High School opened in 1924 to serve the expanding East Side. The school was named after Evansville mayor Benjamin Bosse, who helped finance the school. Even today, it is a linchpin of the historic Lincolnshire neighborhood. This view, looking northwest from the corner of Lodge Avenue, shows streetcar tracks in front of the school along Washington Avenue. (EVPL.)

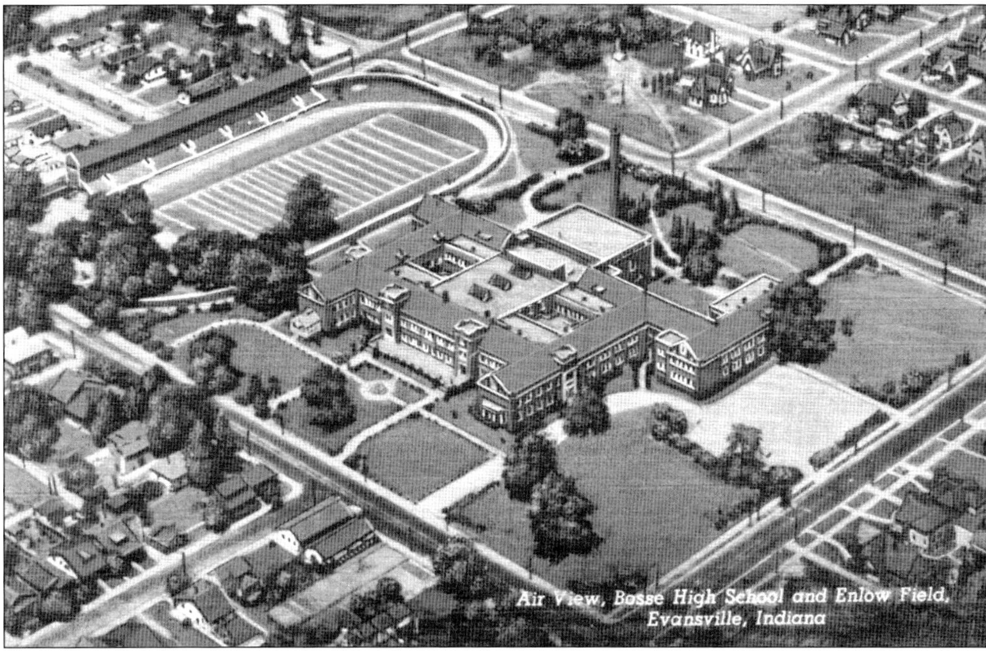

This aerial view shows Bosse High School, with Enlow Field just left of the school. Many of the homes around the school are still standing today. Unlike at Reitz High School, additions to the back of the school have helped Bosse keep its historic front, even through several expansions. (Engler family.)

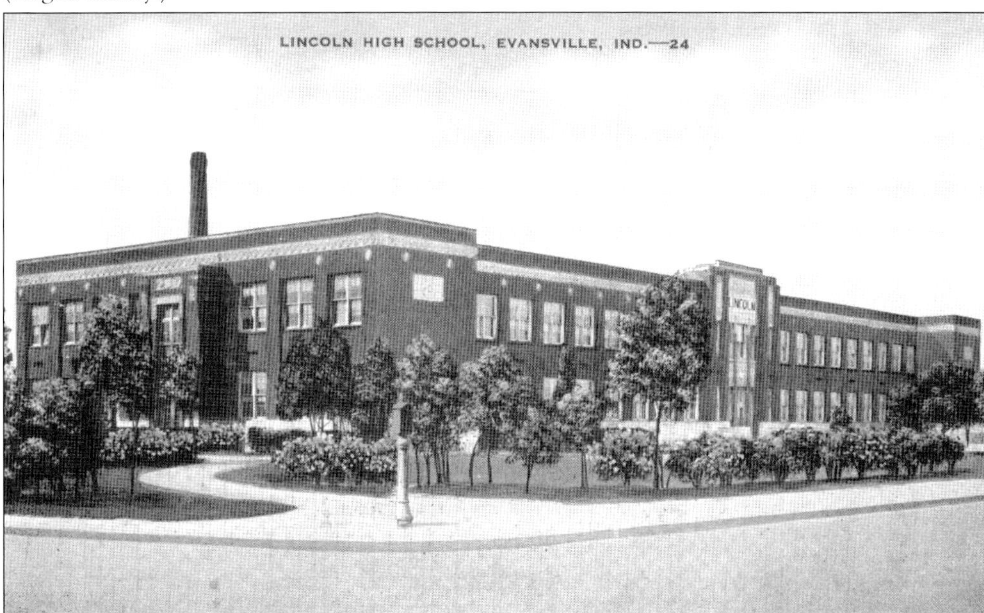

Lincoln High School opened in 1928 to serve the city's African American children, combining several smaller colored schools. In 1962, the high school closed, and it later became a desegregated elementary school. This view of the building, from the corner of Lincoln and Morton Avenues, looks nearly identical to the present-day appearance, thanks to two new well-blended wings added in 2010. (EVPL and the Geiss family.)

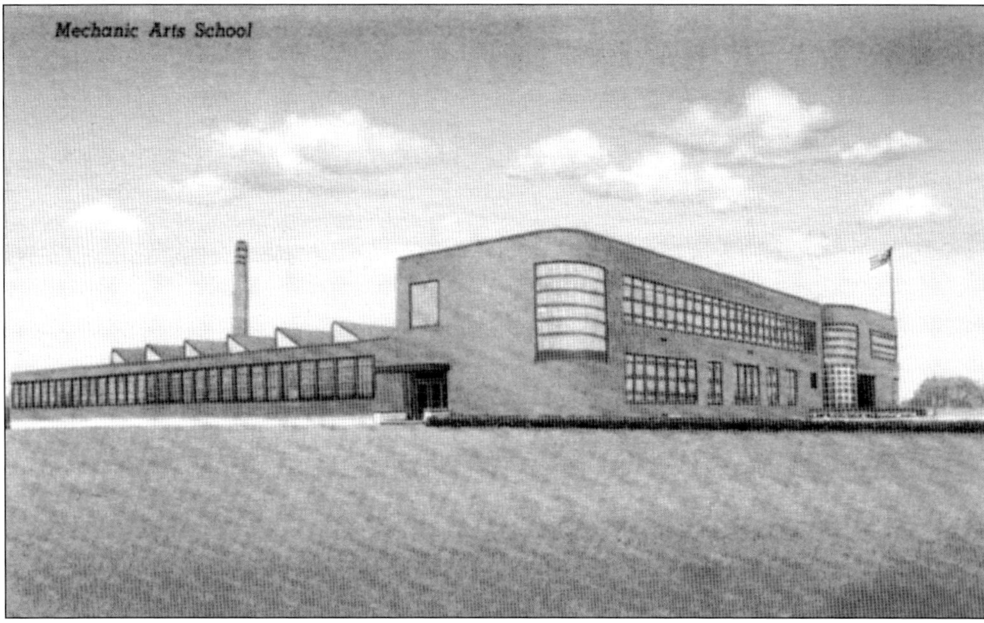

The Mechanic Arts School was built in 1938 along Wedeking Avenue as a trade and industry school. When it became a stand-alone high school in 1956, this building was expanded, and the school was renamed North High School. Several other additions resulted in the school being landlocked, so a new North High was completed in 2012; the school moved, and the old building has remained mostly vacant. (Engler family.)

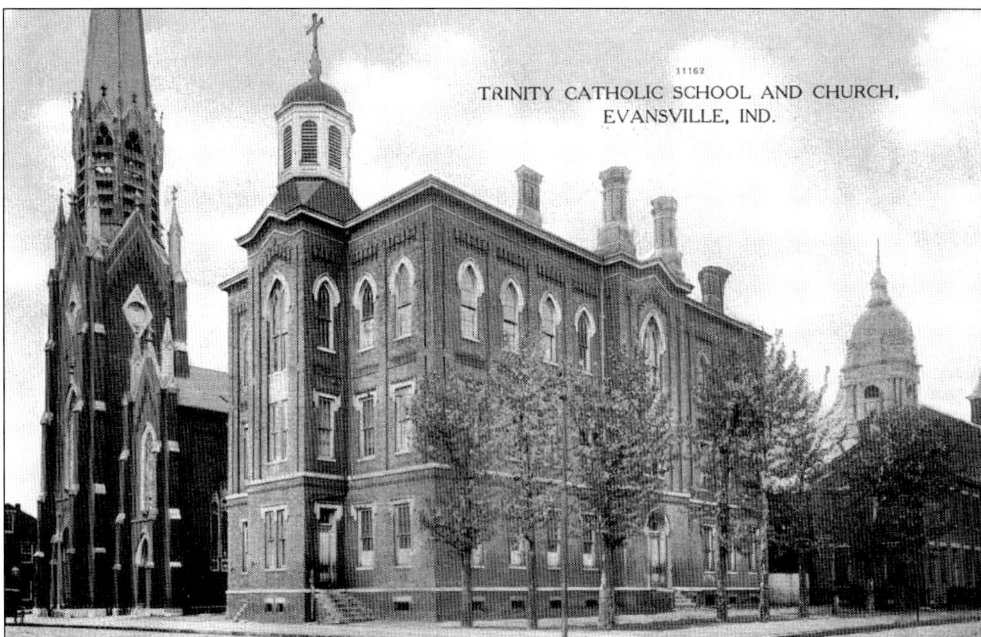

Holy Trinity School was built in 1869 and was the original Catholic high school in the Evansville area. The high school moved when Reitz Memorial High School opened in 1925, and the rest of the school closed in 1948. The building at the corner of Third and Vine Streets was torn down in 1958, and the site is now a parking lot. (Engler family.)

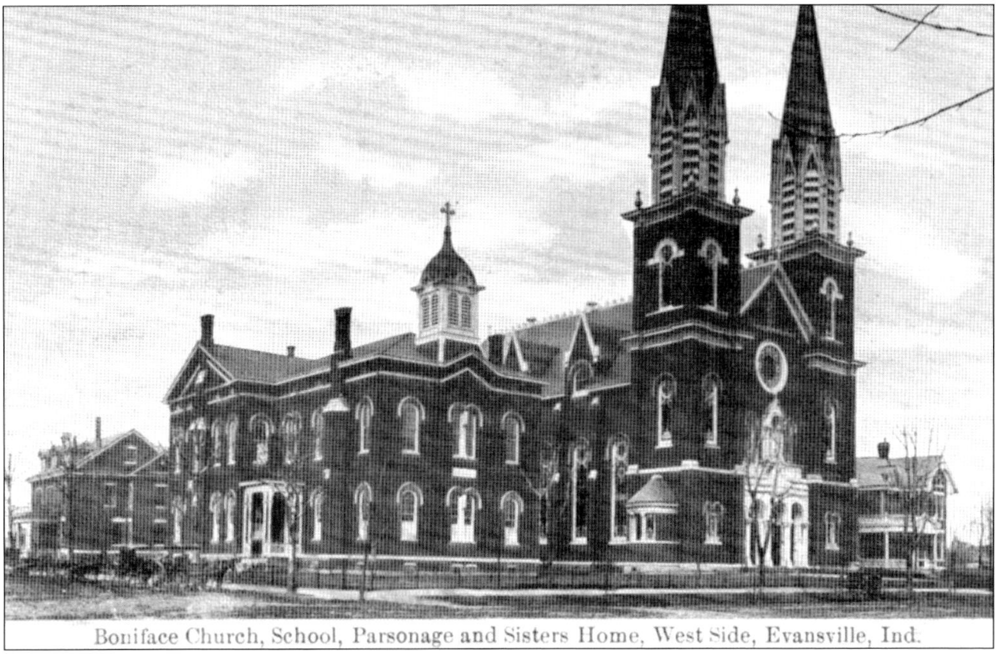

St. Boniface established a permanent school in 1885 when this building was erected on the corner of Wabash Avenue and Michigan Street. It also housed the nuns who taught at the school until the sisters' home was built. When a newer school was built along Tenth Avenue in 1923, this building became surplus. The vacant school was demolished in 1951, and the site was later paved for use as the church's parking lot. (Engler family.)

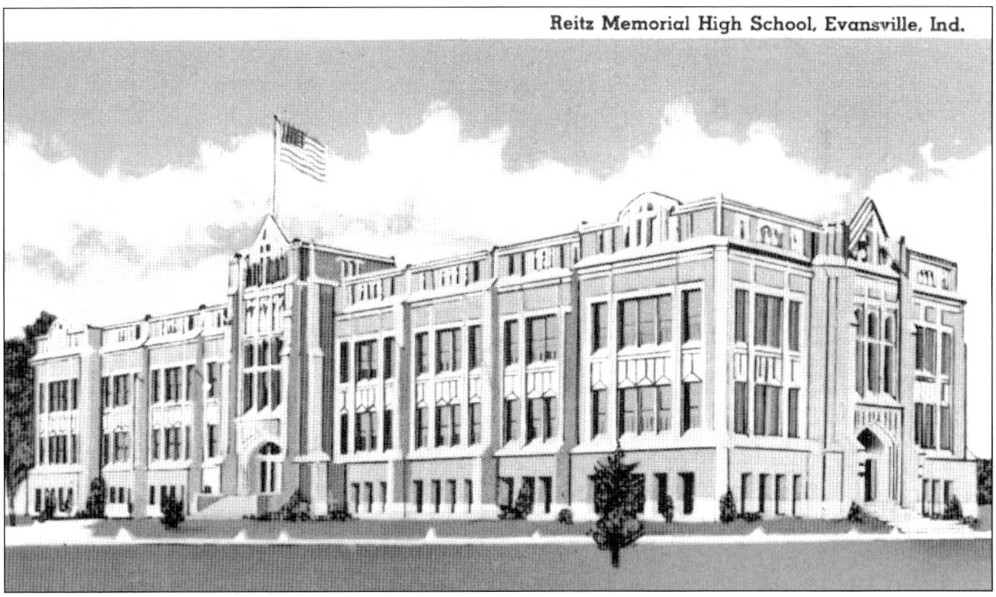

After a year of searching for the perfect site and two years of construction, Reitz Memorial High School opened in 1925 on Lincoln Avenue. It, like the public F.J. Reitz High School on the West Side, was named after Francis Joseph Reitz, who also helped finance the new Catholic high school, often simply referred to as "Memorial." Additions in the back have kept the school's facade much the same as it appears on this postcard. (EVPL and the Topper family.)

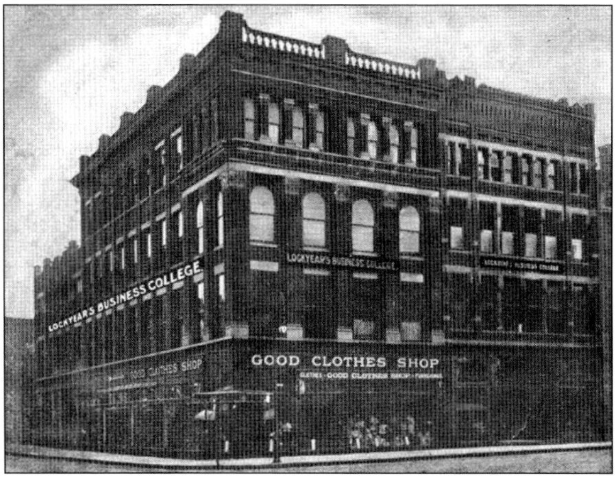

Lockyear's Business College was founded as Columbian Business College in 1893. This c. 1905 image shows the school occupying two buildings at the corner of Main and Second Streets. After Lockyear's moved to its new building (pictured below) in 1911, these buildings later housed the *Evansville Courier*. Both buildings were torn down around 1970 and replaced by the Midwest Federal Building that now houses some Evansville Vanderburgh School Corporation (EVSC) offices. (EVPL and the Topper family.)

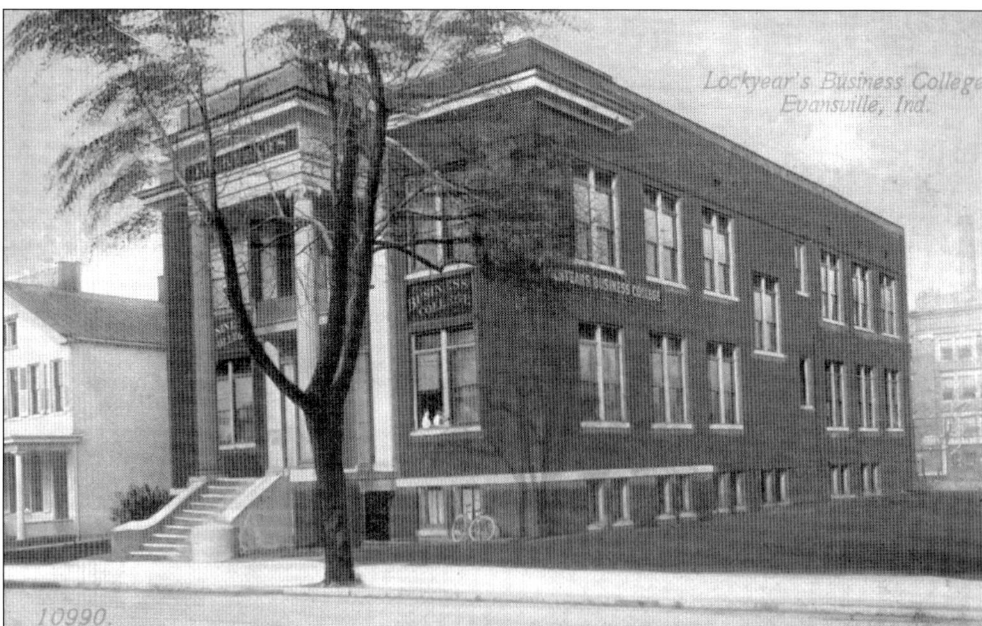

The new Lockyear's Business College building was erected in 1911 on Fifth Street across from the courthouse. This two-story Neoclassical structure was designed by architect F. Manson Gilbert. Lockyear's served the community for many years before going bankrupt and closing in 1991. This building was torn down in 1993, and the site is now a parking lot next to the YMCA (see page 121). (EVPL and the Topper family.)

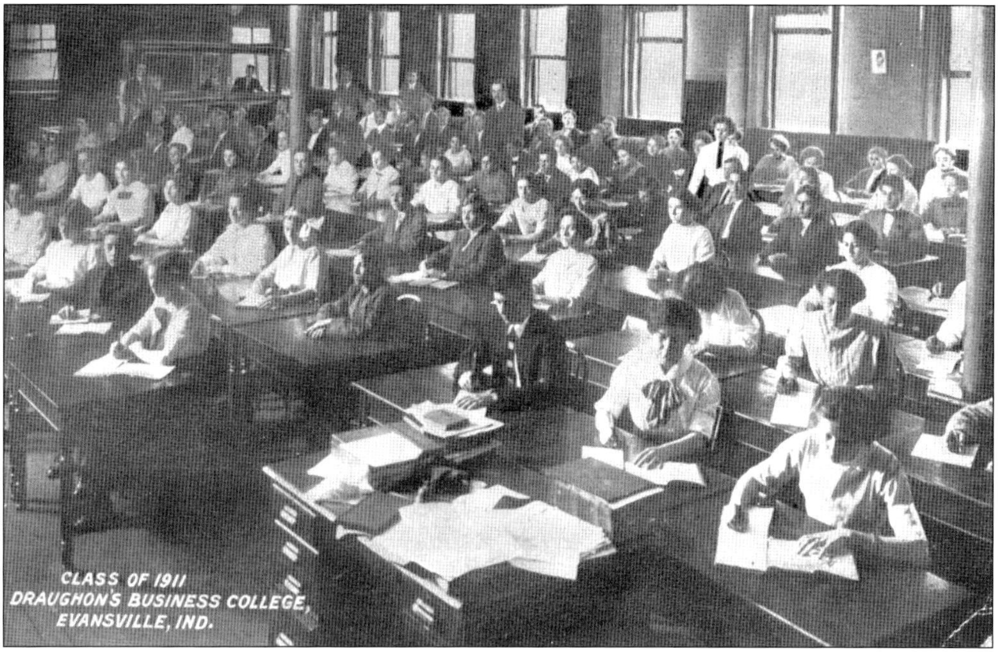

Originally located in the German National Bank Building at Main and Third Streets, Draughon's Business College was another post-secondary school. The postcard above shows the interior, where students learned skills like dictation or typewriting. When the YMCA moved out of its old building in 1914, the school relocated. The postcard below shows the Draughon-Porter Business College (after the school was renamed) in the old YMCA Building (see page 114) at Fourth and Sycamore Streets. This ornate building was torn down in 1928, when the Central Union Bank erected a skyscraper on the site. The new building, often called the Hulman Building, is now home to the Evansville Commerce Bank. (Both, EVPL and the Topper family.)

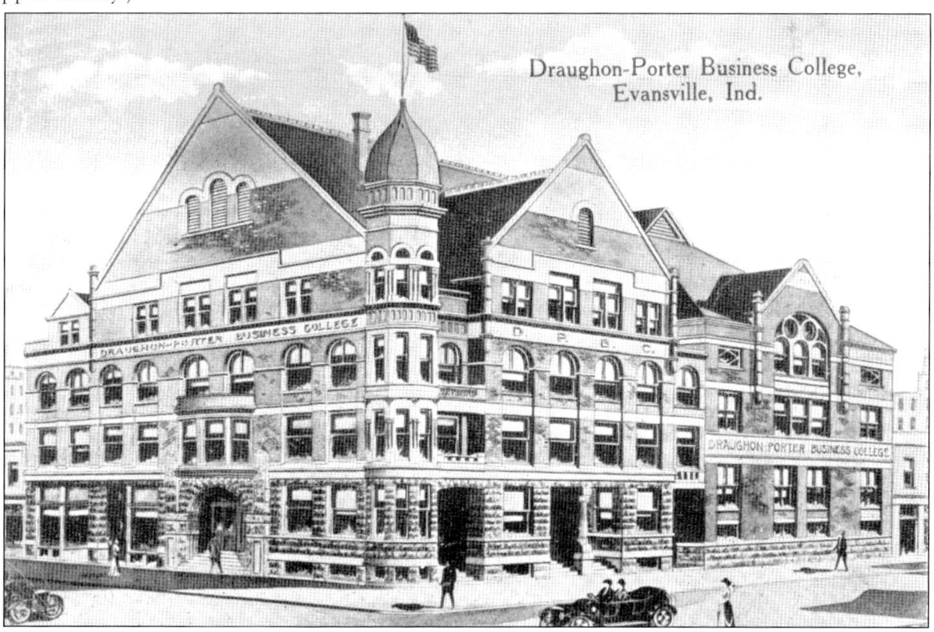

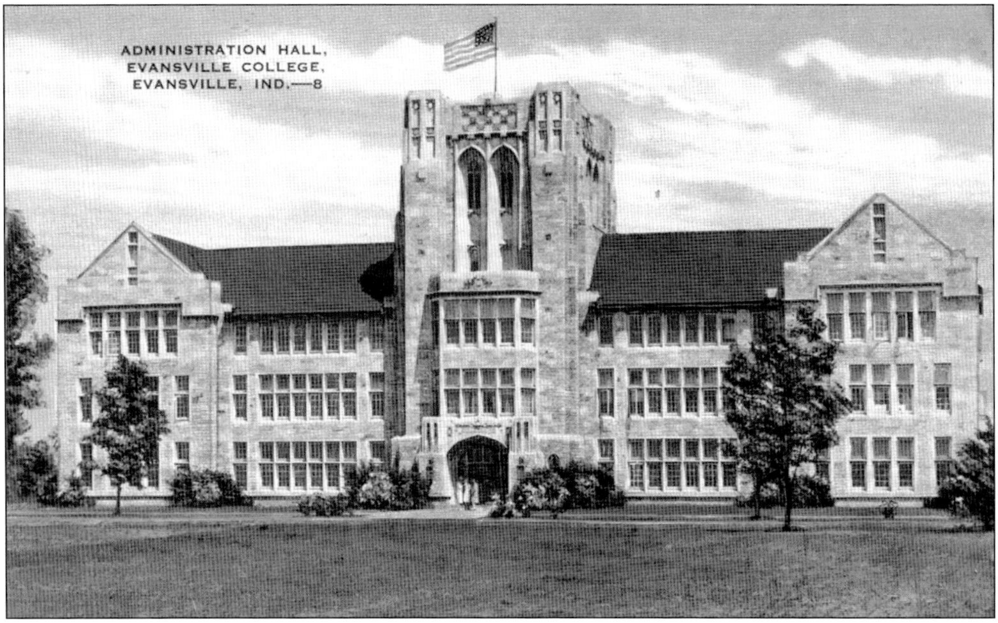

After a push by local bigwigs, Evansville College moved here from southeastern Indiana in 1919. Pictured here is Olmstead Hall, which was completed in 1922. The administration building was the first structure built on the campus and is still the focal point of the horseshoe off Lincoln Avenue. The college continued to grow and was renamed the University of Evansville in 1967. (Engler family.)

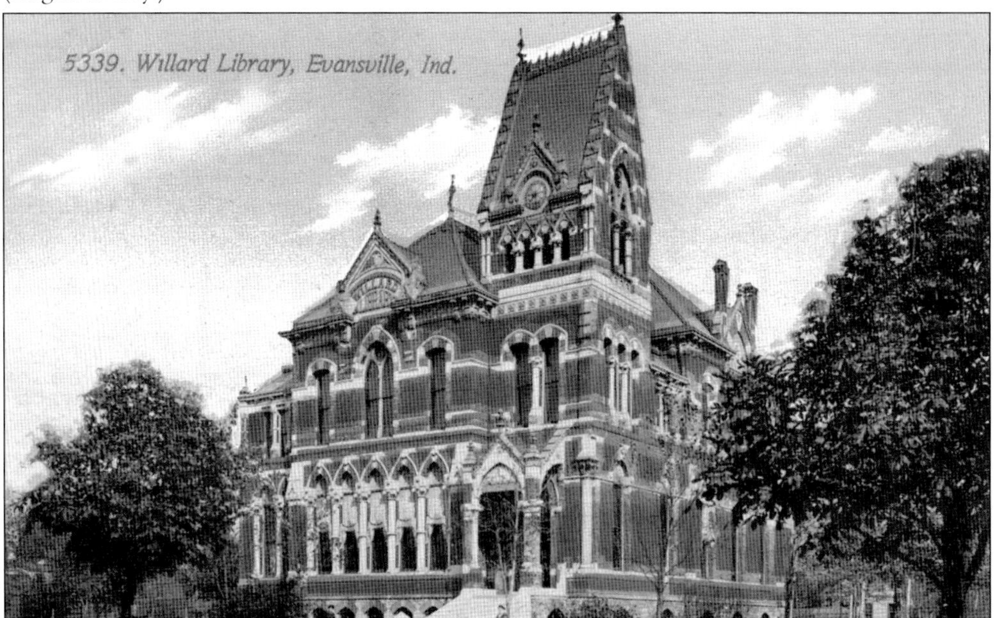

Willard Library, Indiana's oldest library building, opened in 1885. It was the generous gift of Willard Carpenter, who had originally hoped to build a college before a downturn in the economy led to a change of plans. Willard Library, which maintains the region's largest genealogy department, is also home of the famed Grey Lady ghost. (Engler family.)

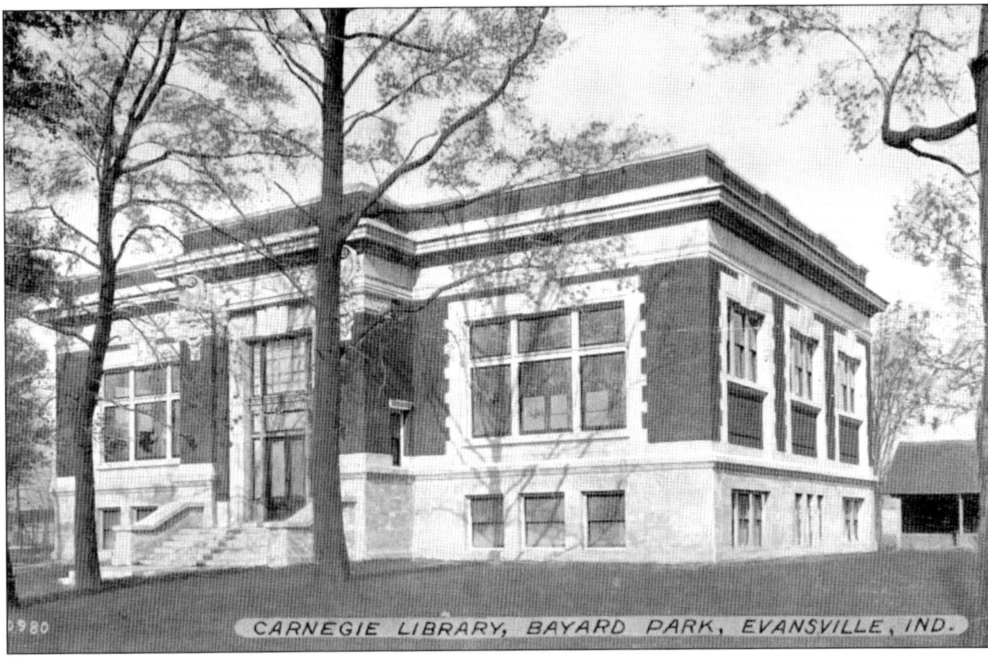

The East Branch (above) and West Branch (below) libraries were funded by steel baron Andrew Carnegie. All across the world, Carnegie would donate money toward the building of a library provided that certain stipulations were met. The twin libraries were constructed simultaneously in 1912 using plans drawn up by Clifford Shopbell & Company. The buildings were Neoclassical and built of redbrick and limestone with terra-cotta ornamentation. Each was situated in a park, close to a quiet place for meditation; the West Branch Library was built on the West Franklin Street Park (see page 110), and the East Branch was nestled near Bayard Park (see page 117). Both libraries were recently restored and still serve a high volume of patrons, just as they did a century ago. (Above, EVPL and the Geiss family; below, EVPL and the Topper family.)

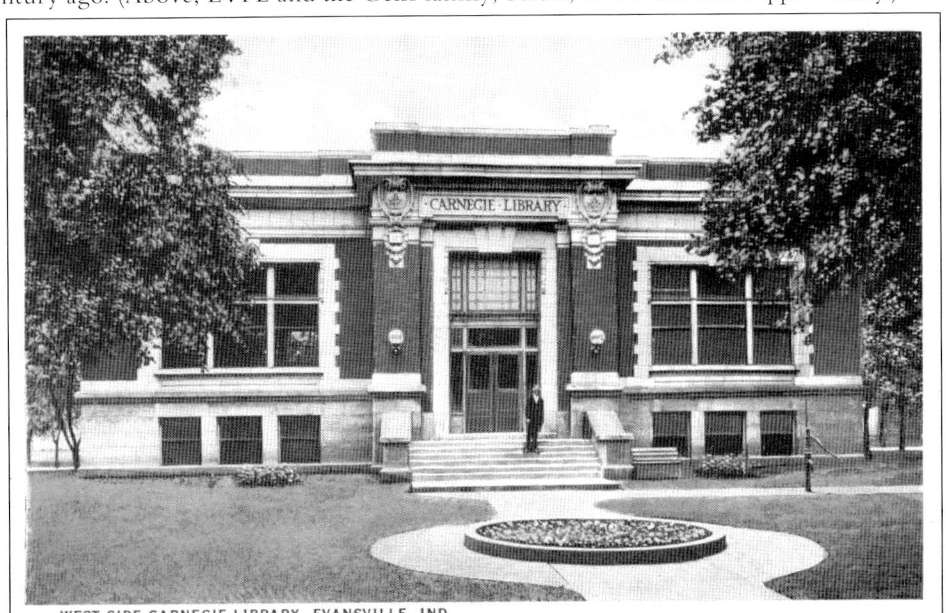

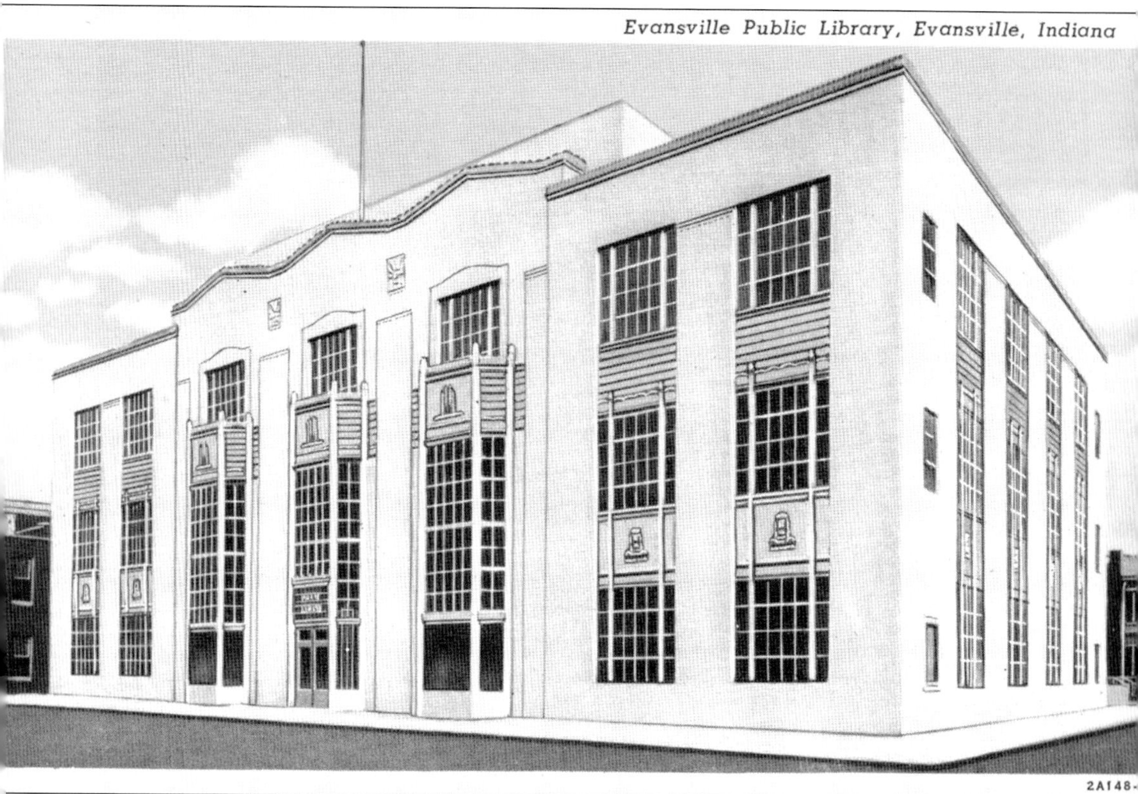

Central Library was built in 1931 on the former site of Evans Hall (see page 110). This Art Deco building at Fifth and Locust Streets served the library for over 70 years, though space was cramped. In 2004, the Central Library moved into spacious new headquarters on Martin Luther King Jr. Boulevard and Walnut Street. Soon after, the Children's Museum of Evansville (CMOE) took over this building. (EVPL and the Geiss family.)

Four

Business As Usual

Evansville's location made it an ideal place for businesses to take root. The Ohio River bolstered the area's economy, and river traffic brought a steady supply of goods to the new city.

From the onset, banks, hotels, and other businesses popped up to support the growing city. A store's proximity to the river ensured success, especially at a time when walking distance meant everything. Main Street was the center of the original city boundaries, and several of the most prominent stores were situated there. As Evansville grew, other streets, like Franklin Street on the West Side and North Main Street to the north, were soon lined with storefronts.

Foundries, breweries, and planing mills were some of the first companies to establish operations in Evansville. Several mills and other large corporations were located along the river or Pigeon Creek, as water was a key source of power. Coal found directly underneath the city also powered the area from the mid-1800s until World War II. Manufacturing ramped up in the late 1800s and early 1900s, and Evansville established itself as a producer of goods. The hardwood forests in the area supplied ample lumber for the furniture industry, which reached its peak here in the 1920s. The city also found a niche as the "refrigerator capital of the world," with three large companies producing units here.

For years, businesses were located in or near downtown, forcing once-residential areas to become commercial. However, space limitations saw several companies move to the outskirts of the city in the mid-1900s, leaving a void still felt downtown. Other businesses left town completely, though Evansville has shown resiliency; even today, the city has a strong economy and is the commercial center of the Tri-State area.

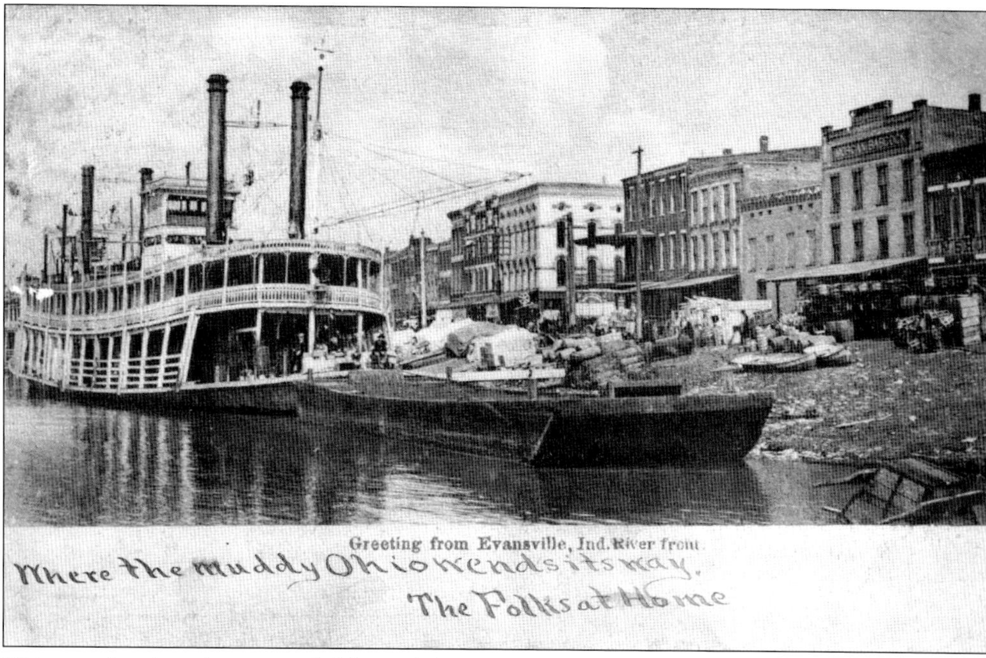

This was the view that greeted ships arriving in Evansville. Several boats along the Ohio River made their way to the wharf near the foot of Main Street. Goods that were brought into the city were transported into the stores pictured above. Location was vital because businesses closer to the riverfront attracted more walk-in traffic. (Engler family.)

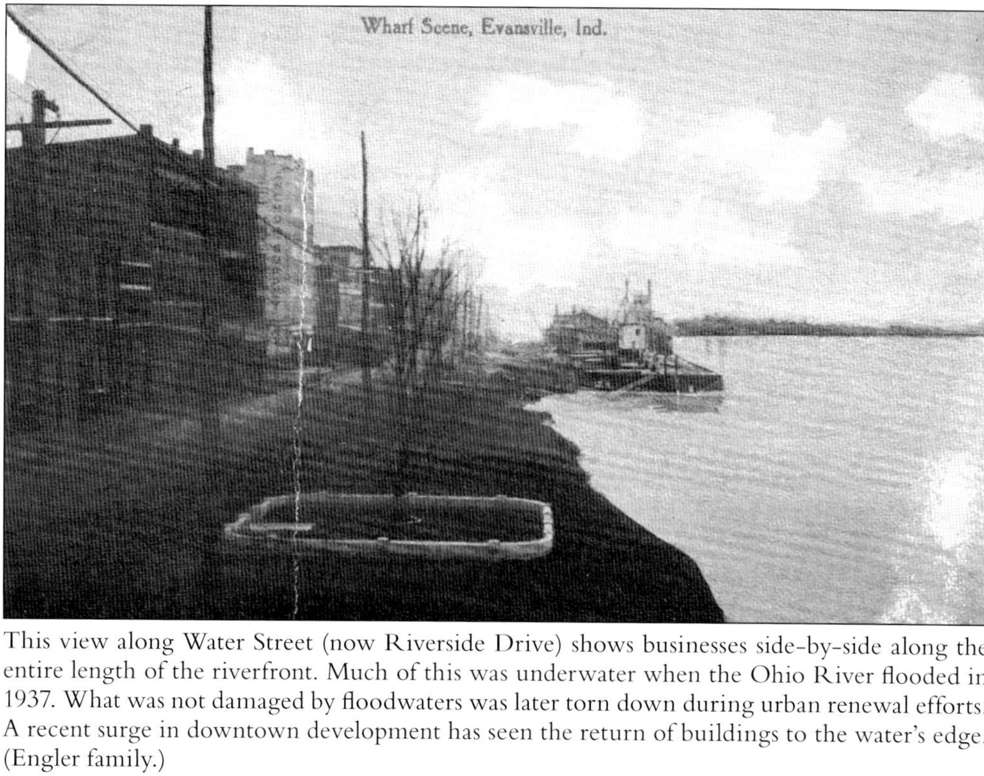

This view along Water Street (now Riverside Drive) shows businesses side-by-side along the entire length of the riverfront. Much of this was underwater when the Ohio River flooded in 1937. What was not damaged by floodwaters was later torn down during urban renewal efforts. A recent surge in downtown development has seen the return of buildings to the water's edge. (Engler family.)

Old State National Bank constructed this building in the 1830s on Main Street near the river. It was remodeled in 1855 to give it this distinctive Greek Revival look. The company, which was renamed Old National Bank in 1883, moved to a newer building farther up Main Street in 1916 (see page 73). The old building served as a Moose Lodge for years but was torn down around 1960. (Engler family.)

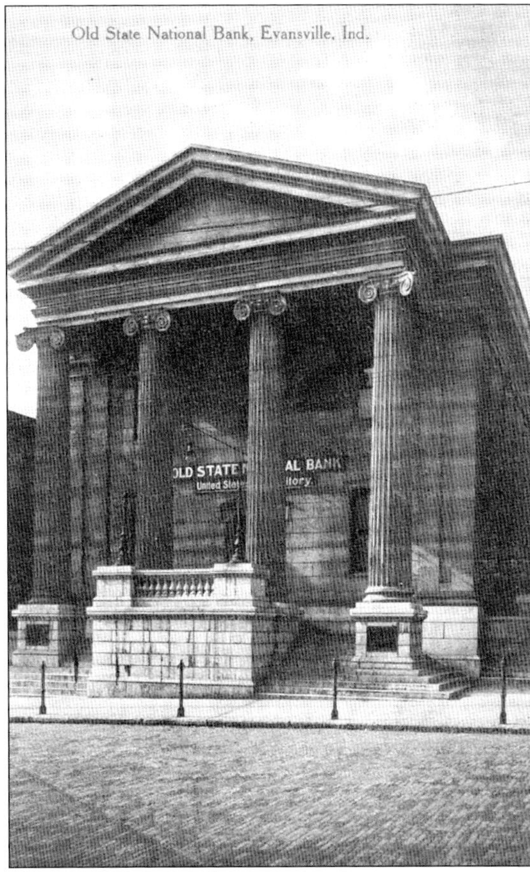

Vulcan Plow, at the corner of First and Ingle Streets, dates back to 1847, when Heilman Plow Works was established. After the company was renamed Vulcan Plow in 1890, a statue of the Roman god Vulcan was placed atop the building. The majority of this building was demolished during urban renewal in the 1950s. A portion of the stables (right) is all that remains from the old plow works. (EVPL and the Topper family.)

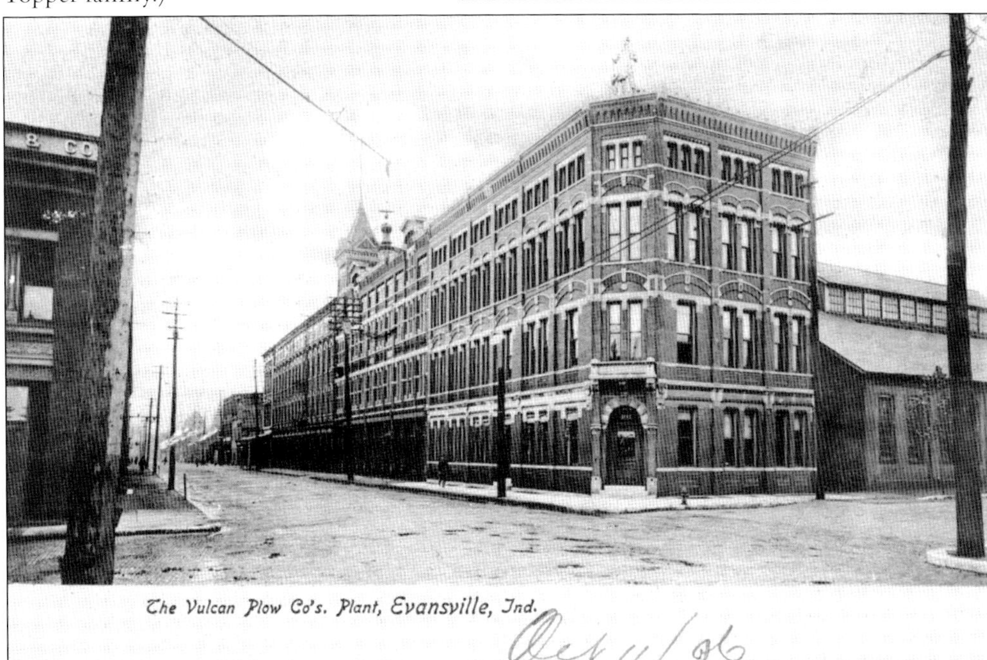

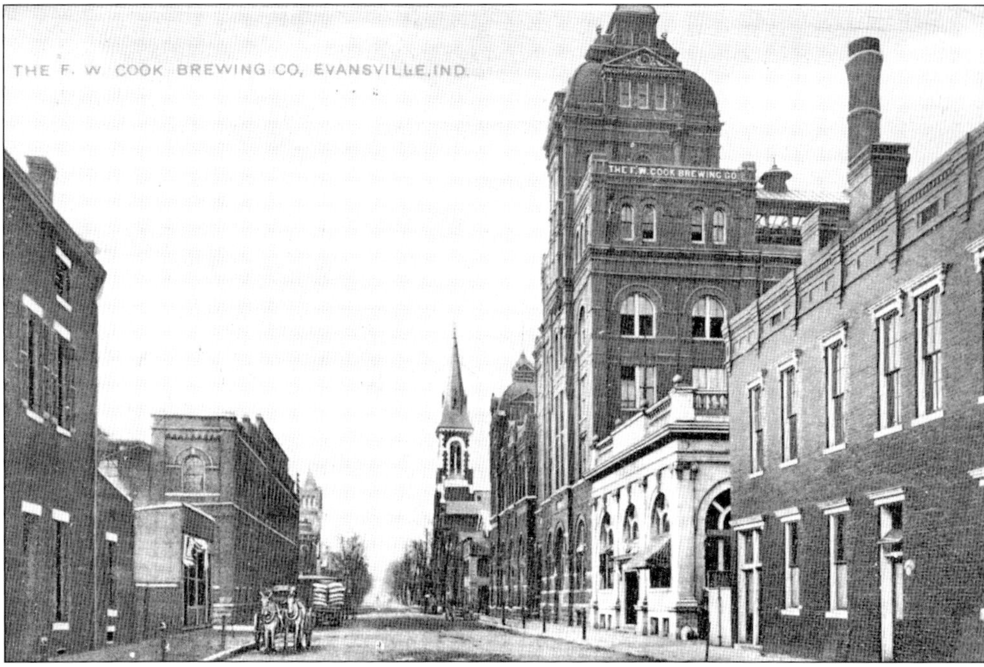

When the Frederick W. Cook Brewing Company opened in 1853 on Seventh Street (now Martin Luther King Jr. Boulevard), it was far removed from downtown. By the time of the above postcard, the brewery was in the thick of urban growth. The office (white building) and brewery (large building at right with dome) pictured above were new structures built in the 1890s after a destructive fire. The German Room (pictured below) was a drinking spot where workers and others could sample the beer. The growing brewery also built a bottling works across the street (left), stables, and a warehouse, occupying much of the adjoining blocks. In 1957, the brewery went out of business, and the entire complex was soon razed for the civic center. (Above, estate of Pam and Dennis Beadles; below, EVPL and the Geiss family.)

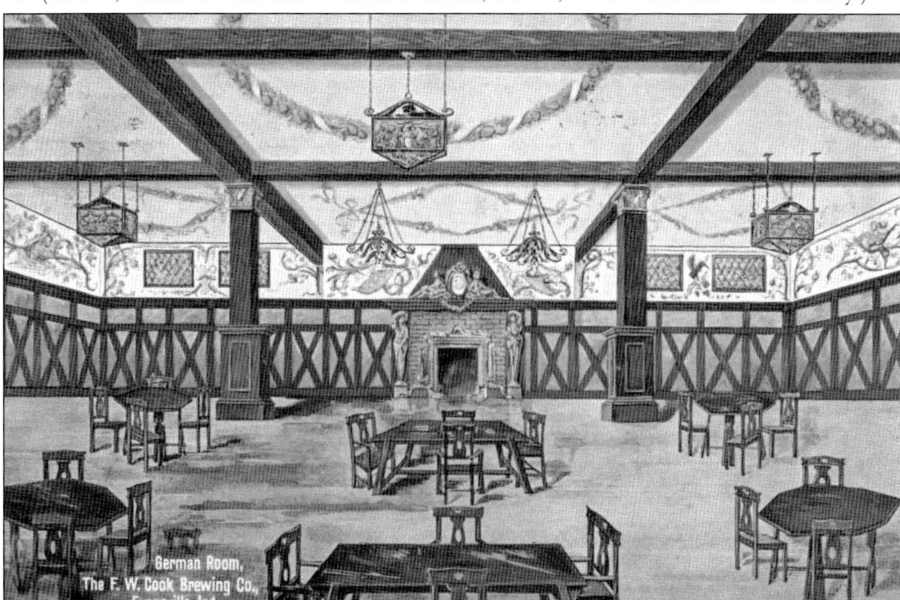

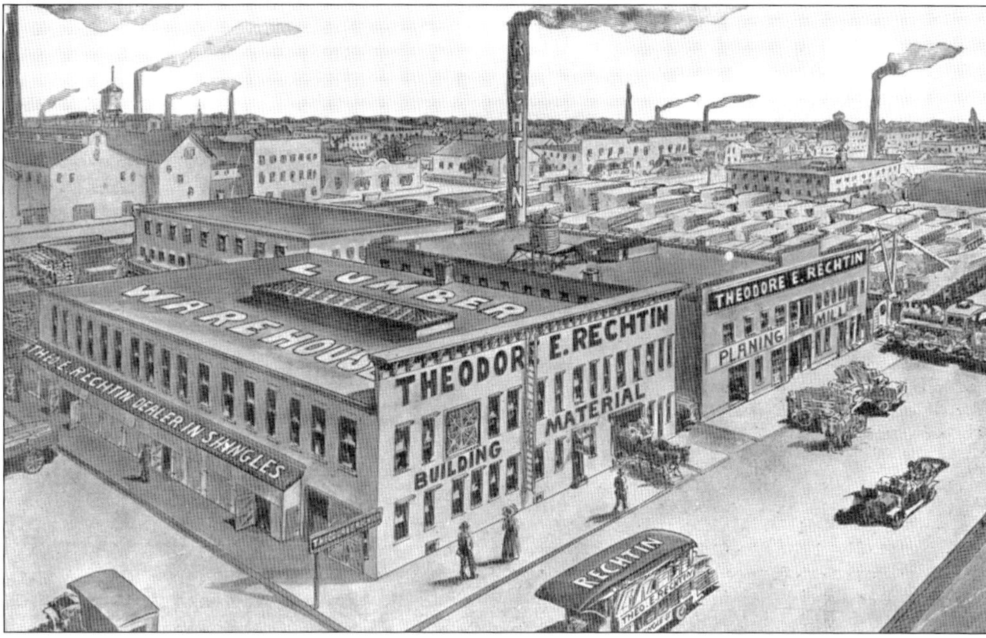

Rechtin Lumber built this mill in 1872 on the east corner of Seventh and Ingle Streets. The company, which supplied lumber for a multitude of Evansville's homes, expanded across Ingle Street around 1905. By 1950, the building had been demolished, and the site was used as an athletic field for Old Central (High School). Nothing remains of the old lumber company since the Lloyd Expressway claimed much of this land. (EVPL and the Topper family.)

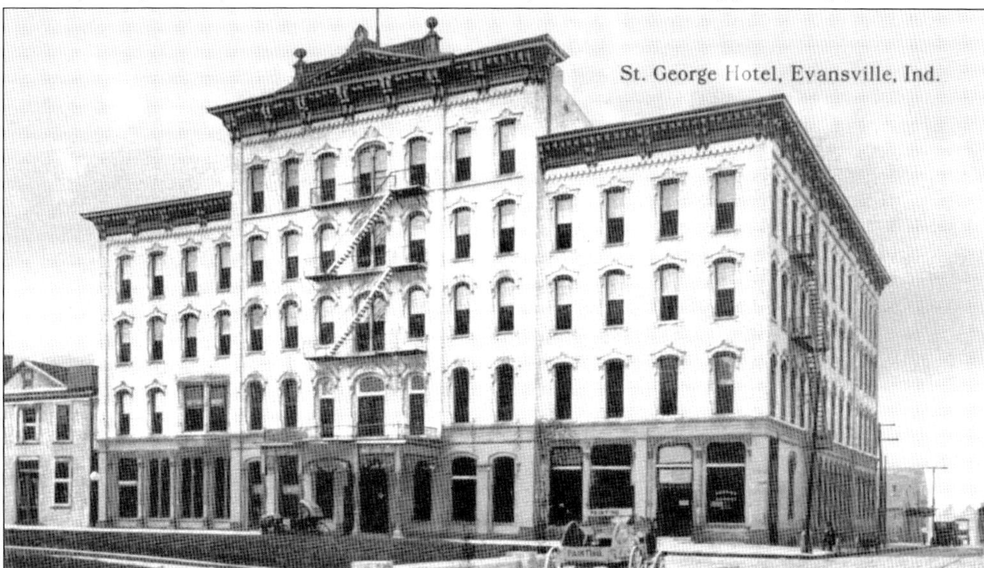

On the same site as the McCurdy (see page 74) was another once-grand hotel, the St. George. It was built by entrepreneur David J. Mackey in 1874 and was Evansville's largest and most exclusive hotel. After prospering for years, the hotel was considered dated and in need of modernization, and in 1915, Mayor Benjamin Bosse spoke at the farewell ceremony, after which the St. George was razed. (Engler family.)

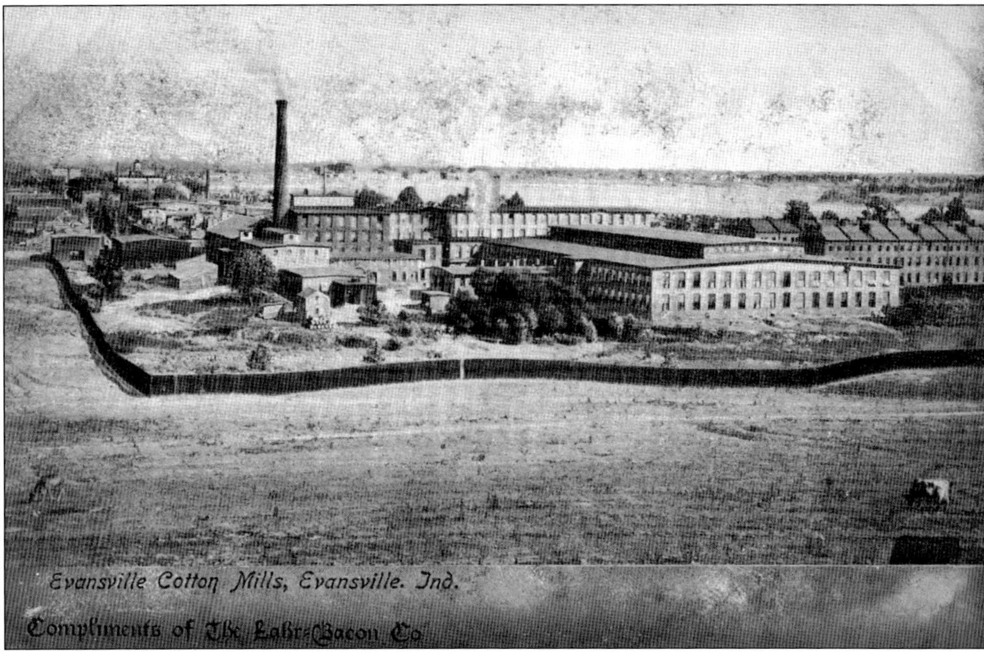

The Evansville Cotton Mill erected a plant in 1875 at the base of Coal Mine Hill on the West Side. The postcard above shows the an eastward view of large facility with the Ohio River and downtown in the background. The mill employed so many people that housing (far right) was built for its employees. The Evansville Cotton Mill closed in 1910, but E. Mead Johnson relocated his company from New Jersey to be nearer to resources. Since operations began in 1916, Mead Johnson Nutrition has been headquartered in Evansville. Several additions make the original mill hard to recognize, but one of the original buildings along St. Joseph Avenue (below) is easily visible from the road. (Above, Engler family; below, EVPL and the Geiss family.)

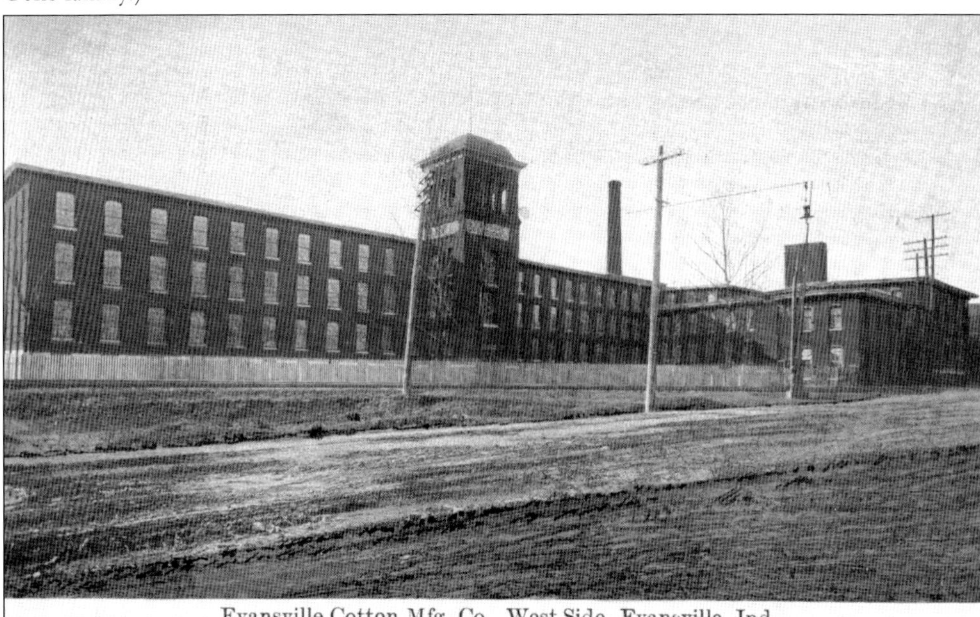

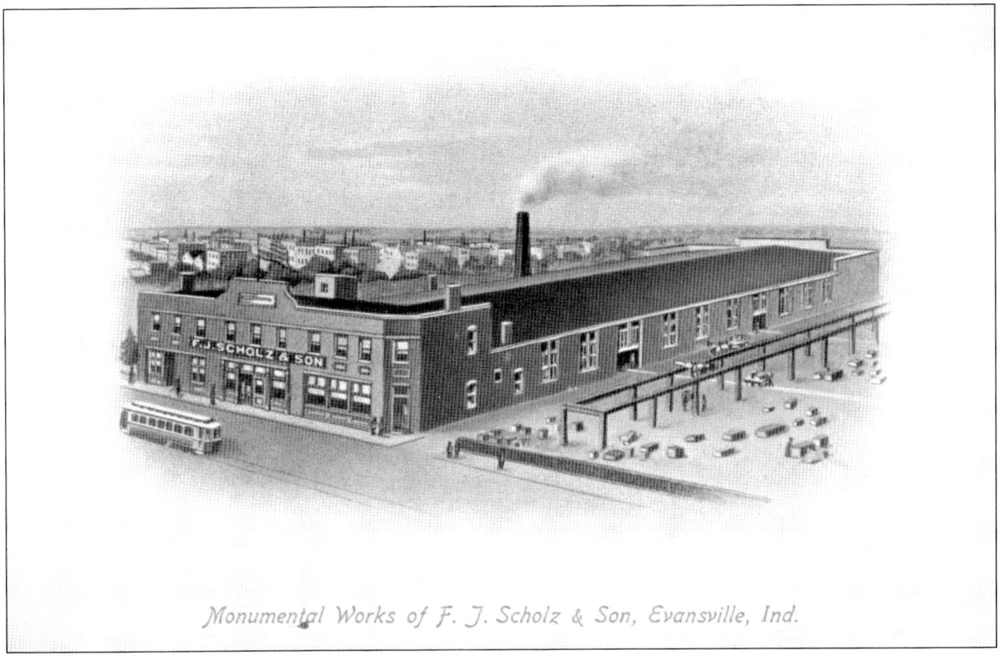

Scholz Monument Works, located on Third Street, was founded by F.J. Scholz around 1870. The company specialized in marble and granite monuments, many of which still stand in Oak Hill Cemetery. By the time it incorporated in 1905, Scholz was reputed to be the largest retail monument dealer in the country. Sometime around 1960, the company closed and was torn down for parking for the neighboring St. John's United Church of Christ (see page 18). (EVPL and the Topper family.)

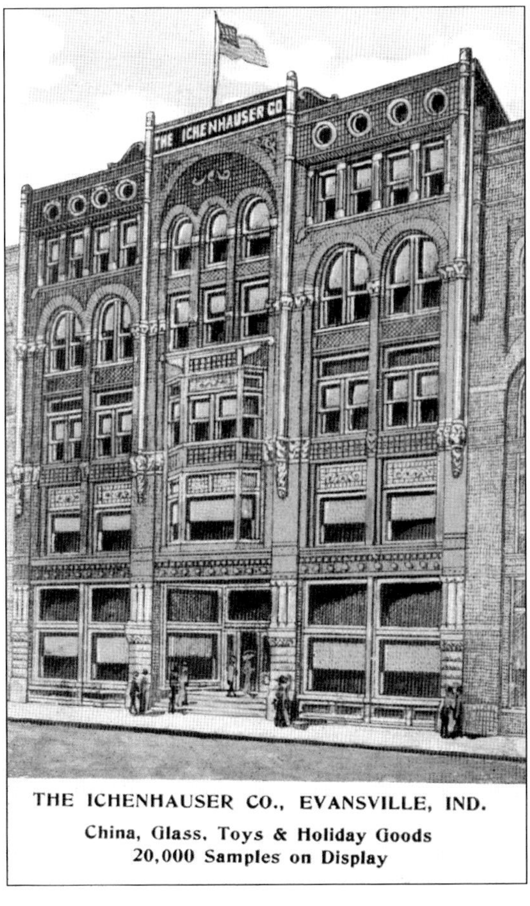

The Ichenhauser Company, established in the late 1800s, was a wholesaler in china, glassware, and other goods. The building itself was the Mackey Building, built by entrepreneur David J. Mackey in 1889. For a while, it also served as the downtown offices and showroom of Armstrong Brothers Furniture. Around 1940, this building on First Street was torn down, and Rose Bowl Lanes was built on the site. (EVPL and the Topper family.)

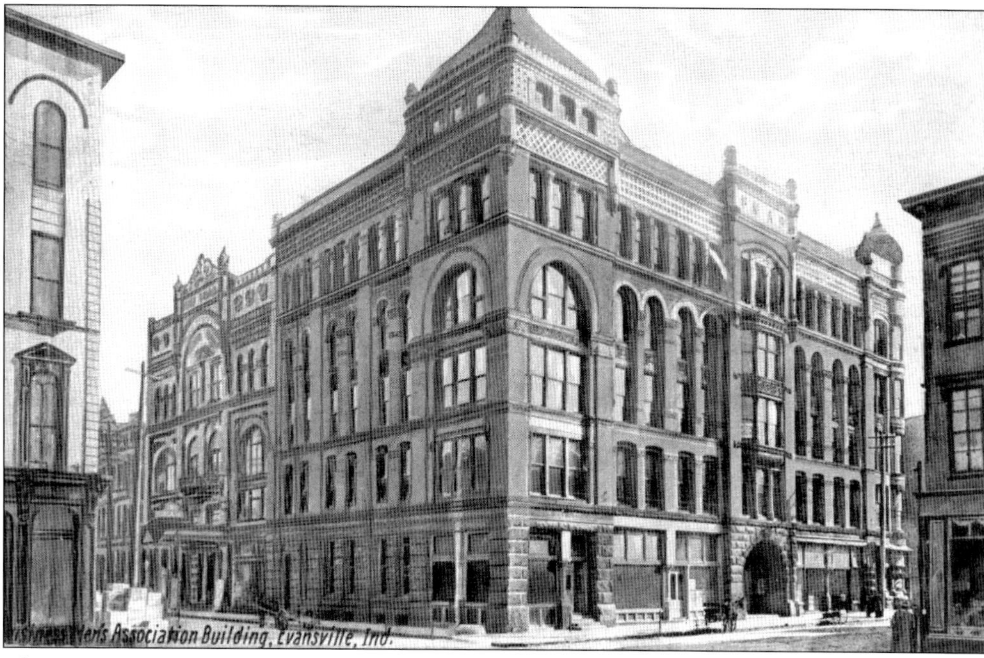

The Business Men's Association (BMA) erected this building around 1890 catercorner from the old post office. Along with the adjoining Grand Opera House (see page 113), the two occupied the quarter block of Sycamore and Second Streets. The building was later known as the Waverly Building and, later still, as the Grein Building. Sadly, it was razed in the 1970s, and this site is now home to the Fifth Third Bank parking garage. (EVPL and the Geiss family.)

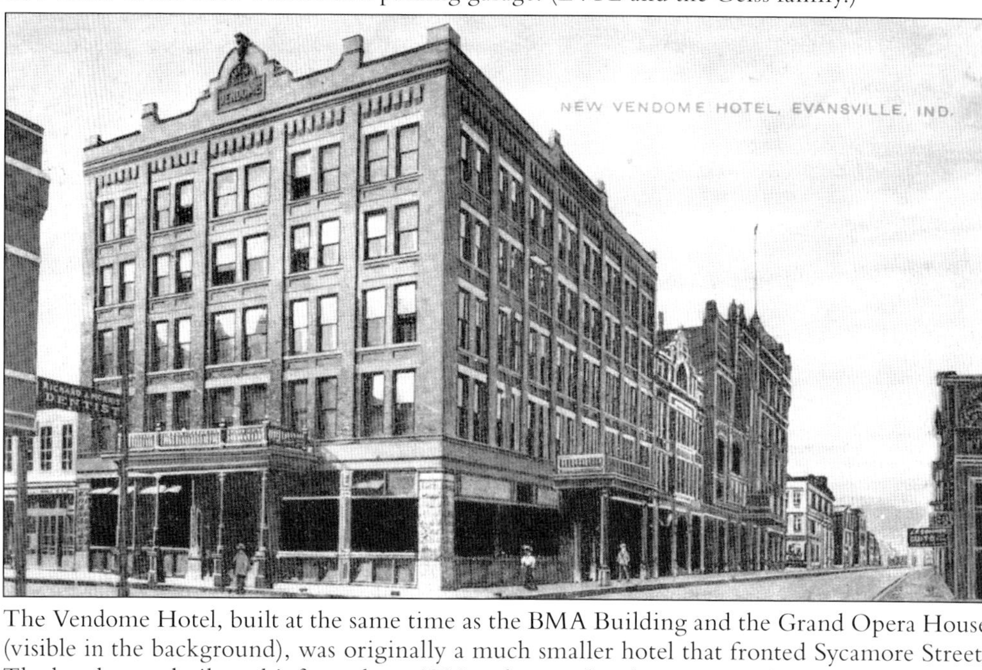

The Vendome Hotel, built at the same time as the BMA Building and the Grand Opera House (visible in the background), was originally a much smaller hotel that fronted Sycamore Street. The hotel was rebuilt to this form about 1908 and opened as the New Vendome Hotel. The new building, which now faced Third Street, claimed to be "one of the finest hotels in the nation." (Engler family.)

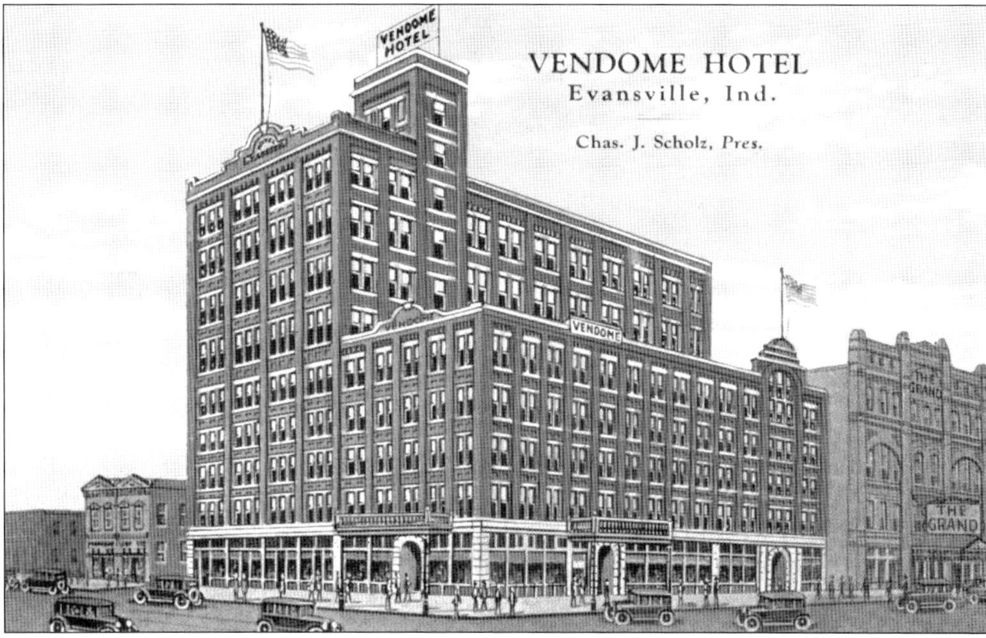

The Vendome Hotel expanded twice more by 1927 and became the behemoth shown here. The nine-story hotel at Third and Sycamore Streets now occupied a quarter block. The Vendome stayed open for years but finally closed about 1970. It was torn down, and the new Citizens Bank Building (now Fifth Third) was built on the site in the 1980s. (EVPL and the Topper family.)

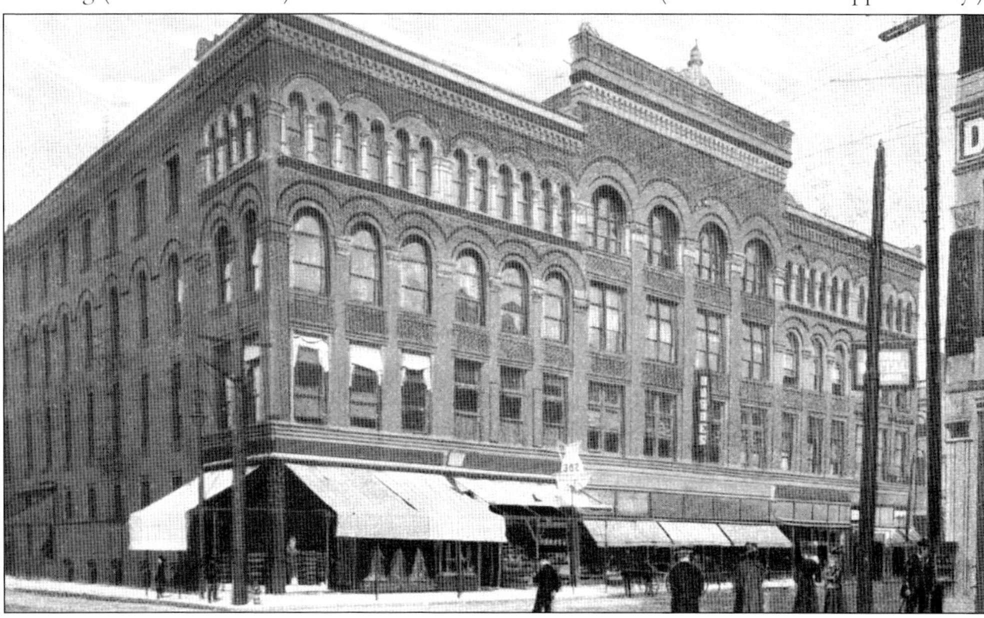
The four-story Eichel Building was erected in 1892 at the corner of Third and Main Streets, on the site of an old courthouse. The corner section of the building was occupied by insurance companies for years. Part of the building was remodeled as DeJong's department store around 1930 after fire damaged the middle section. Large fires in 1951 and 1984 left few remains of the original building. Recently, it has been remodeled as the Meridian Plaza condominiums. (Engler family.)

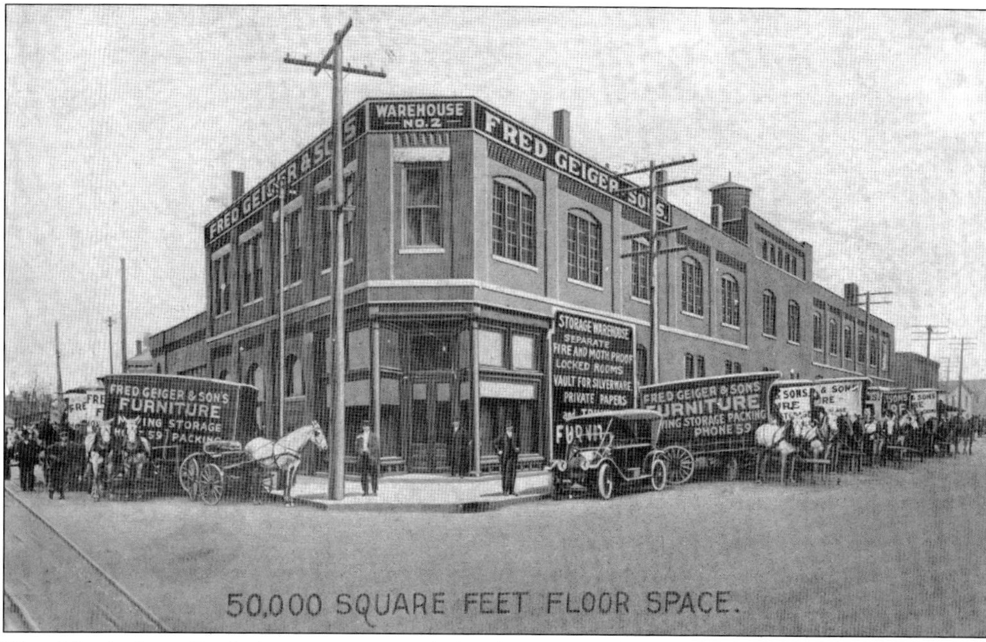

The Marsh-Scantlin Bakery constructed this building, which was designed to contour the angled intersection on the corner of Second and Ingle Streets, in 1894. The bakery was later bought out by the National Biscuit Company (Nabisco). Since the 1920s, Fred Geiger & Sons has occupied this spot, though the company became an affiliate of United Van Lines around 1960. (EVPL and the Topper family.)

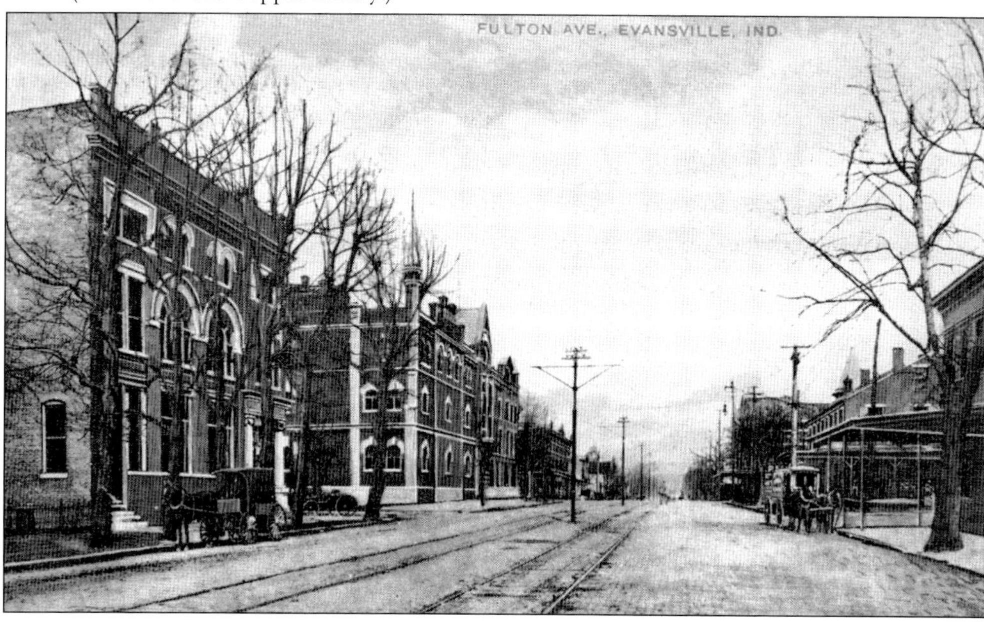

The Fulton Avenue Brewery (later the Sterling Brewery) is at left in this c. 1900 view of Fulton Avenue near Pennsylvania Street. After the Evansville Brewing Co. failed to revive the city's brewing industry, the building was demolished in 1998. Much of this view has been obstructed by the new Lloyd Expressway overpass. The taller commercial buildings in the distance at right are about the only ones still standing. (Engler family.)

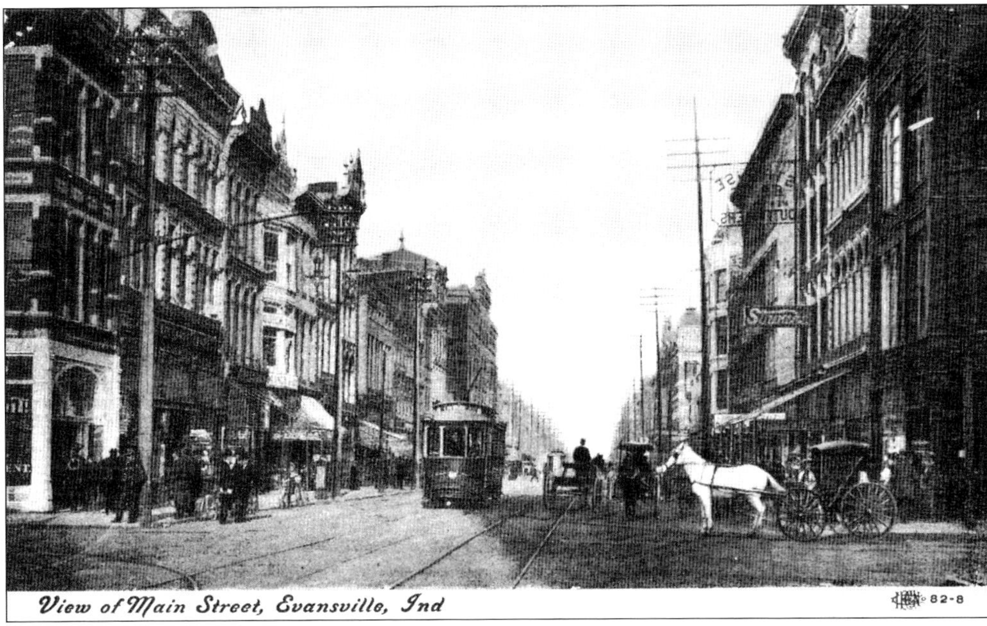

A view of Main Street from Second Street depicts the hustle and bustle of downtown at the beginning of the 20th century. The Bitterman Building (on the corner at left) is still standing and now operates as Salad World restaurant. On the opposite side of the street (at right) is the old Strouse's apparel store; these buildings on the corner were replaced by a contemporary building following a fire in 1945. (Engler family.)

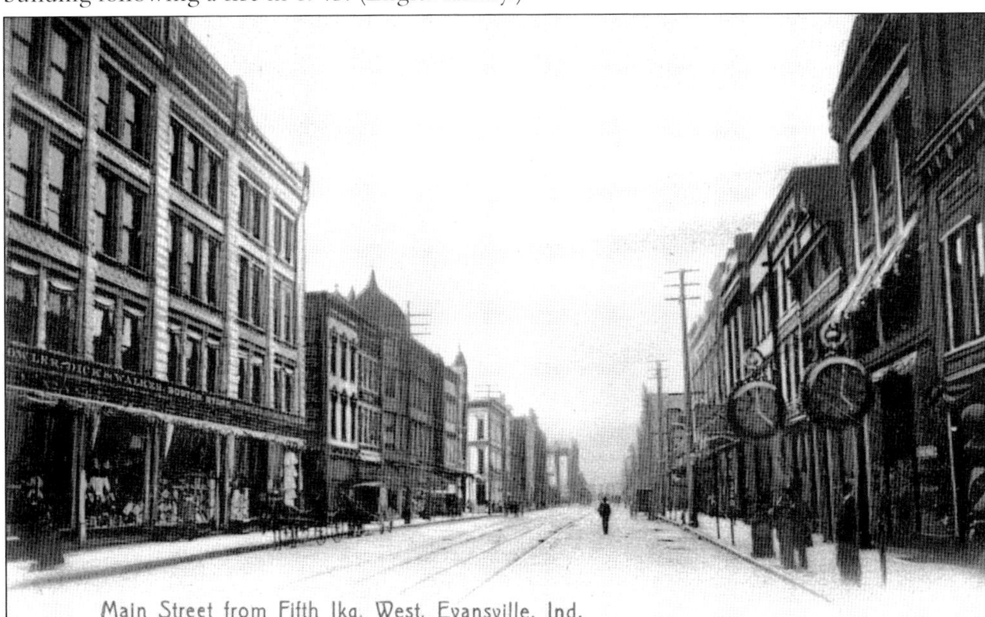

This early-1900s postcard shows a view of Main Street near Fifth Street looking toward the river. The large building at left was the Fowler Dick & Walker Boston Store, erected around 1890 using oolitic limestone. The five-story building, which later became Neisner's, was razed around 1970 and is now a parking lot. Next to it is the Barrett's Britz Building, which most recognize by its present tenant, the Jungle Restaurant. (Engler family.)

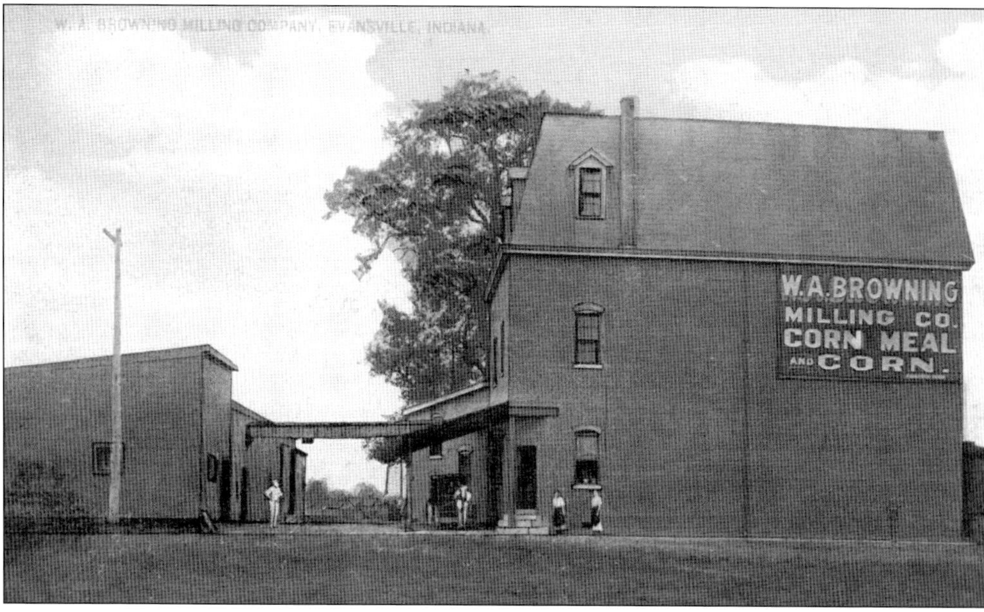

Browning Milling Company was established at the corner of Kentucky Avenue and Canal Street around 1900 and specialized in the manufacturing of cornmeal. In 1935, the mill became the Wittekindt Brewing Company, and a rear addition was built. The brewery closed just six years later, a victim of the Depression. Although the rear portion still stands, the original building has been razed, most likely when Highway 41 was rerouted around 1970. (EVPL and the Topper family.)

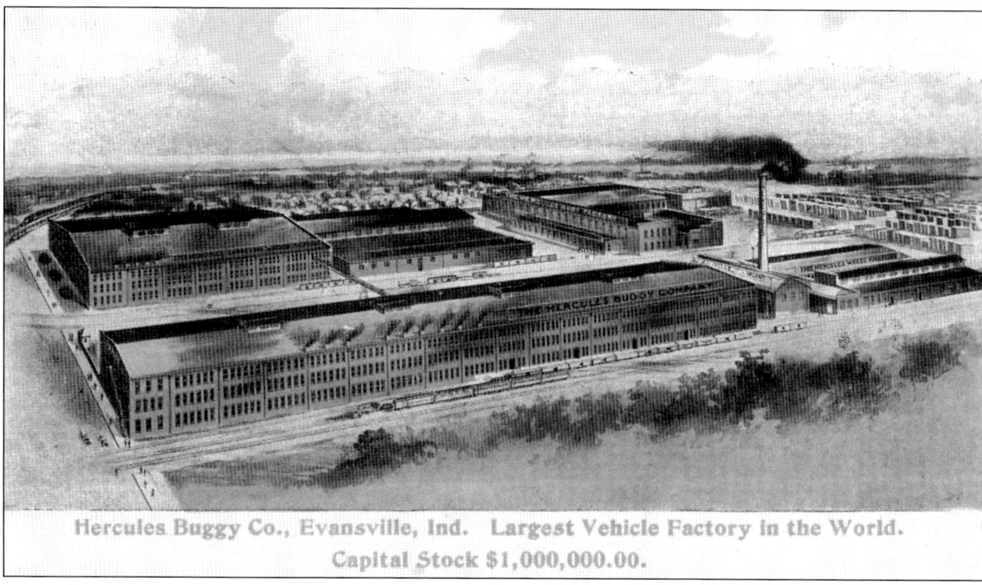

Hercules Buggy Company moved from Cincinnati in 1902 and built this factory on Morton Avenue. The company experienced substantial growth while adapting to the automobile industry. In 1925, the facility became home to Servel, producer of refrigerators. Servel, which produced wing panels and gun casings during World War II, went bankrupt in 1957. The complex is now the Morton Avenue Warehouse, which provides warehousing and services for small- and medium-sized businesses. (EVPL and the Topper family.)

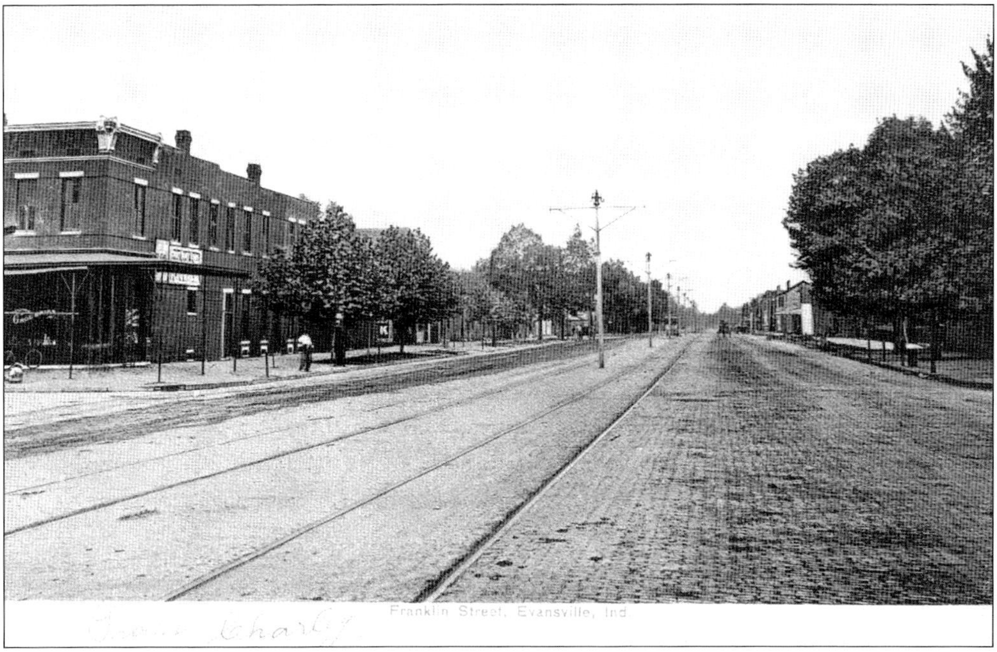

Streetcar service helped the city to expand, and businesses began to pop up around town to support growing neighborhoods. This view shows a route along Franklin Street in the early 1900s. At left, on the corner of Sixth Avenue, is Peter Detroy's grocery store, which is now home to Lamasco Bar and Grill. (Engler family.)

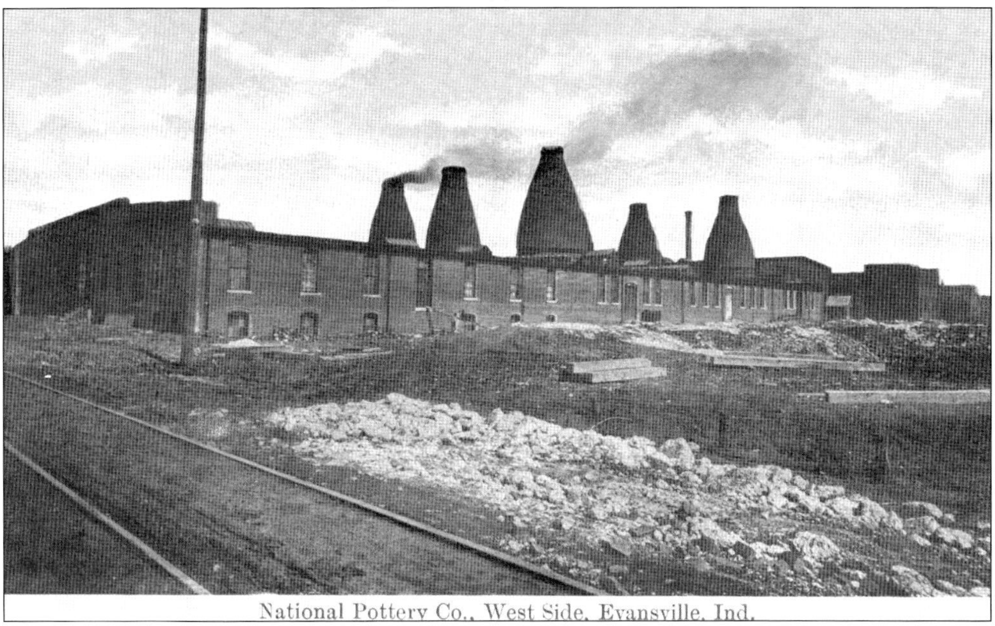

National Pottery established this plant on St. Joseph Avenue around 1902. The company was later renamed National-Helfrich Potteries Co. and, later, Peerless Pottery. After closing in 1978, Peerless was bought by Bootz Industries, which still uses much of the plant. The original building was torn down, however, and a McDonald's was built on this site. (EVPL and the Topper family.)

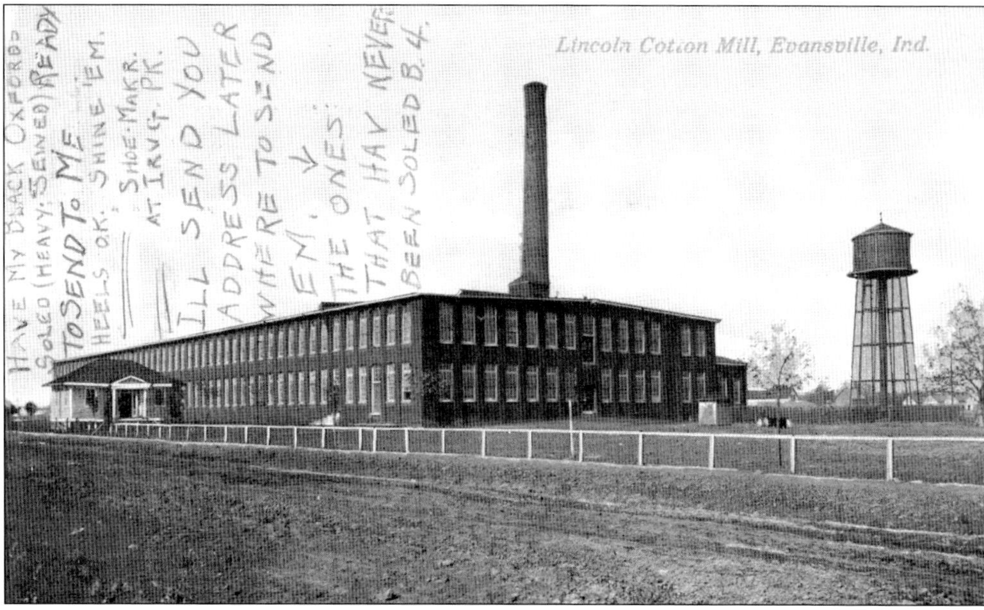

Lincoln Cotton Mill incorporated in 1902 and built this mill on Park Street near the Belt Railroad. The small office building in the side yard at left was originally a house in Howell that was moved to this site. By 1960, the company had closed, and its building became part of Whirlpool's facilities. The old mill was recently used by Metal Classics, Inc., but has since been abandoned. (EVPL and the Topper family.)

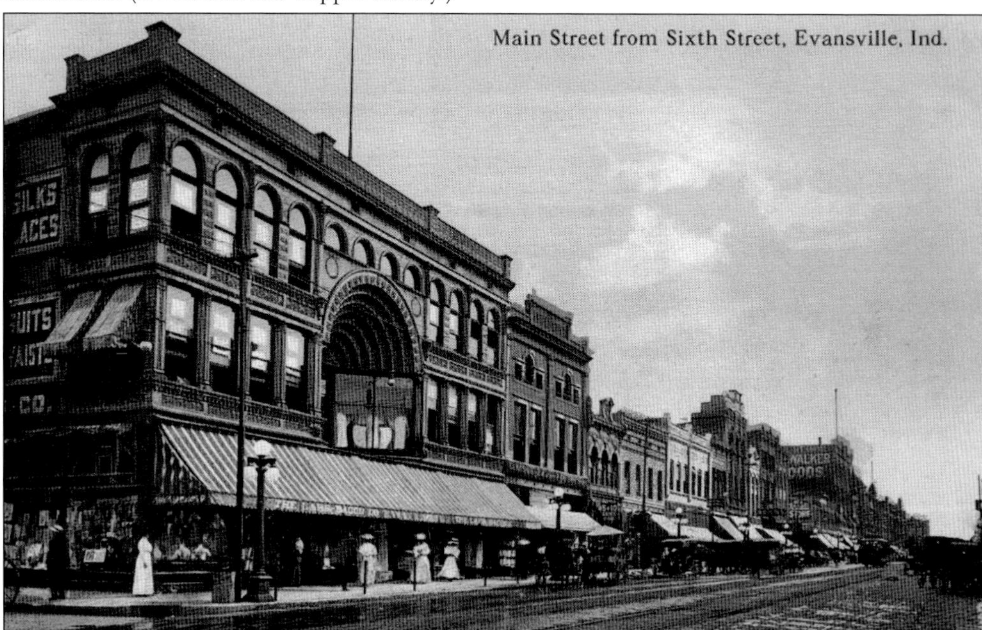

This view of Main Street near the start of the 20th century shows the Lahr-Bacon Department Store at the corner of Sixth Street. It later became the H.E. Bacon Department Store and was remodeled in the 1930s as a Woolworth's. The Keck Building next door still stands, but many of the other stores along the 500 block were razed in the 1960s to make space for the Union Federal Building. (Engler family.)

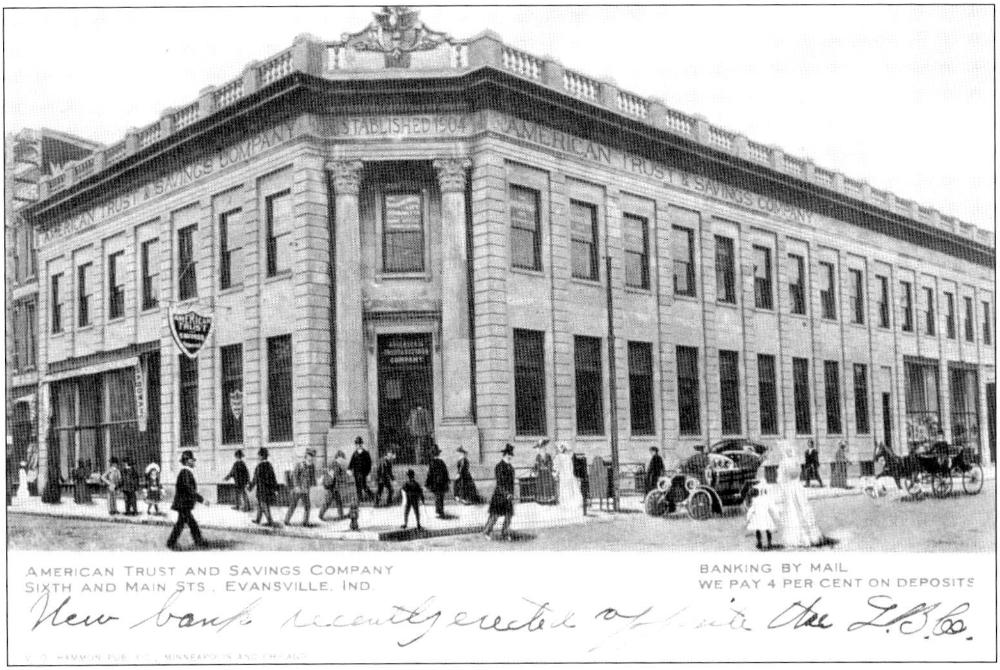

The American Trust & Savings Bank built this two-story structure in 1904 across from the Lahr-Bacon Department Store. It was designed by Harris & Shopbell in the Beaux-Arts style and is full of detail. Two Corinthian columns adorn the entrance, and the name, date, and motto of the company are carved into the stonework at the top. The bank at the corner of Main and Sixth Streets prospered, and in 1913 two additional floors were added to the top. The new American Trust Building also leased office space. In 1931, the Depression caused the bank to close. The building now houses offices, including the main office of the Evansville Icemen hockey team. (Above, EVPL and the Topper family; below, EVPL.)

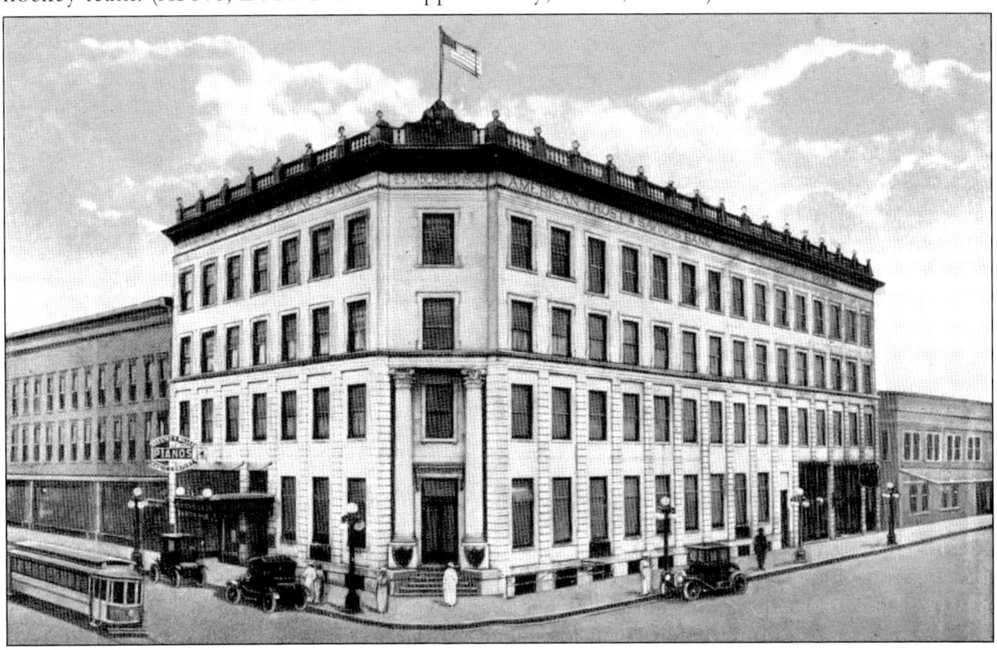

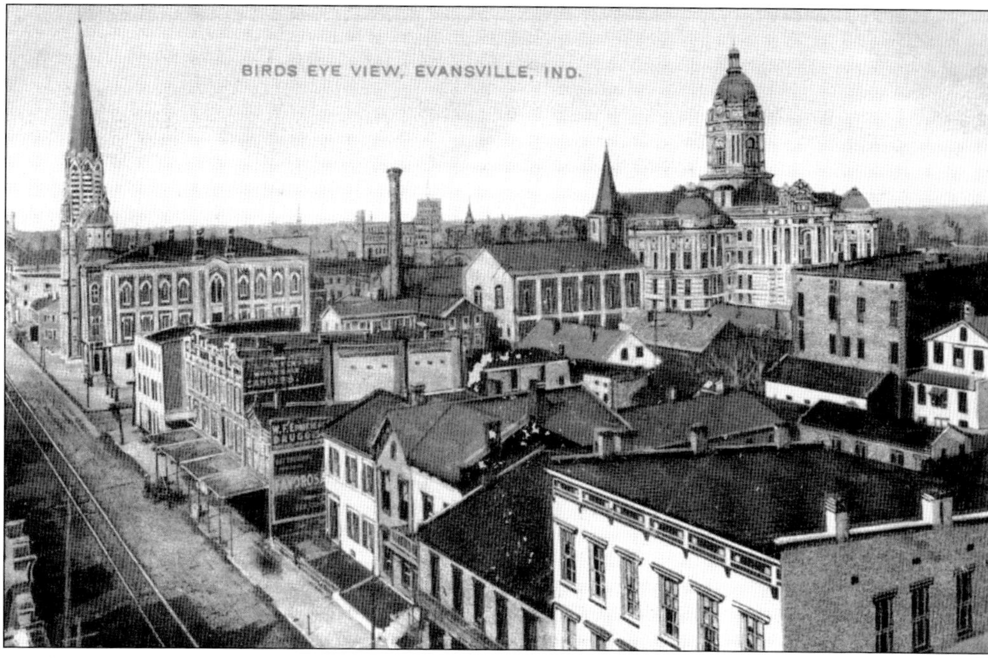

By the early 20th century, commercial buildings had phased out residential ones downtown, as seen in this bird's-eye view from the Vendome Hotel. Holy Trinity Church and the old courthouse frame this view, with Third Street running along the left side of the image. The second building from right at the bottom of the image will be familiar to many as Café Venice. (Engler family.)

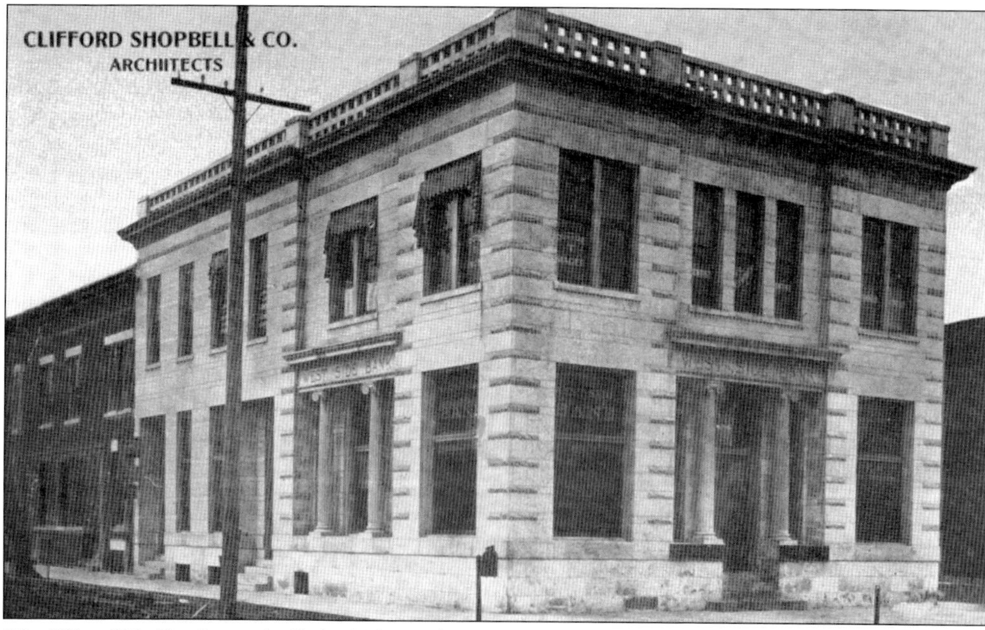

The West Side Bank was built in 1906 at the corner of Franklin Street and Eleventh Avenue. A c. 1920 addition seamlessly blended the old and new and nearly doubled the size of the bank. A victim of the Depression, West Side Bank closed in 1932. First Federal Bank opened a branch office here in 1935, which still operates today. (EVPL and the Topper family.)

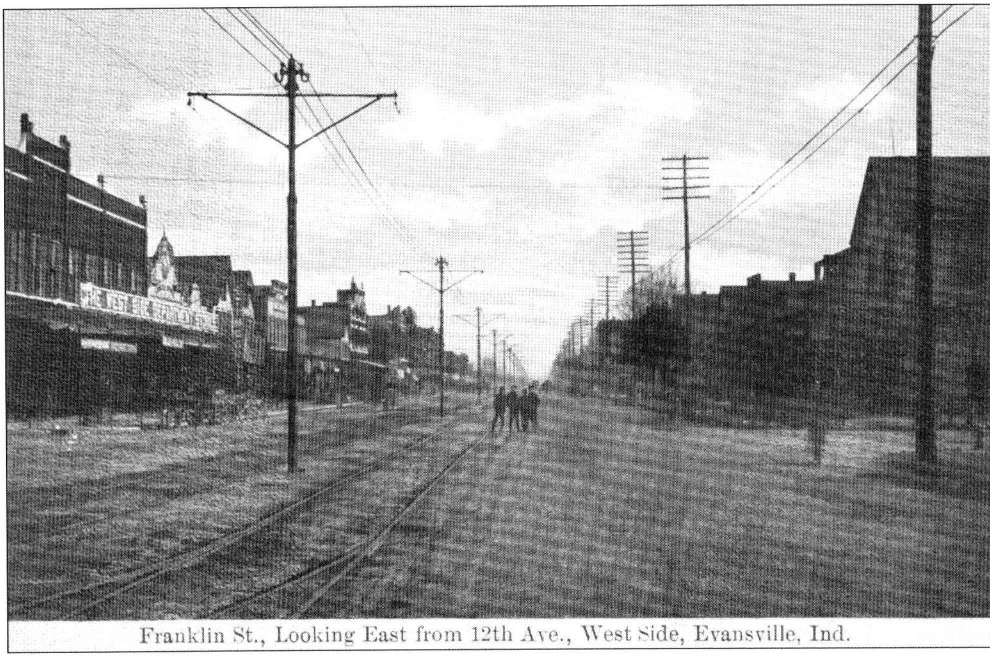

Continuing on the West Side, this is Franklin Street looking east from Twelfth Avenue. The West Side Department Store is the large building at left. It was built as an investment property by Jacob Folz Jr. in 1904 and is shown here after a 1905 addition. Streetcar tracks run down the middle of Franklin Street, and several boys pose in the center for the picture. (Engler family.)

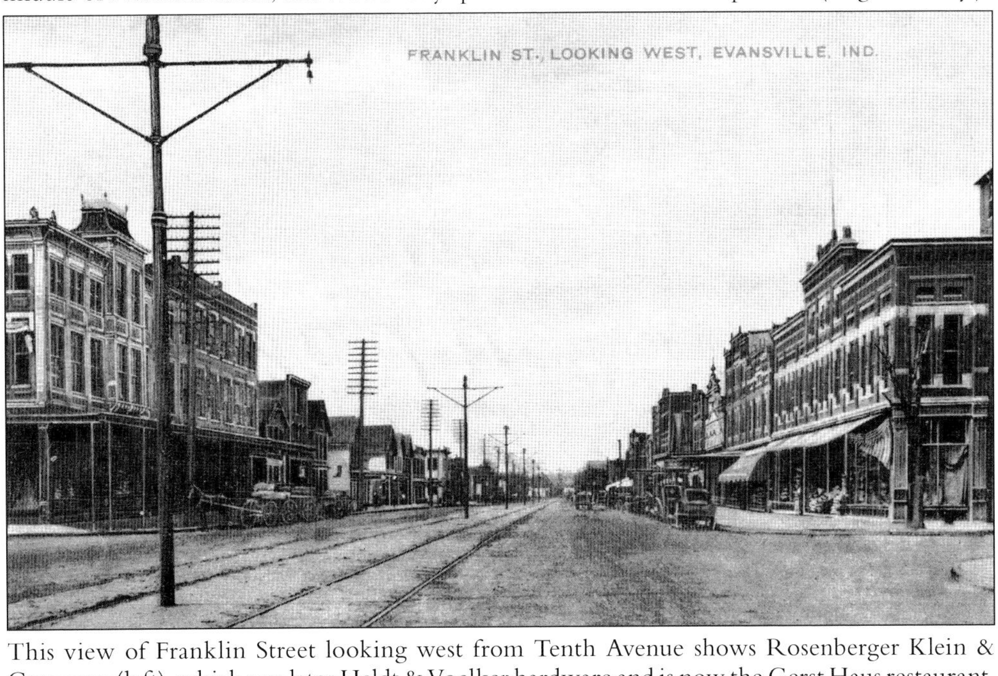

This view of Franklin Street looking west from Tenth Avenue shows Rosenberger Klein & Company (left), which was later Heldt & Voelker hardware and is now the Gerst Haus restaurant. A warehouse of similar proportions once stood next to it but has since been removed. On the opposite corner is the Scherffius Building, which later became a Kroger. It burned down in 1957, was later replaced by Jerry's Market, and is now a parking lot. (Engler family.)

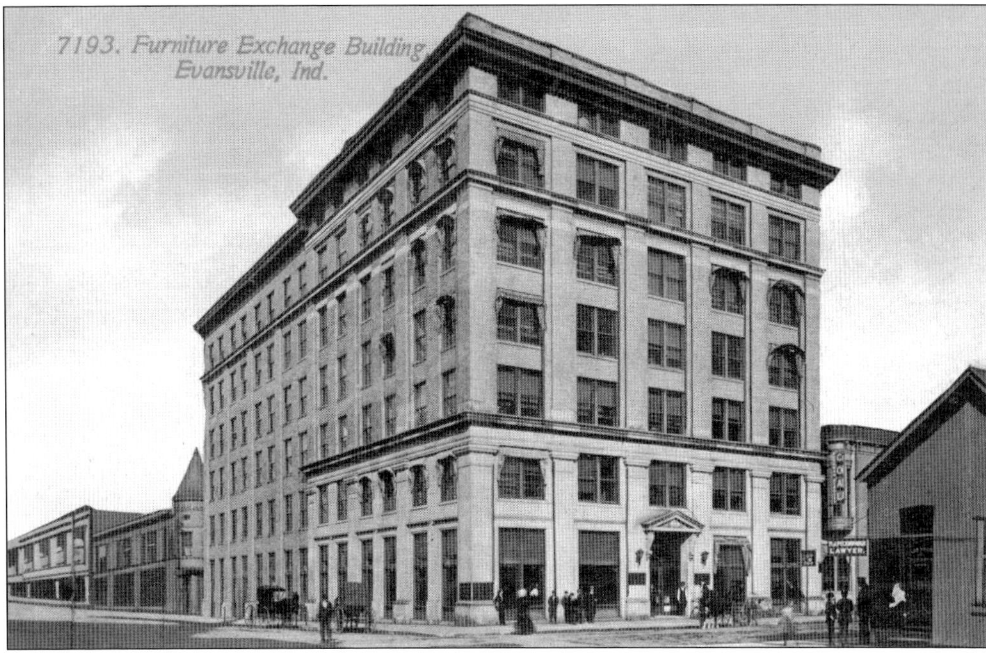

The Furniture Exchange Building was constructed in 1909 to showcase the products of local furniture companies. The buff brick building was designed by the architectural firm Harris & Shopbell and featured 60,000 square feet of display space. Situated at the corner of Fourth and Vine Streets, it has gone by the name Court Building since 1940. The owners of the building now lease it for office space. (EVPL and the Topper family.)

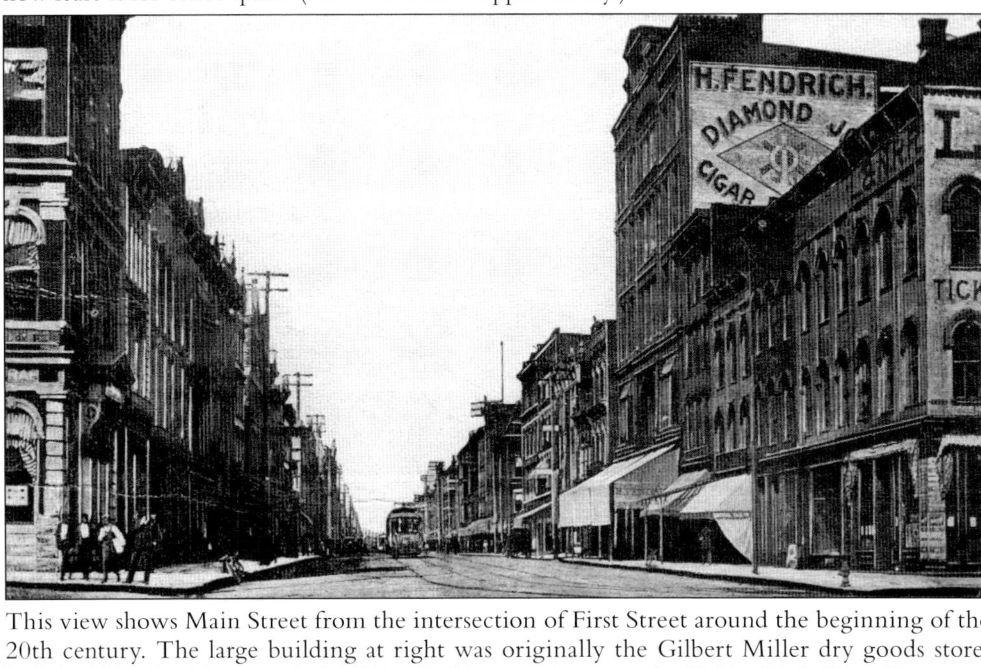

This view shows Main Street from the intersection of First Street around the beginning of the 20th century. The large building at right was originally the Gilbert Miller dry goods store, built in 1885. By this time, the building had become home to the H. Fendrich Cigar Company. The Merchants' National Bank (on the corner at left) was built in 1874 and served as the headquarters for the Royal Order of Lions in the 1920s. (Engler family.)

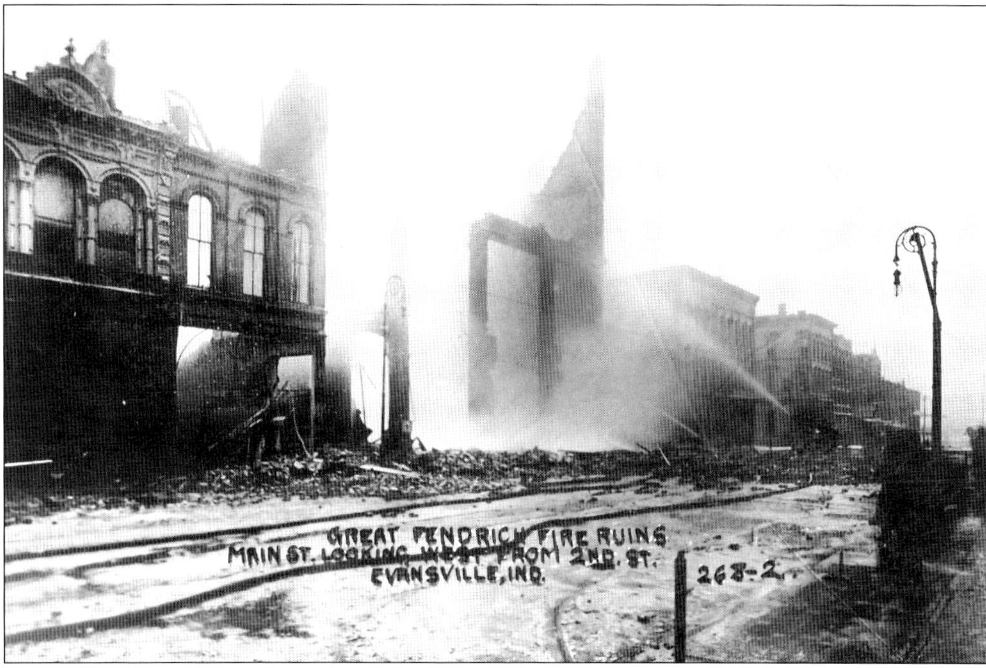

Here is the H. Fendrich Cigar Building after it was destroyed by fire on December 6, 1910; an old fire pump is still hosing down the ruins. The damage extended to several of the surrounding buildings, which all had to be rebuilt. The Buckskin Breeches Company constructed a new building on this site in 1912. (EVPL and the Topper family.)

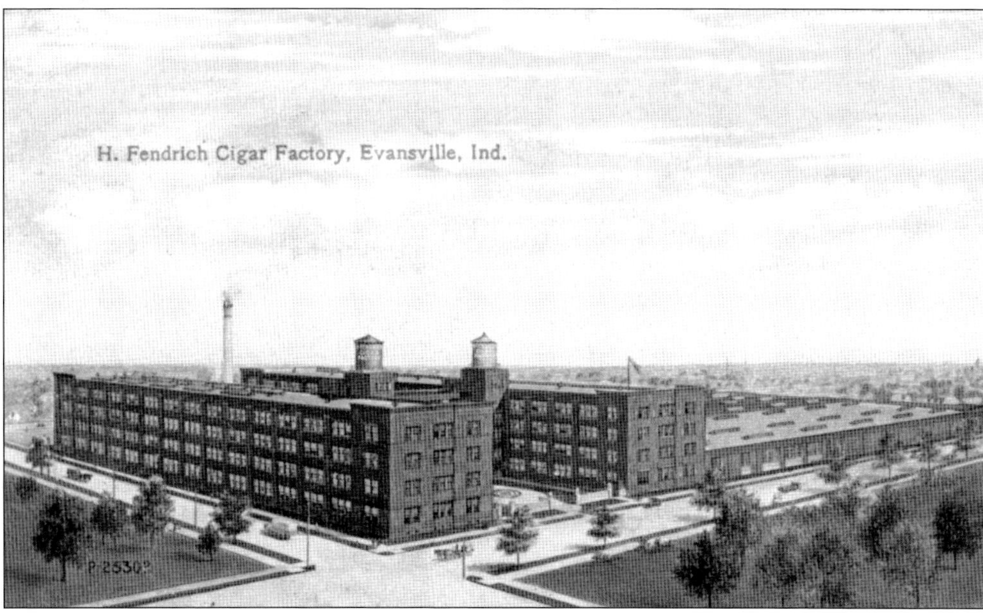

H. Fendrich Cigar opted to build a new plant away from downtown after the 1910 fire. A spot was chosen on Oakley Street near Illinois Street, and construction soon began. The "world's largest cigar factory under one roof" opened in 1912. After Fendrich closed in 1969, Imperial Plastics (which was later renamed Berry Plastics) moved in. Subsequent expansions by Berry have claimed several city blocks that were once residential. (EVPL and the Geiss family.)

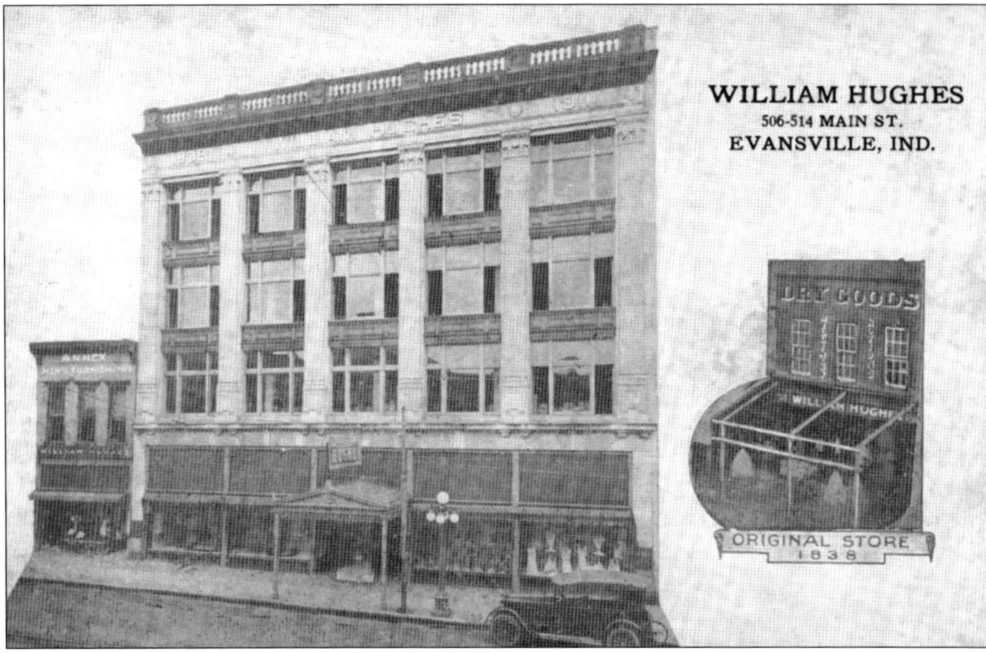

Hughes Department Store was built in 1911 on the 500 block of Main Street. It was later the Evansville Dry Goods store, but most will remember this as the JCPenney building, with its covered up facade. The company, one of last to abandon the downtown area, moved to Eastland Mall in 1981. After several years of sitting vacant, the Hughes Building was converted into the Renaissance on Main condominiums in 2006. (EVPL and the Topper family.)

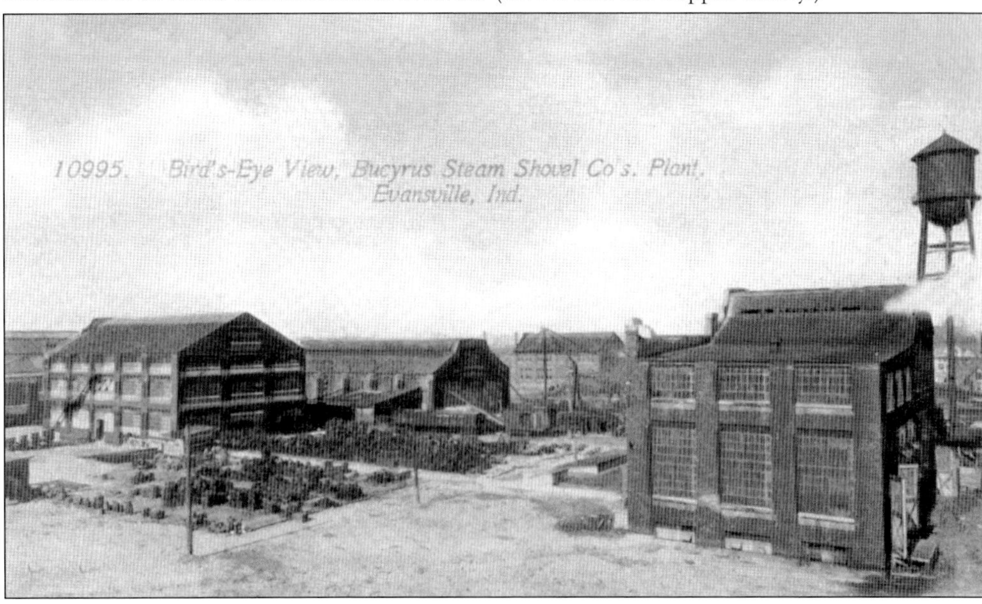

Bucyrus Steam Shovel Co. built this plant on Decker Avenue (now Claremont Avenue) and opened for operations in January 1912. The company employed a large number of people and spurred residential growth west of Reitz Hill. It was renamed Bucyrus-Erie in 1928, and the bulk of the complex still stands. The main office building, which was added later, once housed a nightclub and is now home to a church. (EVPL.)

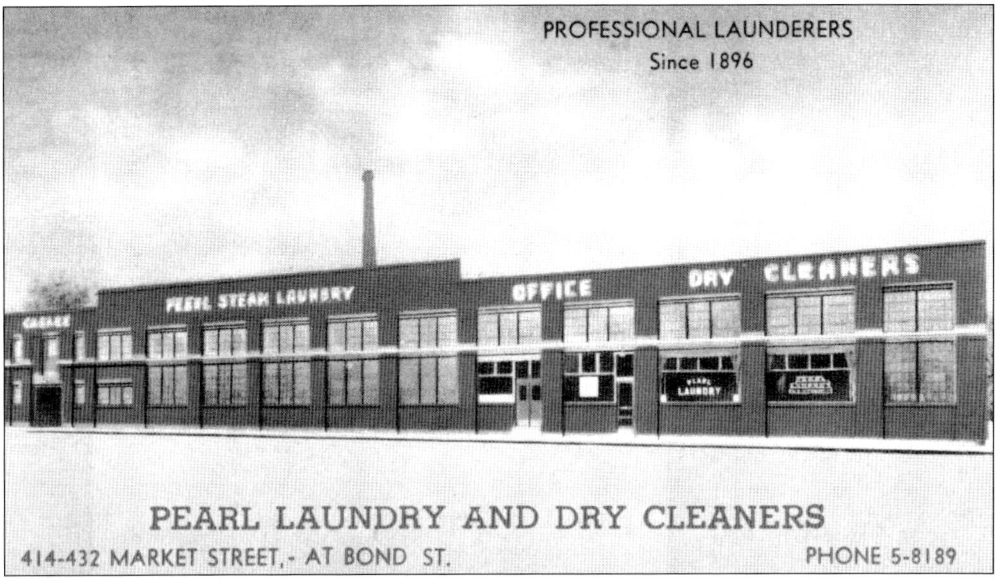

Formerly in an old building on Riverside Drive, Pearl Steam Laundry built this new facility in 1912. Located on Market Street (now Third Street) between Bond and Ingle Streets, the redbrick structure had many windows and touted that it was the best-lit building in the city. The company, which now goes by Pearl Laundry, still operates out of this building. (EVPL and the Topper family.)

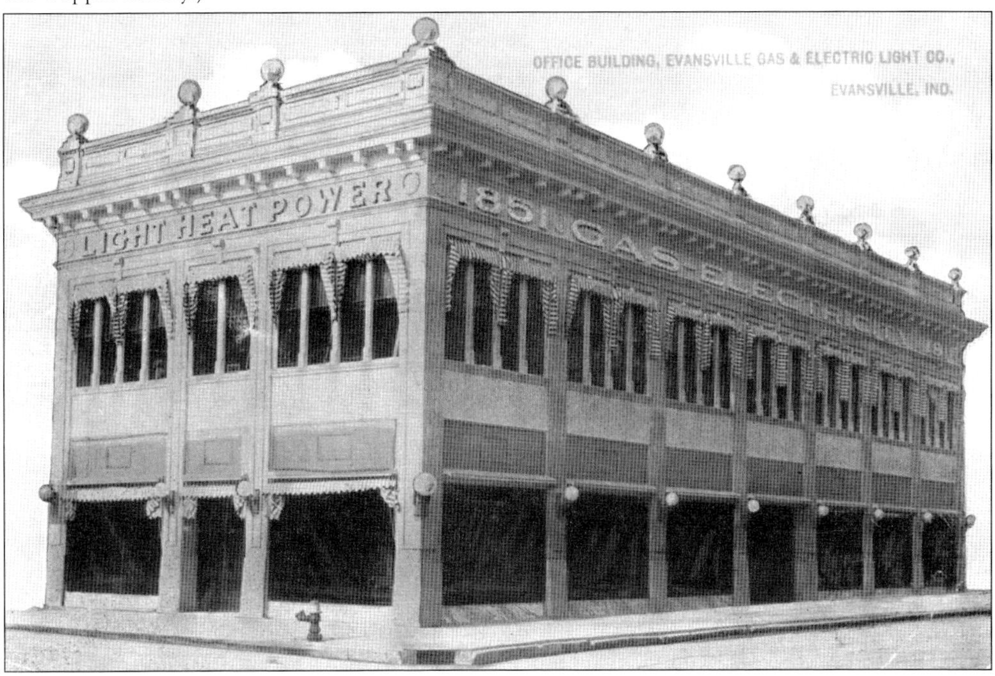

Evansville Gas & Electric Light Co., the predecessor of Vectren, completed this office at the corner of Second and Sycamore Streets in 1913. The Skora Building, as it was commonly called, served as town offices for the LST Shipyard during World War II. After failed renovations, the building was torn down despite being listed in the National Register of Historic Places. The empty lot has been proposed as a location for a multiuse park. (EVPL and the Geiss family.)

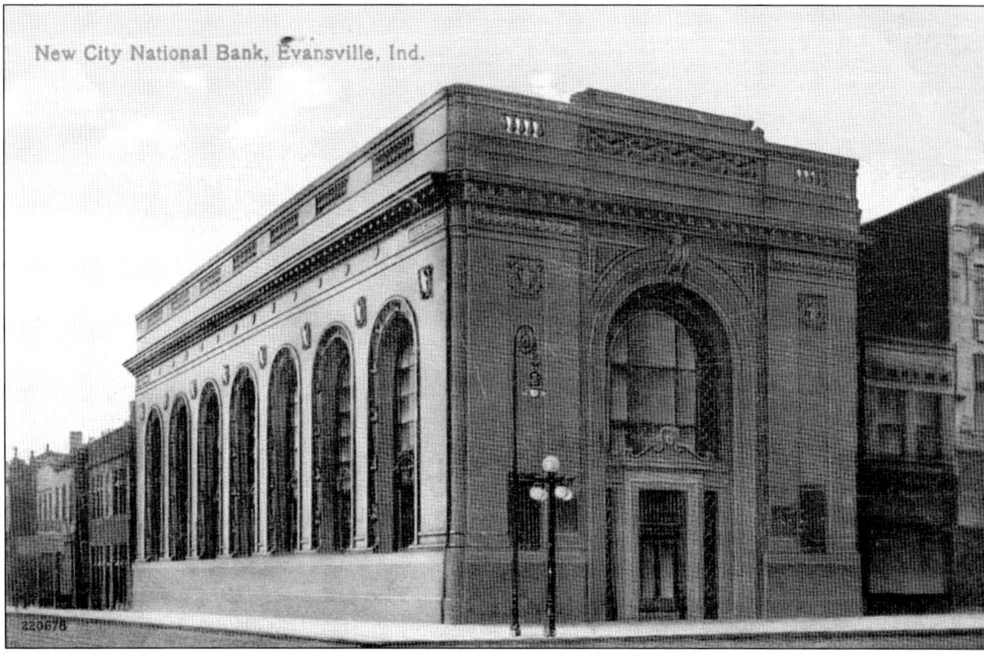

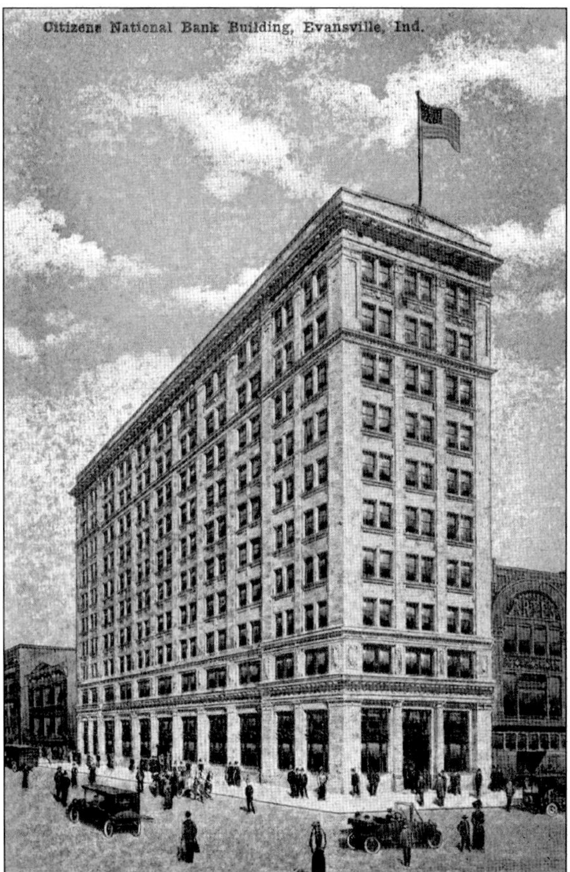

City National Bank completed this building at Main and Third Streets in 1913. It was designed in the Neoclassical style and built using marble from Marble, Colorado. The bank was renamed National City Bank in 1922 and served as the headquarters for the Evansville-based company. The bank became Integra in the early 2000s, then closed in July 2011 when it was taken over by the Federal Deposit Insurance Corporation (FDIC). (Engler family.)

Citizens National Bank followed the trend of banks moving up Main Street in 1916 when it moved into this building, dubbed the city's first skyscraper. Citizens Bank moved into new buildings in 1959 and again in the 1980s and now operates as Fifth Third Bank. The old building on the corner of Fourth Street was recently home to Hilliard Lyons financial planners and is slated to become condominiums. (Engler family.)

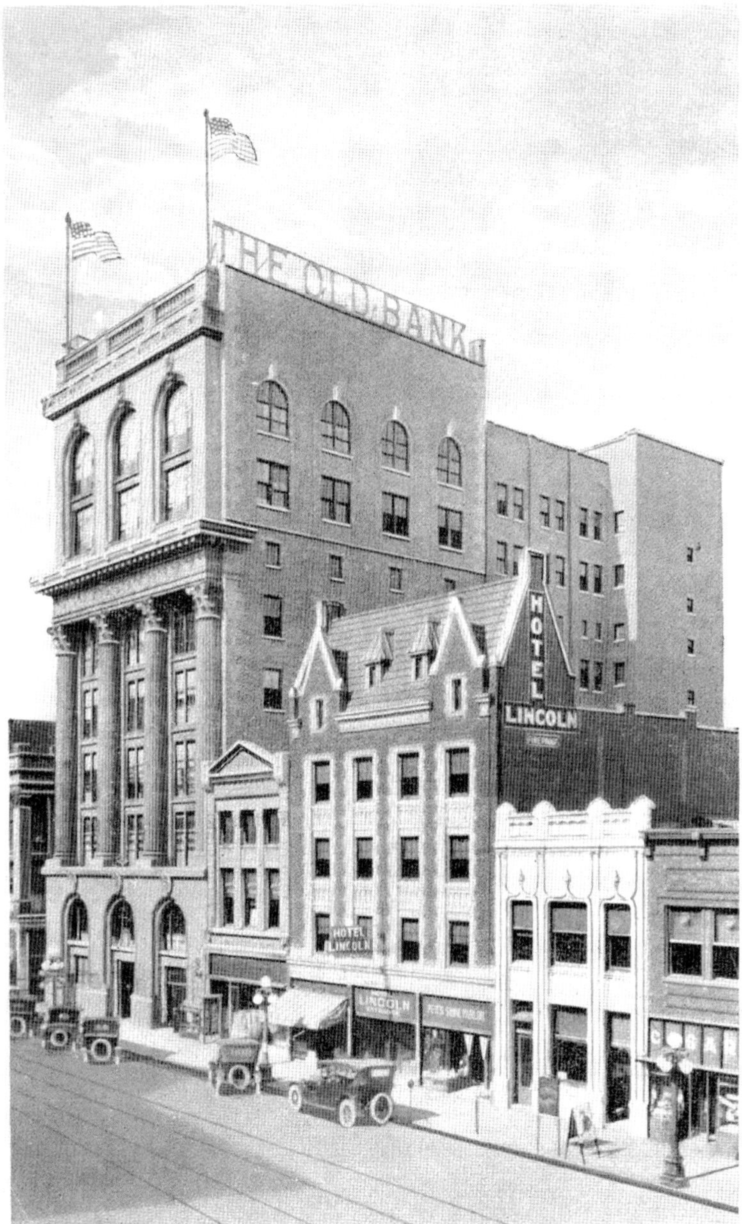

OLD STATE BANK AND LINCOLN HOTEL, EVANSVILLE, IND.

In 1916, the Old National Bank also moved up Main Street and into the large building at left. The new bank featured a polished red granite exterior and was seven stories tall. About the same time, Hotel Lincoln tore down older commercial buildings to erect a new entrance on Main Street. Together, these two structures dwarfed the other buildings on the 400 block of Main Street and made it a busy location for the next 50 years. Old National decided to build an even taller bank next to the old one, and by the late 1960s, the rest of the block was cleared to Fifth Street. After the new structure (still standing and known as the 420 Building) was completed in 1970, the bank moved, and the old building was razed for an addition. Old National now has a new riverfront building. (EVPL.)

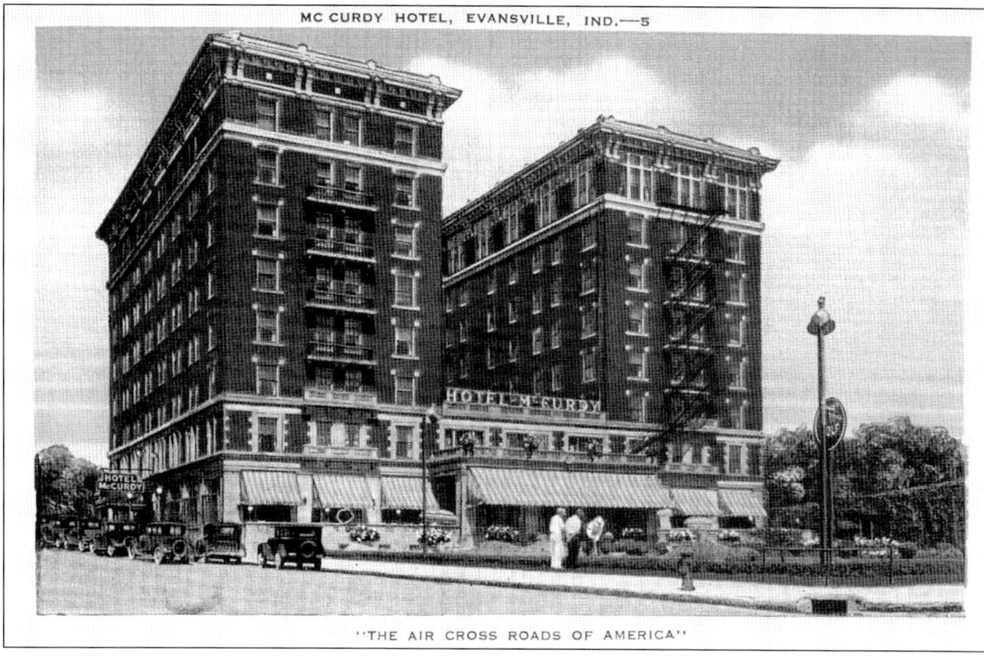

The Hotel McCurdy, with its commanding view of the Ohio River, is one of the last historic structures on the riverfront. The eight-story hotel opened in 1917 and replaced the equally large St. George Hotel (see page 55). St. Louis architect H. Ziegler Dietz designed the U-shaped hotel so that all rooms would have a view. Dietz included a top-floor ballroom and an opulent lobby (below) to dazzle guests. The hotel survived the major 1937 flood and hosted famous guests, such as Katharine Hepburn and Clark Gable, over the years. As business dwindled, the McCurdy was forced to close in 1969. Soon after, the hotel became a retirement home and served as a healthcare center until it closed in 2011. Although the building was still abandoned in 2012, plans are underway to restore the McCurdy for use as condominiums. (Above, Engler family; below, EVPL and the Geiss family.)

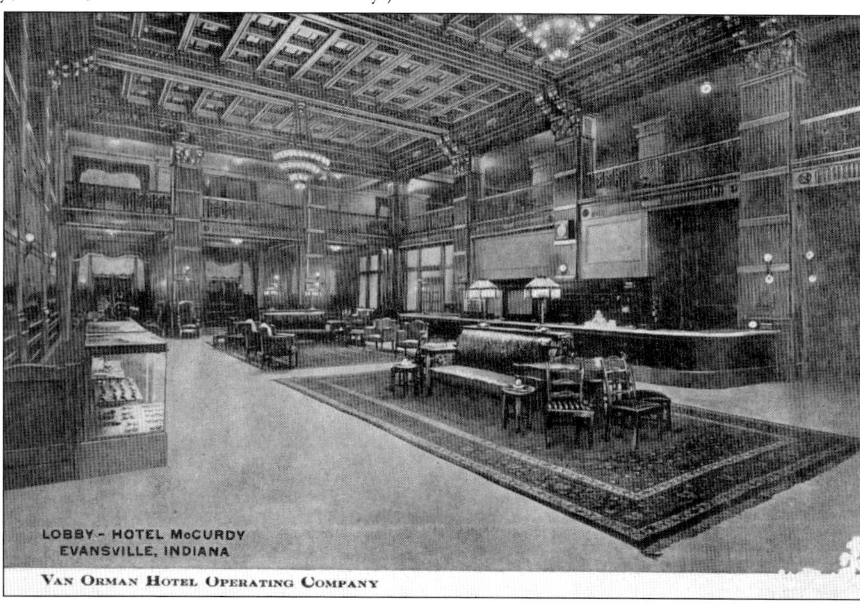

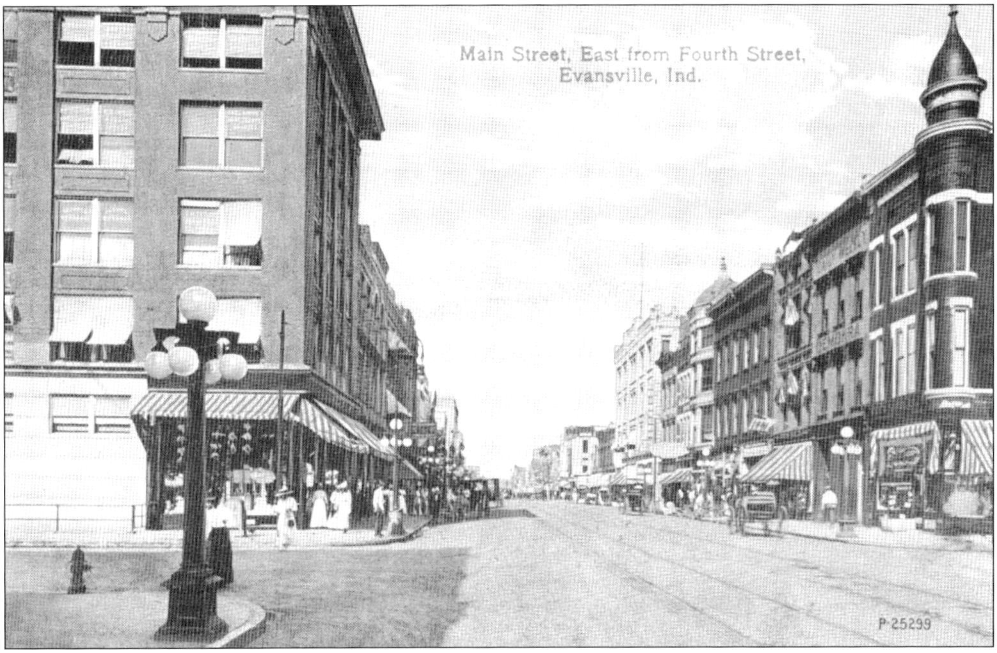

The postcards on this page contrast the view from the corner of Main and Fourth Streets over time. The c. 1915 scene above shows the newly completed Woods Building (left) and the Boston Store across the street as the only sizeable buildings. Below is the same view at night about 25 years later. The Woods Building was occupied by Salm's Department Store, the Old National Bank Building up the street had been completed, and the tower was removed from the building on the corner at right. Salm's went out of business in 1968 and was razed in 1971; the site was converted into a park. Most of the buildings at right were torn down for an S.S. Kresge store, which opened in 1948. That Art Moderne building, which later housed Stratman's Pharmacy, is now mostly vacant, though the second story contains renovated lofts. (Both, Engler family.)

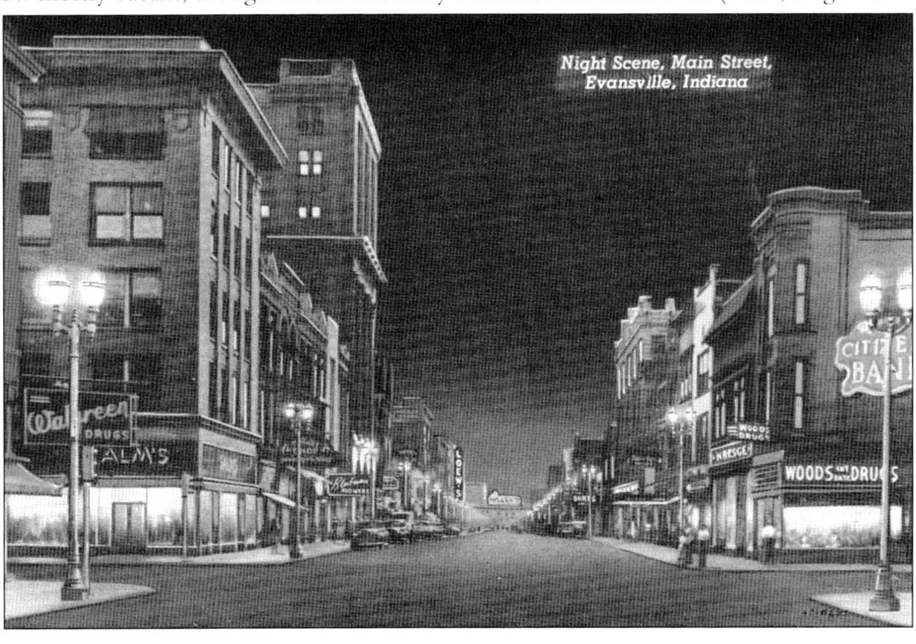

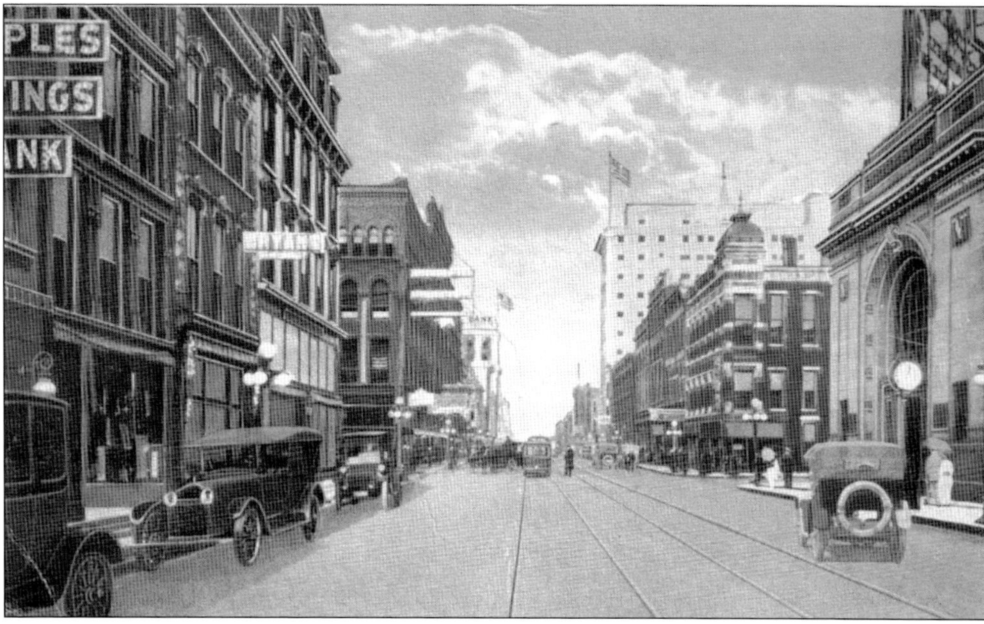

The intersection of Main and Third Streets, shown here around 1920, was one of the busiest spots in Evansville. It was originally called the "public square" because a courthouse once stood on the north corner, where the Eichel Block (see page 59) was located. The Washington House (left), German National Bank (domed structure at right), and National City Bank (right) occupy the remaining corners. The German National Bank was recently restored as apartments with a Subway restaurant on the ground floor. (Engler family.)

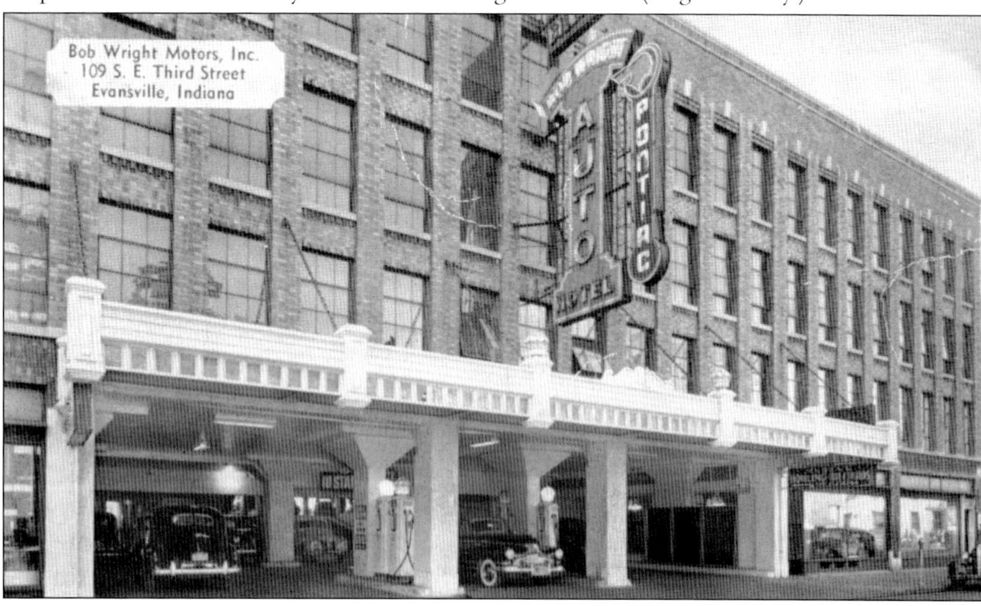

Constructed in 1929 and 1930, the Auto Hotel Building was designed by local architect Harry E. Boyle as a parking garage. It was built on Third Street on the site of the old Strand/Wells-Bijou Theater. In 1941, Bob Wright Motors sold Pontiacs and Cadillacs out of this building. Since about 1980, the Auto Hotel has been the home of Citizens Realty and Insurance (now Fifth Third Insurance). (EVPL and the Topper family.)

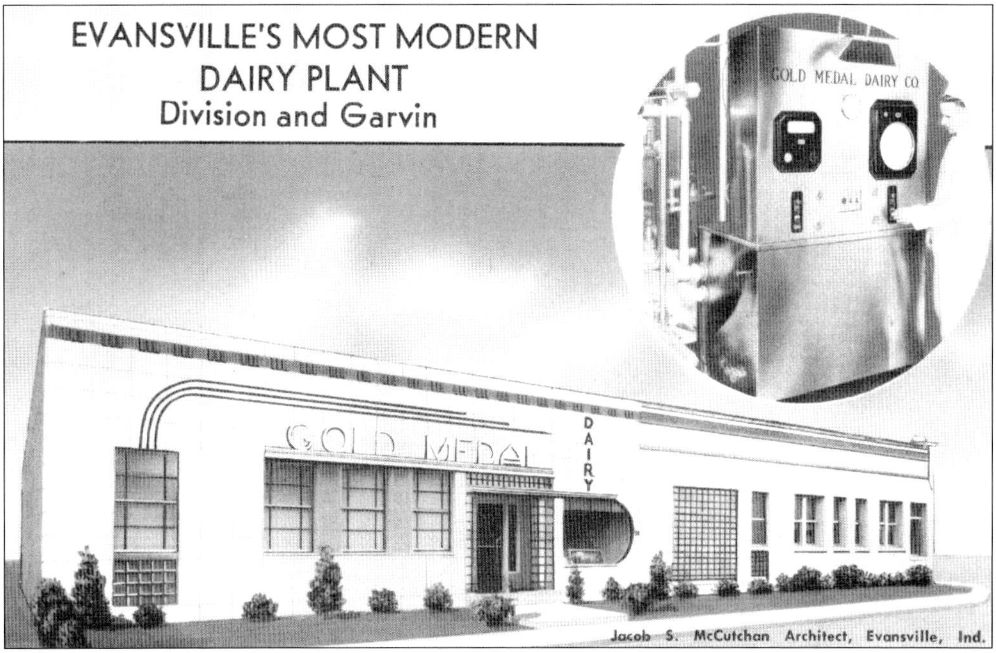

Gold Medal completed this facility on the corner of Division and Garvin Streets around 1930. The company merged with American Dairy in 1954 and relocated. The old Gold Medal Building is no longer standing; it was most likely razed sometime around 1980 during Lloyd Expressway construction. (EVPL and the Geiss family.)

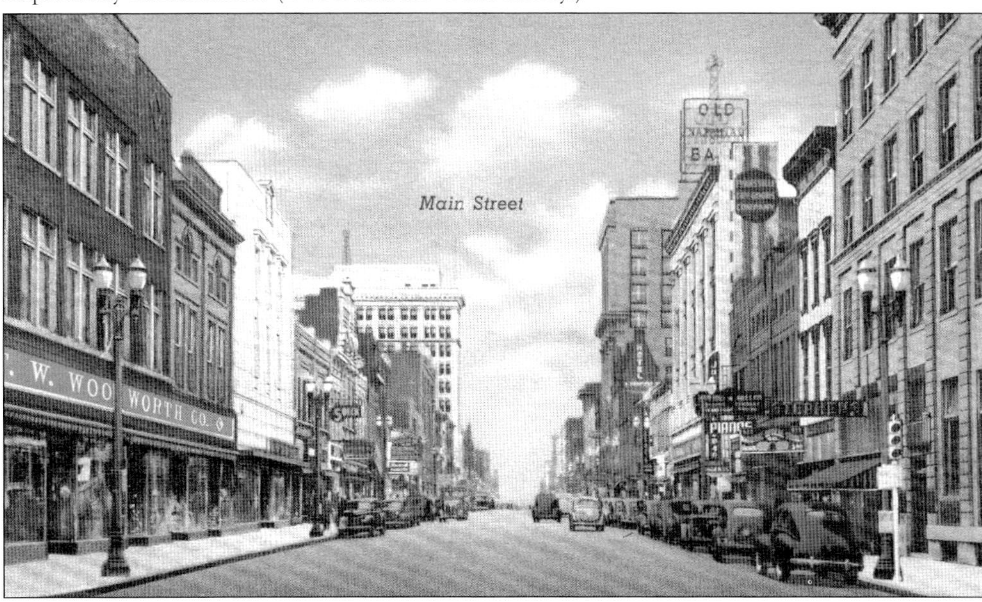

This is Main Street as viewed from Sixth Street sometime around 1940. Today, this view would approximately be looking out from the new Ford Center toward the river. The old Lahr-Bacon Department Store on the corner had been remodeled as a Woolworth's. Other key buildings in this image include Montgomery Ward (the white building next to Woolworth's), Hughes Department Store, and American Trust & Savings Company. Aside from the Woolworth Building, which burned down around 1990, much of this scene is still intact. (Engler family.)

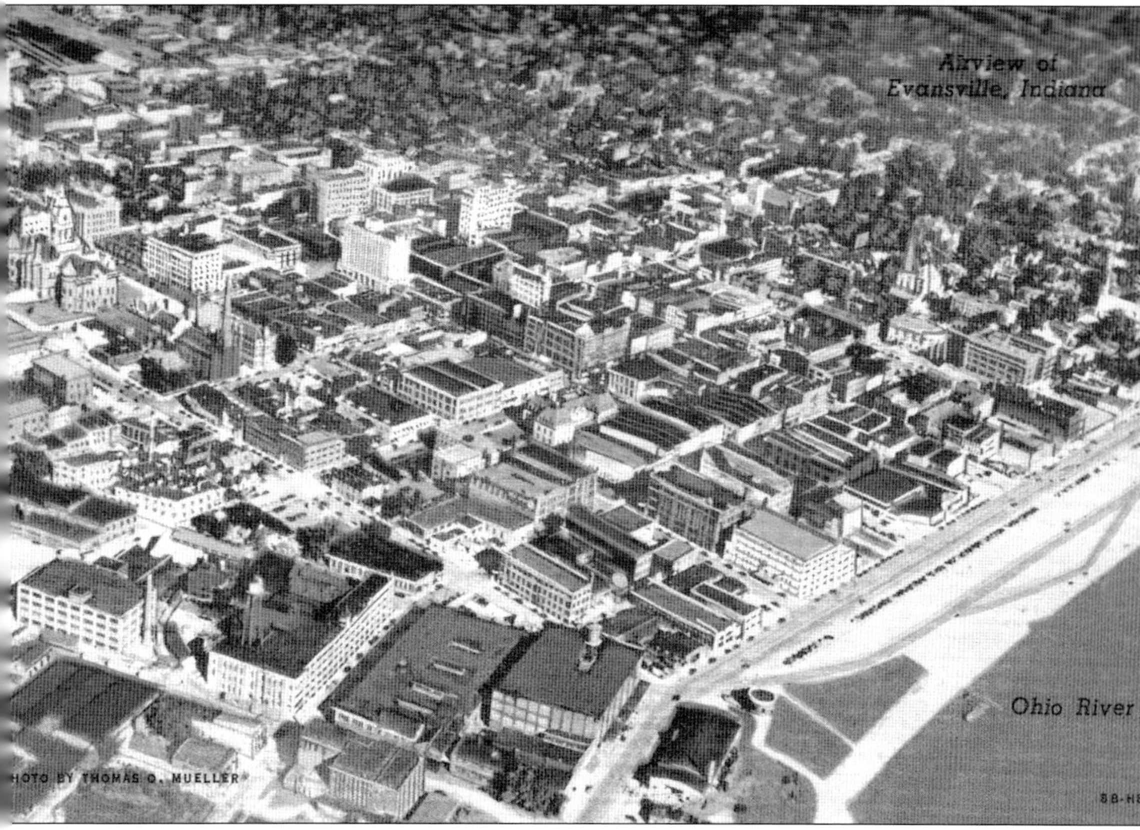

This 1940s aerial view shows downtown Evansville as the commercial center of the city. A number of these buildings still stand today, but several—especially those closer to the riverfront—have been razed in the name of urban renewal. The densely populated downtown area in this image contrasts with the scores of empty lots that exist today. (Engler family.)

Five

Is There a Doctor in the House?

The health of a city corresponds to the well-being of its citizens, and Evansville has been a leader in the health care field since the early years. Originally, medical care consisted mostly of doctors making house calls and dispensing elixirs or home remedies. As Evansville grew, so did the number of practitioners administering to the sick. The Evansville Medical College was established in 1846 as one of the first medical schools in the Midwest. The college operated a small outpatient health facility to treat city residents, though it was primarily used for the students' education. The first official hospital was the US Marine Hospital, built in the 1850s to treat sick passengers traveling along the Ohio River. Additional sanitariums and hospitals followed soon after, including St. Mary's Hospital (now St. Mary's Health System), founded in 1872, and a city hospital established in the 1880s. Of these facilities, some were operated wholly by the government, and others were tied to religious organizations.

Today, large hospitals may have replaced the small-scale operations depicted in some of these postcards, but their aim is the same: to provide health care to ensure the welfare of Evansville.

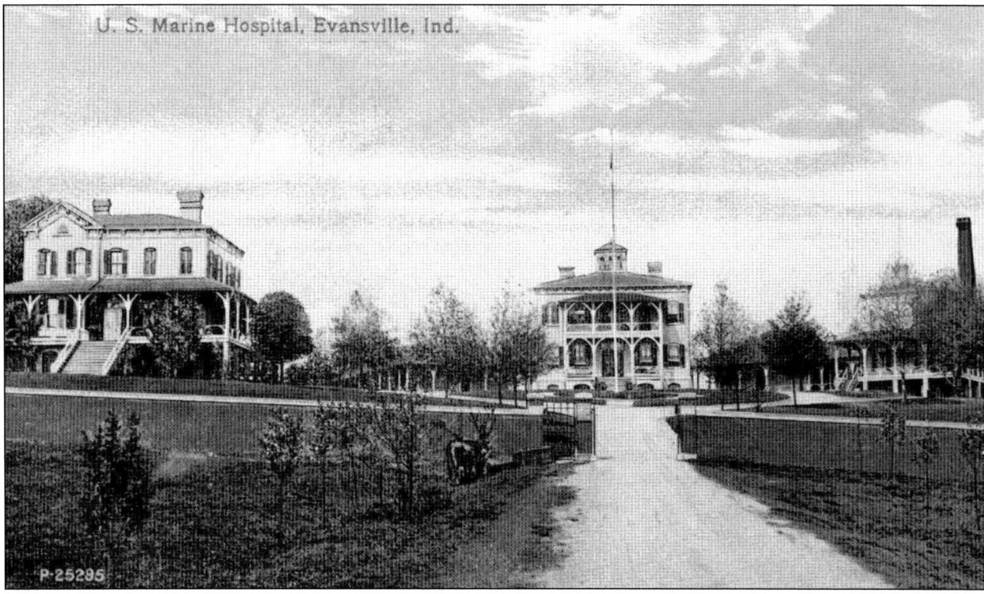

The US Marine Hospital was established in Lamasco in 1856 at the foot of Wabash Avenue. This is the second US Marine Hospital, which was built around 1890 at the western end of Illinois Street. The hospital closed in 1947, and the facility became a training center for the US Navy and the Marine Corps. After failed redevelopment, the old hospital was torn down around 1984. (Engler family.)

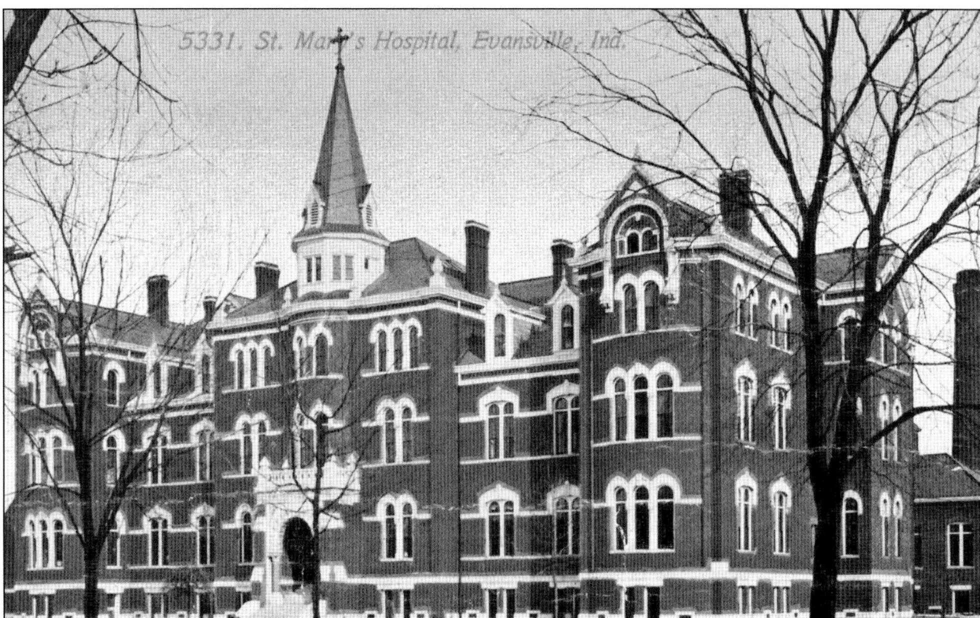

St. Mary's Hospital, established in 1872 by the Daughters of Charity, was initially situated in the first US Marine Hospital. In 1894, this building was erected on First Avenue across from St. Anthony Catholic Church. The hospital was just a stone's throw from the new Deaconess Hospital, which was completed in 1899, and the two operated in close proximity for the next six decades. (EVPL and the Geiss family.)

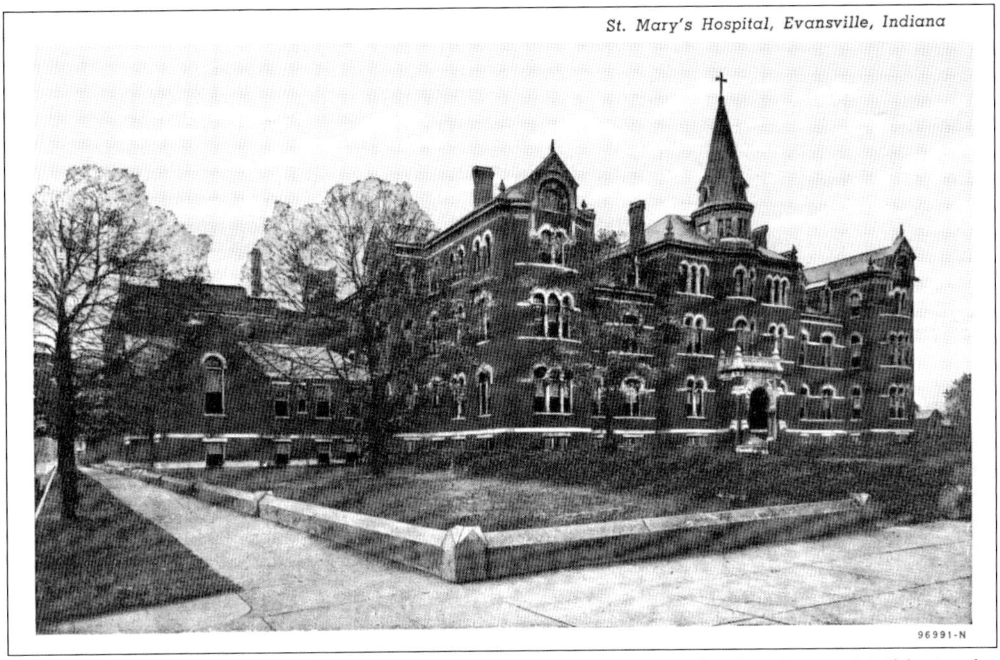

In 1922, St. Mary's Hospital built a four-story annex along Columbia Street (visible in the background at left). Even with the addition, the hospital eventually outgrew the old facility and moved in 1956 to a new hospital (pictured below). The main building was torn down in 1960, and Hacienda Mexican Restaurant now occupies the site. The addition, which was converted into the Tri-State Medical Center, is now utilized as mixed-use office space. (Engler family.)

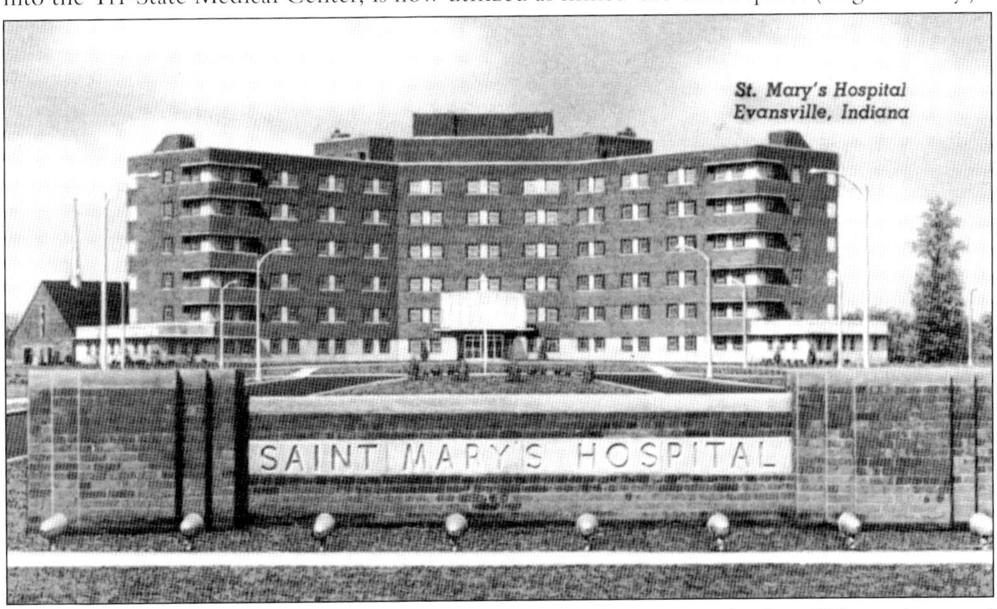

St. Mary's Hospital selected a new site on Washington Avenue on the East Side, and ground was broken in 1953. The new, modern building was completed three years later, and the entire hospital—patients and equipment—was moved on March 10, 1956, with the help of 800 volunteers from the community. The St. Mary's campus has continued to expand and is now one of the biggest health care facilities in the area. (EVPL and the Topper family.)

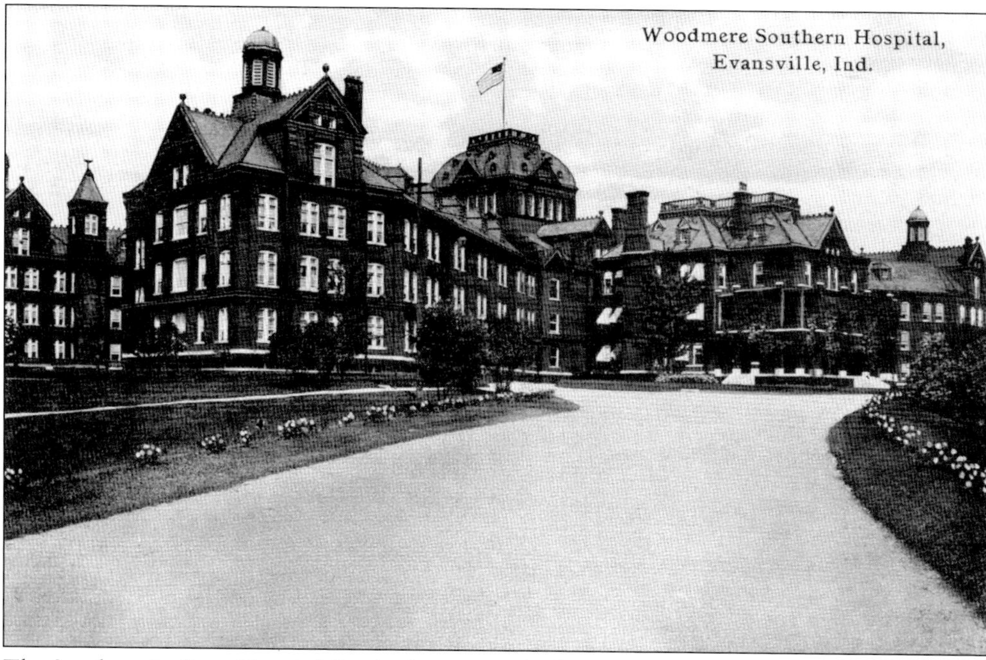

The Southern Indiana Hospital for the Insane was built in 1886, along with one in Indianapolis and another in Logansport in northern Indiana. Nicknamed "Woodmere," the asylum was situated on tree-covered grounds on an old farmstead in Knight Township off Lincoln Avenue. In the early 1900s, an office, laundry facilities, a chapel (below), and several other auxiliary buildings were built to support the growing hospital. The main building burned down in 1943 and was replaced with the new Evansville State Hospital. In 2006, much of this historic district—the newer hospital and the older buildings surrounding it—was torn down as the Evansville State Hospital began to modernize. (Both, Engler family.)

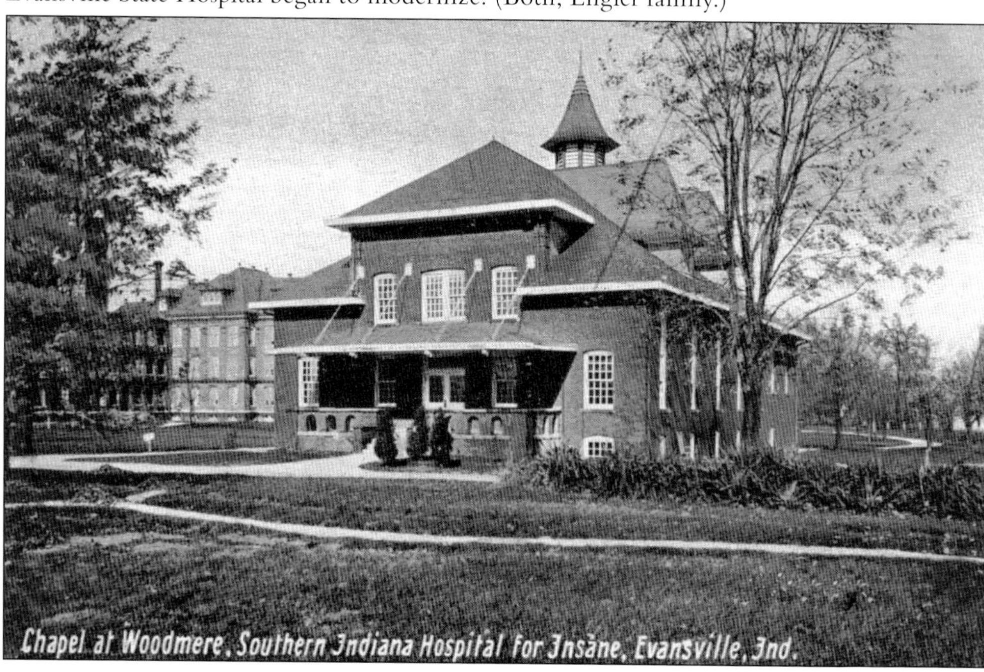

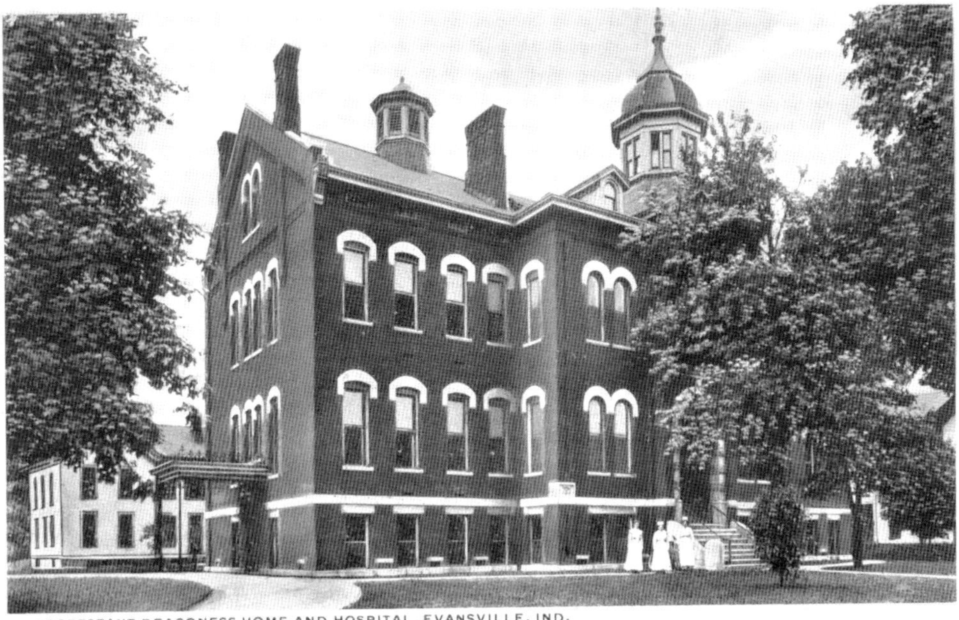

Protestant Deaconess Hospital was founded in 1893 in a house at the corner of Mary and Iowa Streets. Deaconess relocated the old home (visible in the background at left) and built this three-story brick hospital on the same corner in 1899. The building had beds for more than 60 patients and boasted three operating rooms. The postcard below shows Deaconess in the 1920s, after a top story was added and additions to the back and right side were completed. The hospital kept expanding, and subsequent additions took over most of the block. The original building was still integrated in the Deaconess complex until it was demolished around 1971. The Deaconess Physician Center, which contains a Subway restaurant, is now located here. (Above, EVPL; below, EVPL and the Topper family.)

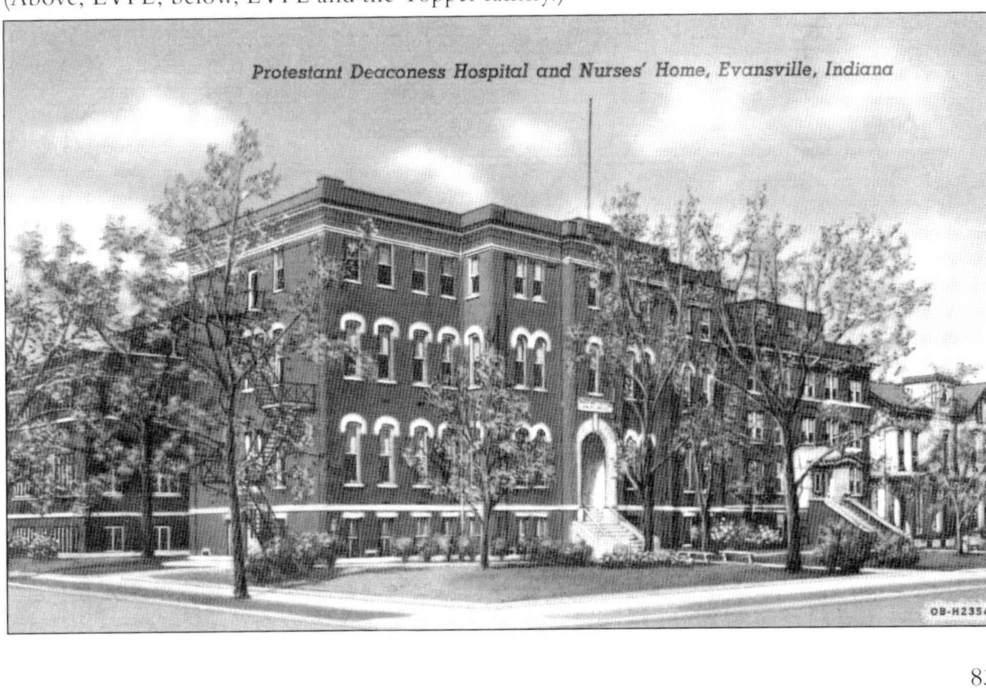

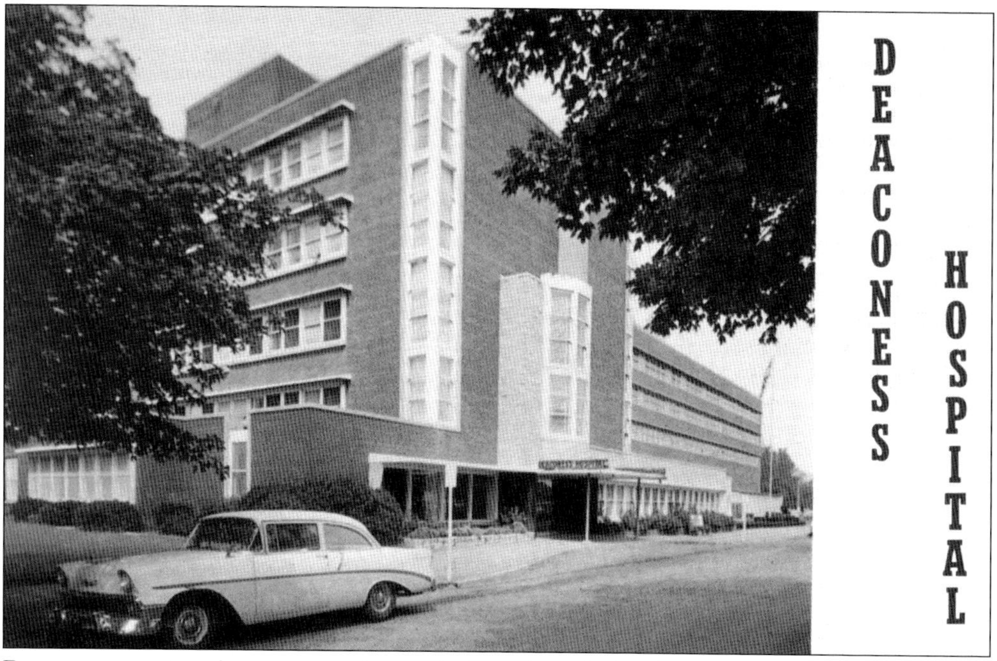

Deaconess continued to grow and extended north to Columbia Street after a large addition was built to the right of the old hospital. This is the hospital as it appeared around 1960 from Mary Street. The lobby and a large addition now jut out from this view, and Mary Street is now closed off. Deaconess Hospital now occupies several of the surrounding blocks, which were once residential. (EVPL and the Geiss family.)

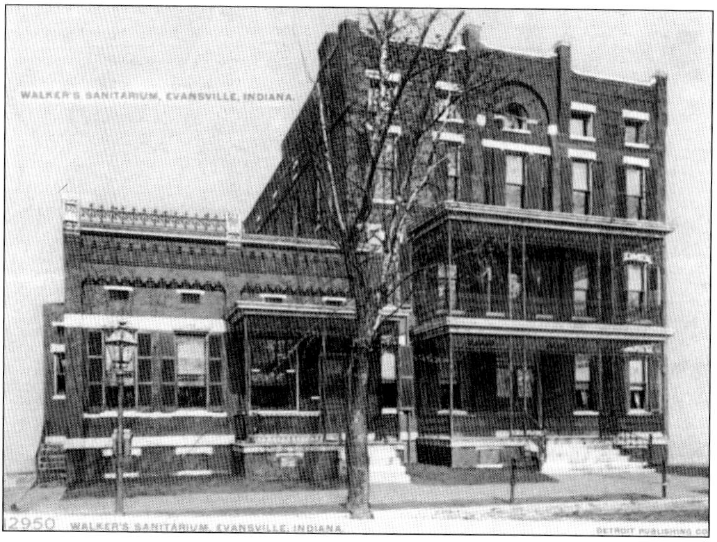

Dr. Edwin Walker split from the old city hospital to establish the Evansville Sanitarium, which eventually grew to become Welborn Hospital. A three-story brick building was completed on Fourth Street, and the hospital opened in January 1894. The hospital, also called the Walker Sanitarium, is pictured here after offices were added in 1895. (EVPL and the Topper family.)

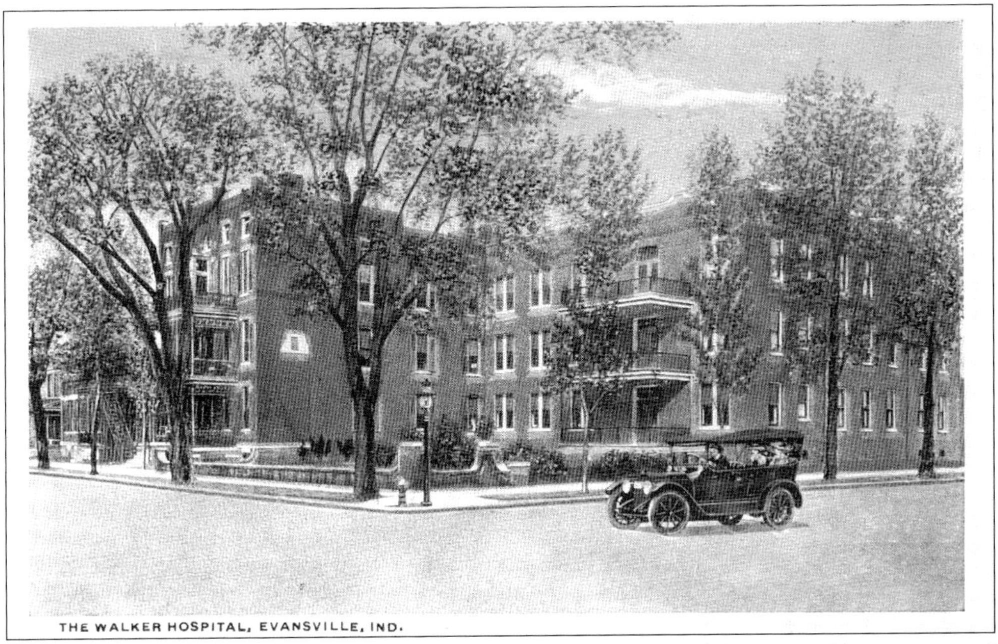

In 1914, a large addition extended the Evansville Sanitarium to Oak Street, and it was renamed Walker Hospital. In 1943, the First Baptist Church bought the facility, and it was renamed Welborn Baptist Hospital. When the original building was replaced in 1947, the hospital took up most of the block. Further expansions saw the closure of Fifth Street as the hospital continued to grow. Welborn was purchased by St. Mary's in 1999 and gradually phased out; the old facility is still being used for a variety of purposes. (Engler family.)

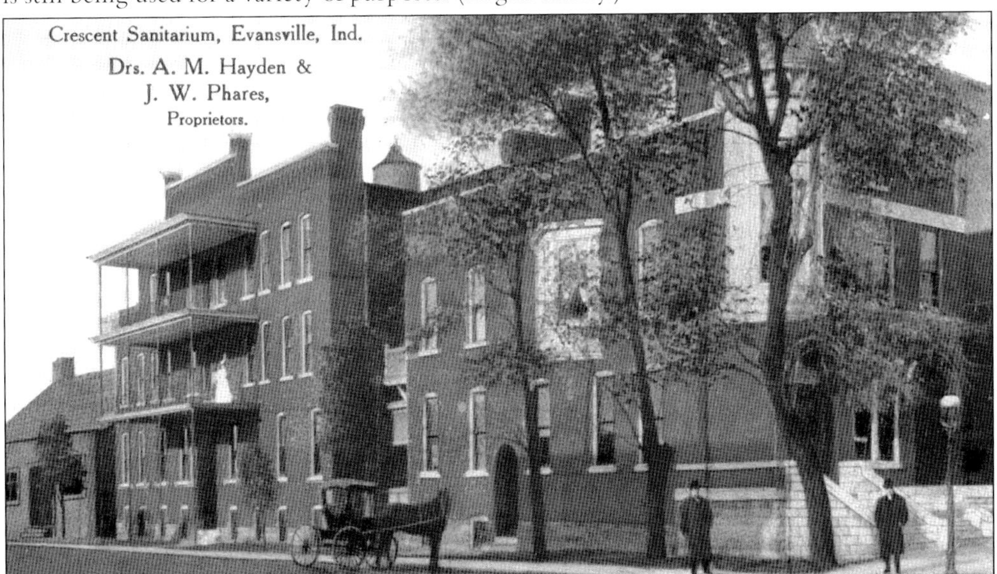

Dr. A.M. Hayden established the Crescent Sanitarium about 1899. He expanded his personal practice from his residence and erected this building at the corner of First and Walnut Streets. In 1912, a three-story addition (visible at left) was built in the rear along Walnut Street. The hospital was razed around 1960 and replaced by the Jackson House (later known as the River House Hotel). (EVPL and the Topper family.)

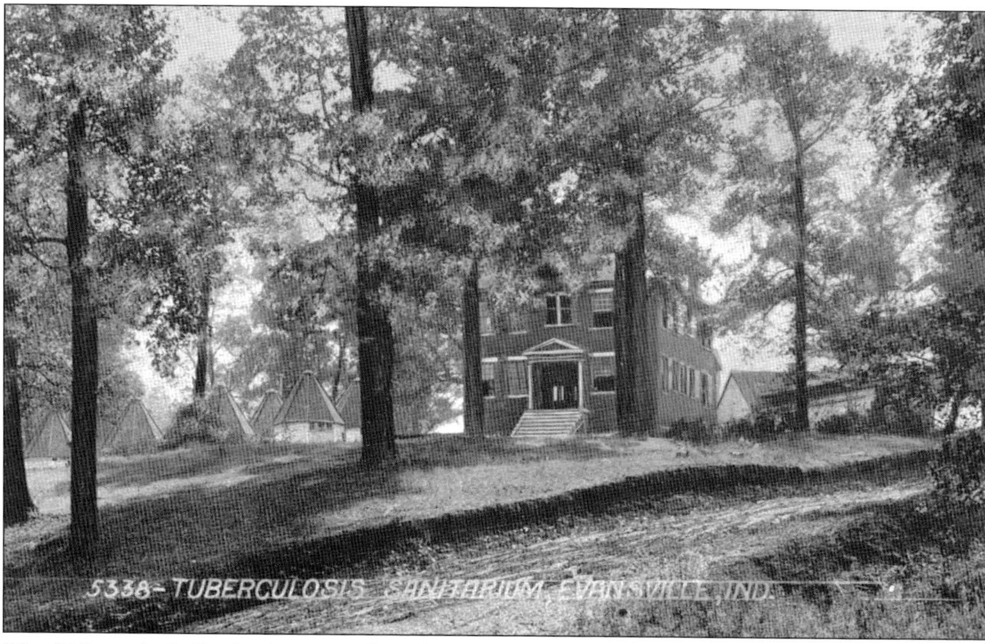

The Tuberculosis Sanitarium was founded in 1908 in response to a tuberculosis epidemic. It was renamed the Boehne Tuberculosis Hospital when the county took over operations in 1924 (hence the name "Boehne Camp Road"). The hospital closed in the 1960s and later housed a drug rehabilitation center. The nurses' residence and the main office (recently remodeled as apartments) remain, but the old hospital building has been demolished. (Engler family.)

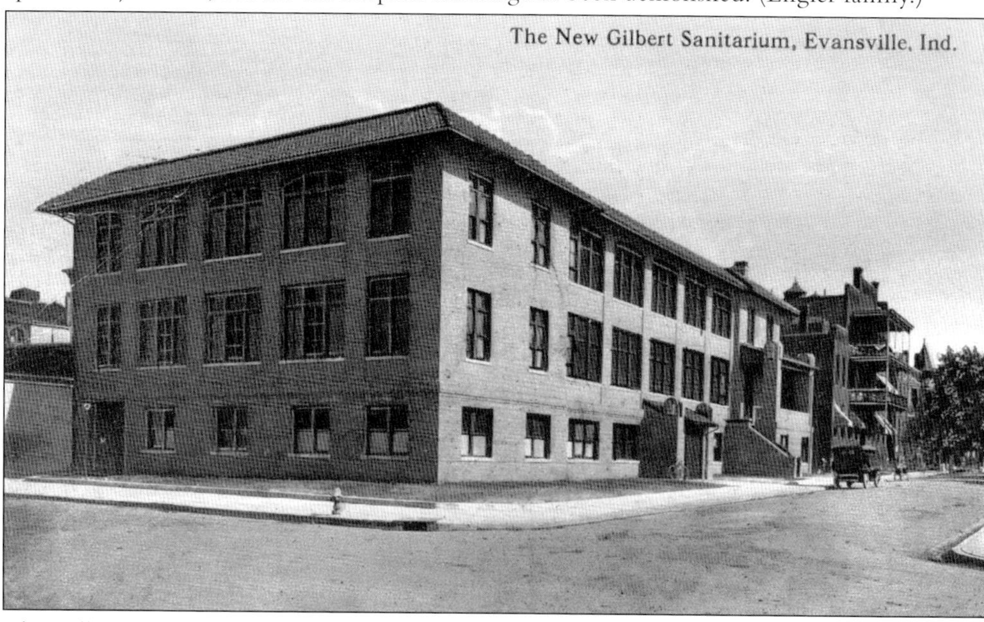

The Gilbert Sanitarium, founded in 1897, was located near Deaconess. It soon outgrew the old facility on Harriet Street (which now houses apartments) and built this structure in 1910 at the corner of Walnut Street and Riverside Drive; however, the sanitarium closed soon after the move. In 1923, the Shriners bought the old hospital and turned it into the Hadi Shrine Temple. The Crescent Sanitarium is visible in the background. (Engler family.)

Six

From Point A to Point B

A city needs to be connected to the larger world to survive, and its transportation and infrastructure can determine a lot. Evansville's access to the Ohio River ensured its early success, and its ability to adapt through the years has made it a strong city today.

When the railroad arrived around 1850, it initially worked with the trade of the river but eventually replaced it. The city's status as a terminus on the Wabash and Erie Canal helped in its selection as a railroad destination. With several railways connecting through Evansville, the railroads helped facilitate the area's growth.

Within town, streetcars began to provide faster transportation than walking and made suburban living a reality. Bridges and roadways were improved to allow accessibility to all points in the city.

Later still, the automobile became a part of everyday life, and buses replaced streetcars. Cars and state highways—as well as air travel—all but eliminated the need for passenger trains. Larger projects such as the West Side Expressway (now part of the Lloyd Expressway) and US Highway 41 altered neighborhoods but have helped the city to grow.

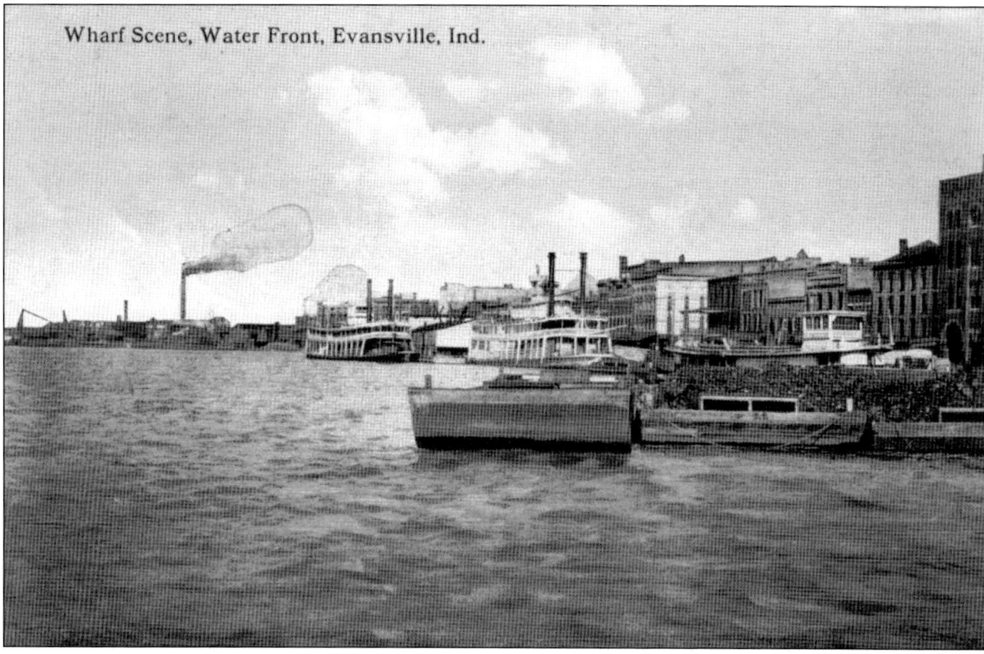

Since the city's founding in 1812, boats have transported goods to and from the Evansville riverfront. The scene in the postcard above shows the high volume of shipping traffic on the Ohio River. Increased commerce and shipping interests corresponded with the city's growth. For early travelers, ferries were the primary means of crossing the river. (Engler family.)

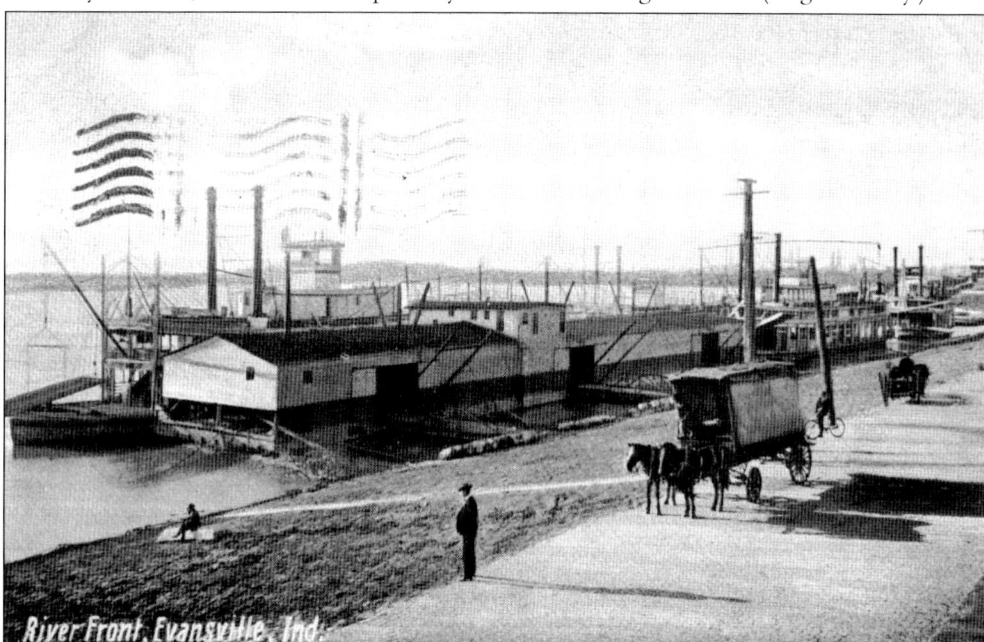

To ease the loading and unloading of goods, in 1848, the riverbank was graded and a wharf was built. The first wharfmaster was P.G. O'Riley, and he built the City Canal and Railroad Wharf (pictured) in the 1860s. Further improvements, including a second wharf on Lamasco's bank (the present-day site of Mulzer Crushed Stone), soon followed. (Engler family.)

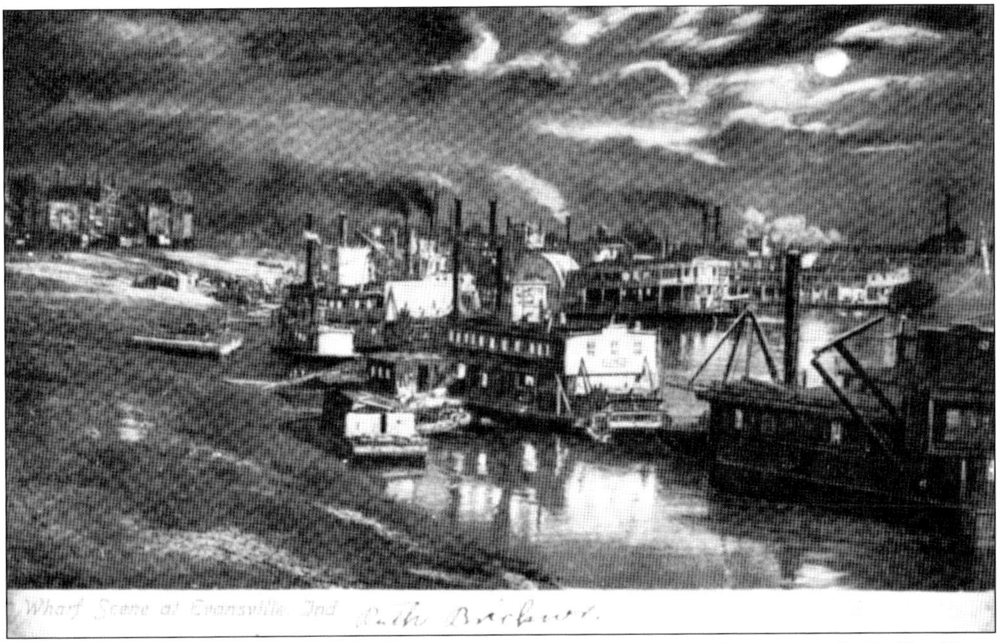

Evansville's wharf was busy at all times, as illustrated in this busy night scene. The bulk of boat traffic along the Ohio River would soon give way to the railroad. The Mead Johnson River-Rail-Truck Terminal (now the Port of Evansville) was built around 1930, and the continuous flow of barge traffic still emphasizes the importance of the city's riverfront. (Engler family.)

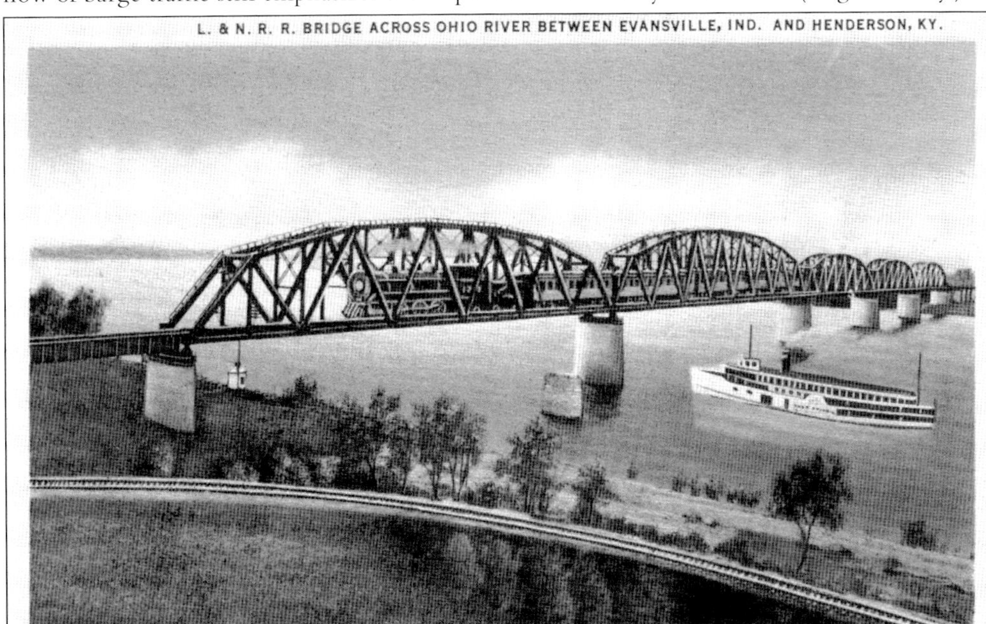

The Louisville & Nashville (L&N) Railroad reinforced Evansville's strategic location when it built the bridge between Evansville and Henderson, Kentucky, in 1885— the first in the area to span the Ohio River. A new railroad line crossed into Union Township. The bridge is pictured sometime after it was rebuilt in 1932; it is still heavily used today. (Engler family.)

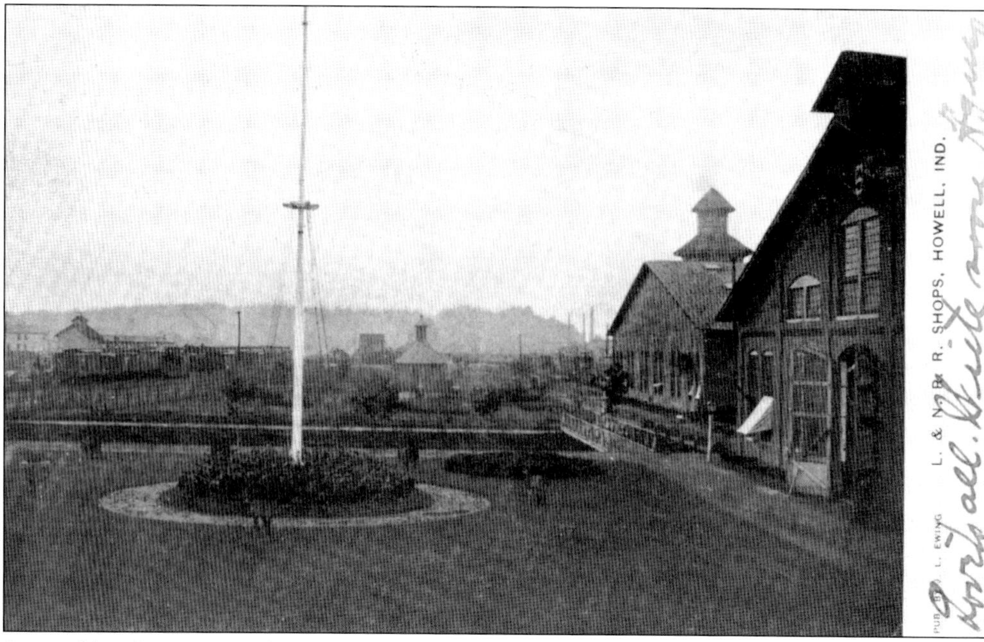

Spurred by the success of the Henderson Bridge, the Louisville & Nashville (L&N) Railroad opened these repair shops in 1889, which helped establish the town of Howell, Indiana, located just southwest of Evansville. Often called the Howell Yard, the shops employed locals and helped give rise to churches and a school for the community. The area was ultimately annexed in 1916, but it retains a distinct identity as a neighborhood. (EVPL and the Topper family.)

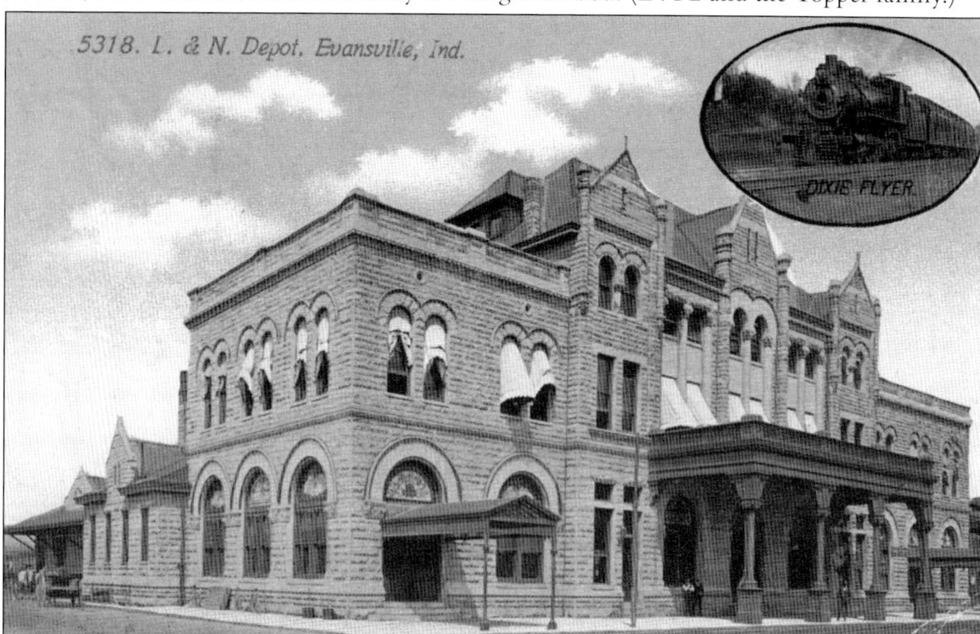

The L&N Depot was built in 1902 on Fulton Avenue. For years, this stone structure greeted travelers arriving in Evansville. As the popularity of passenger rail service waned, the depot became a relic. It was vacated in 1975, and the historic landmark was torn down in February 1985 after plans to convert the space stalled. (Engler family.)

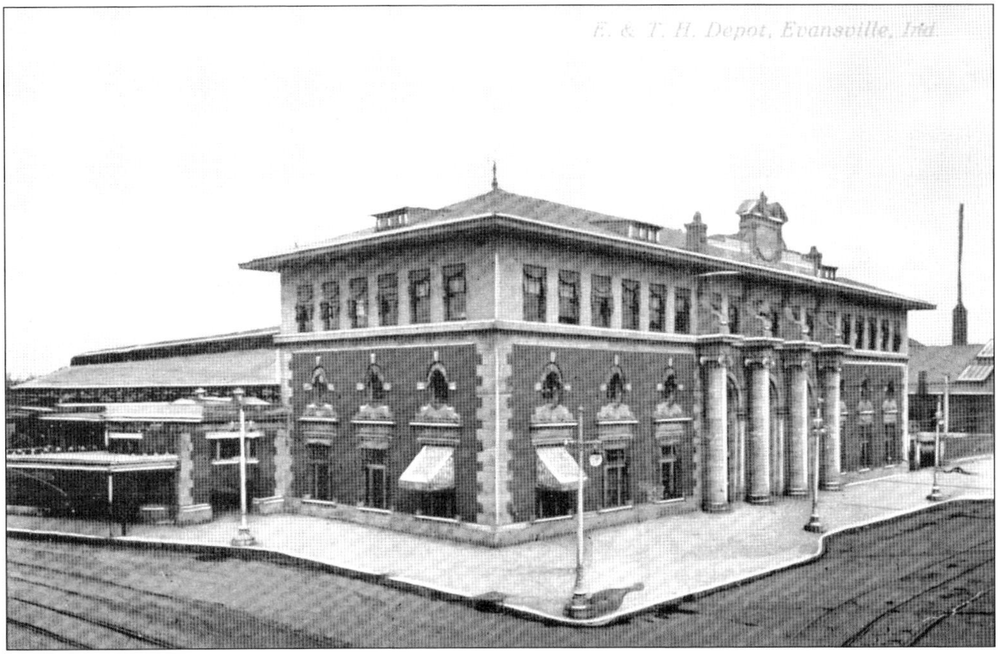

The Evansville & Terre Haute (E&TH) Railroad depot at Eighth and Main Streets was built in 1903 and 1904 and replaced the old Union Station on the corner of Eighth and Main Streets. It was later renamed the Chicago & Eastern Illinois (C&EI) Depot after the E&TH was bought out. In the early 1930s, when the C&EI was taken over by the Louisville & Nashville (L&N) Railroad, this depot became redundant. It subsequently served as a USO Club, a community center, and even a car dealership. When the site was chosen for the new Evansville civic center complex, the depot's time was up. The four Ionic columns in front of the depot were salvaged when the depot was razed in the 1960s; they were integrated into the Four Freedoms Bicentennial Monument located on the riverfront, just beyond the foot of Walnut Street. (Both, Engler family.)

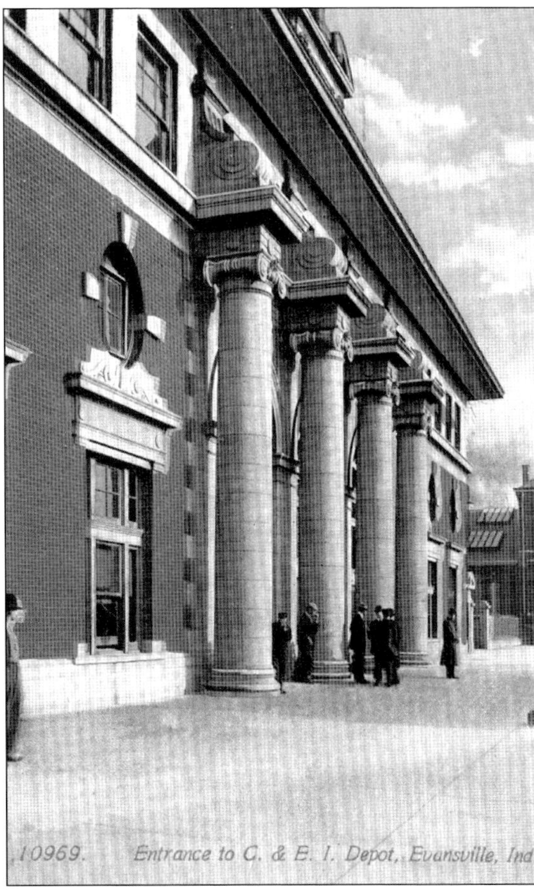

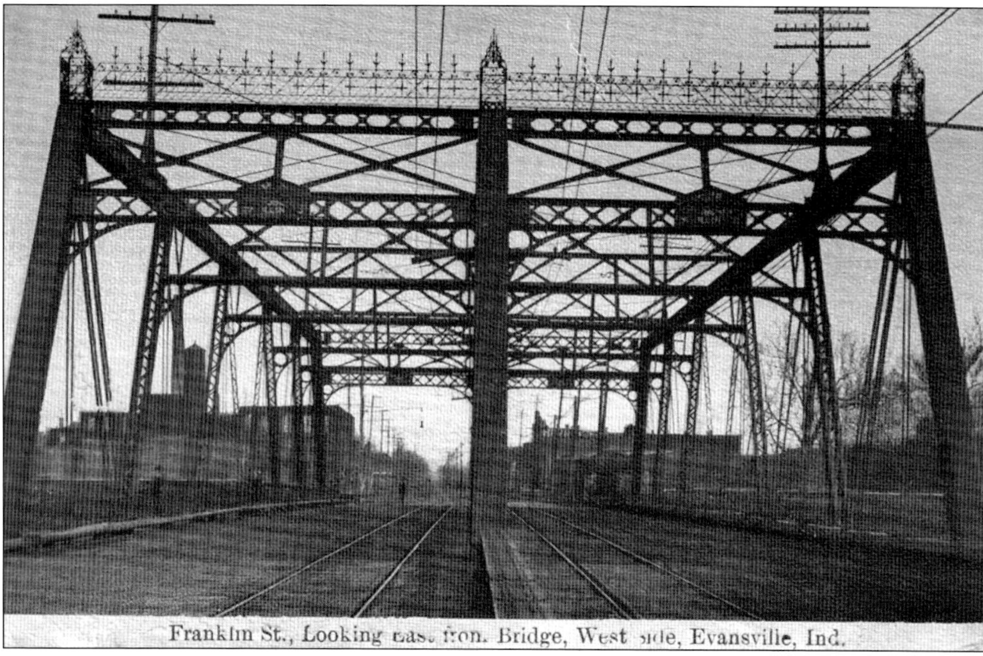

This is a view of the original steel bridge on Franklin Street looking east from Pigeon Creek. The bridge served as a link to the isolated West Side. The Armstrong Brothers Furniture factory is at left, and the Franklin House hotel, currently being converted into the Tin Man Brewing Company, is at right. This bridge was replaced with the current concrete one in the 1930s. (Engler family.)

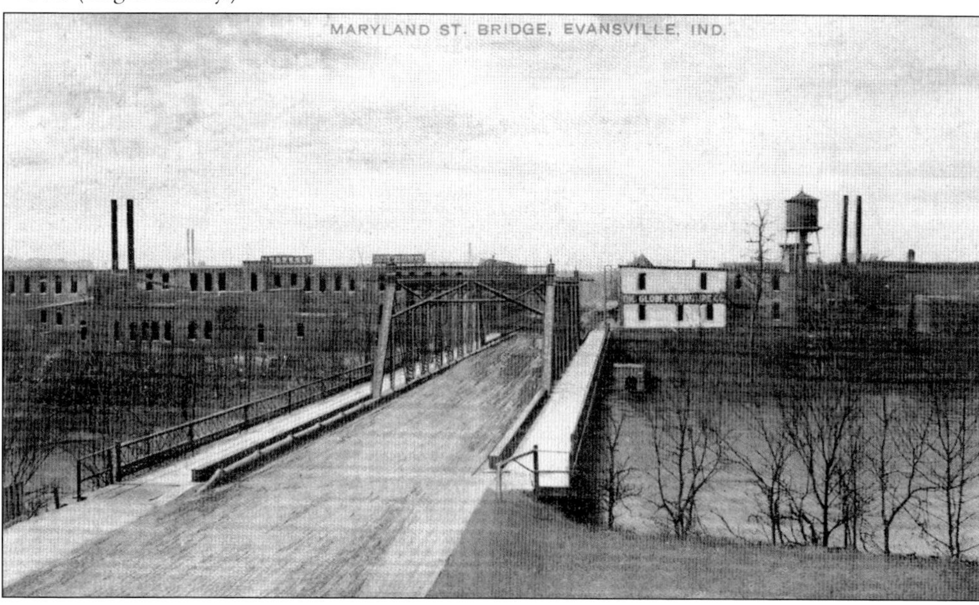

The Maryland Street Bridge, another vital passageway over Pigeon Creek to the West Side, is shown here in 1910 in its new steel guise. After being deemed structurally unsafe, this bridge was replaced in 1984 with the existing concrete one. Across the creek are Globe Furniture (right) and World Furniture (left), which later merged with Bosse Furniture to form the Globe-Bosse-World Furniture conglomerate. (Engler family.)

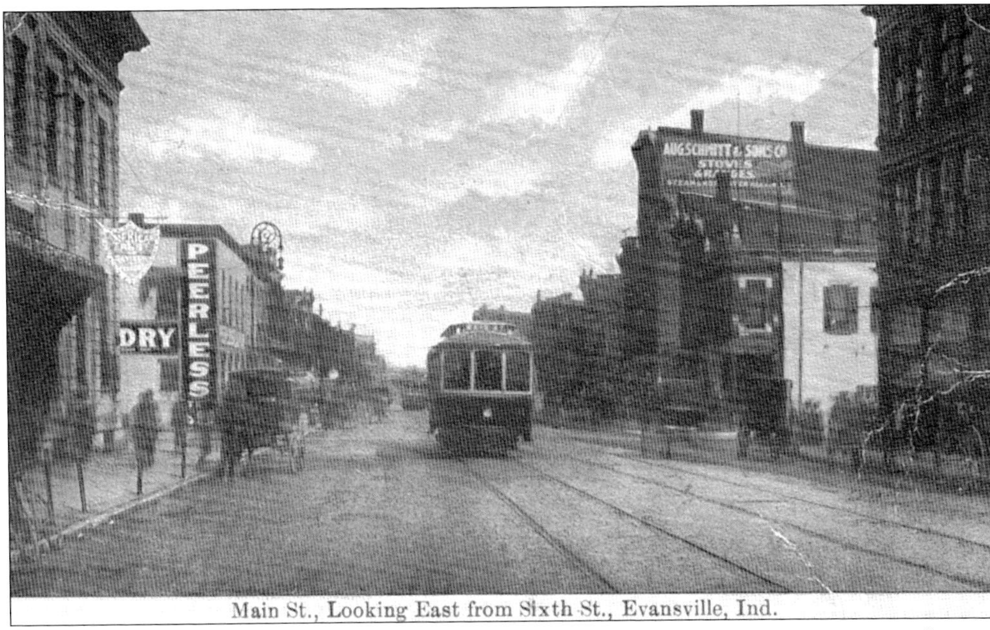

Streetcars once provided quick travel downtown as well as to the suburbs. A maze of routes connected most of the town and made transportation easier. This postcard shows a streetcar traveling down Main Street near Sixth Street. The buildings in the background at right were torn down in 2010 to make way for the new Ford Center. (Engler family.)

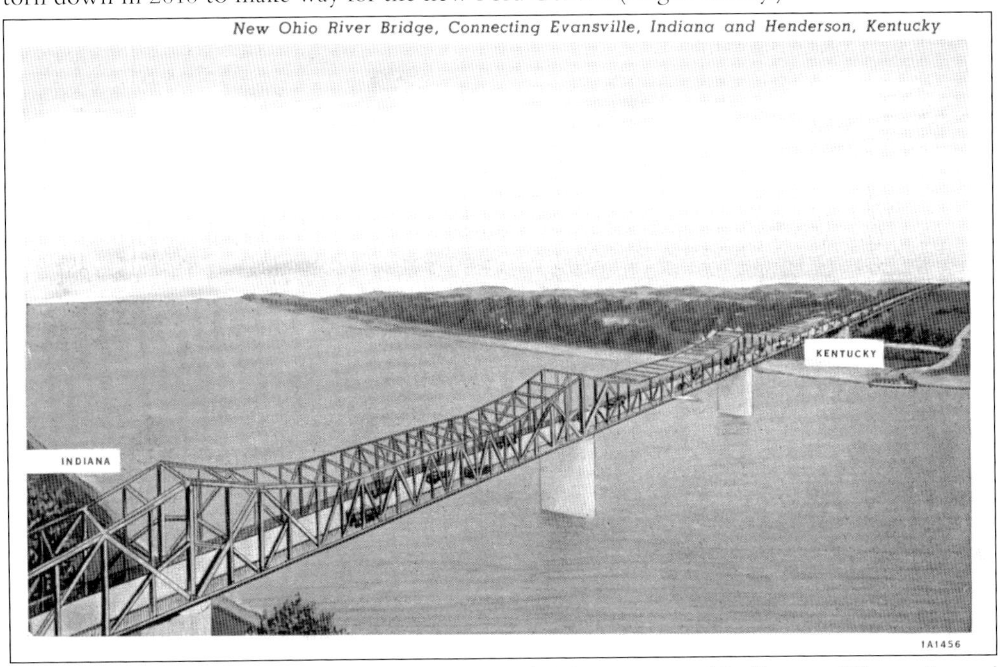

The Audubon Memorial Bridge, built in 1931 and 1932, connected Indiana and Kentucky and became part of the Dixie Bee Highway (now known as US Highway 41). In 1966, another span was added to the right of this one. The old bridge was designated northbound, and the new one handled southbound traffic. The pair became known as the Twin Bridges, though viewers can spot the more ornate metalwork on the original bridge. (EVPL and the Geiss family.)

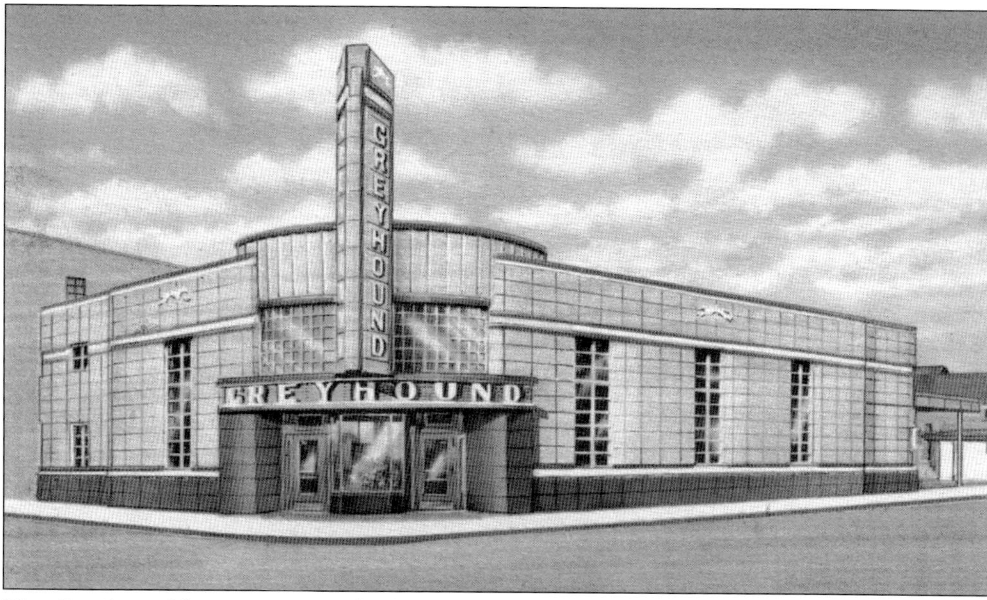

The Greyhound bus station was built in 1939 in the Art Moderne style. As buses replaced passenger rail, the station at the corner of Third and Sycamore Streets became a busy location. Greyhound stopped running buses here in 2007 and relocated to its current location on Sixth Street. The vacant building is now owned by Indiana Landmarks, a statewide preservation organization, and will become its regional office. (Engler family.)

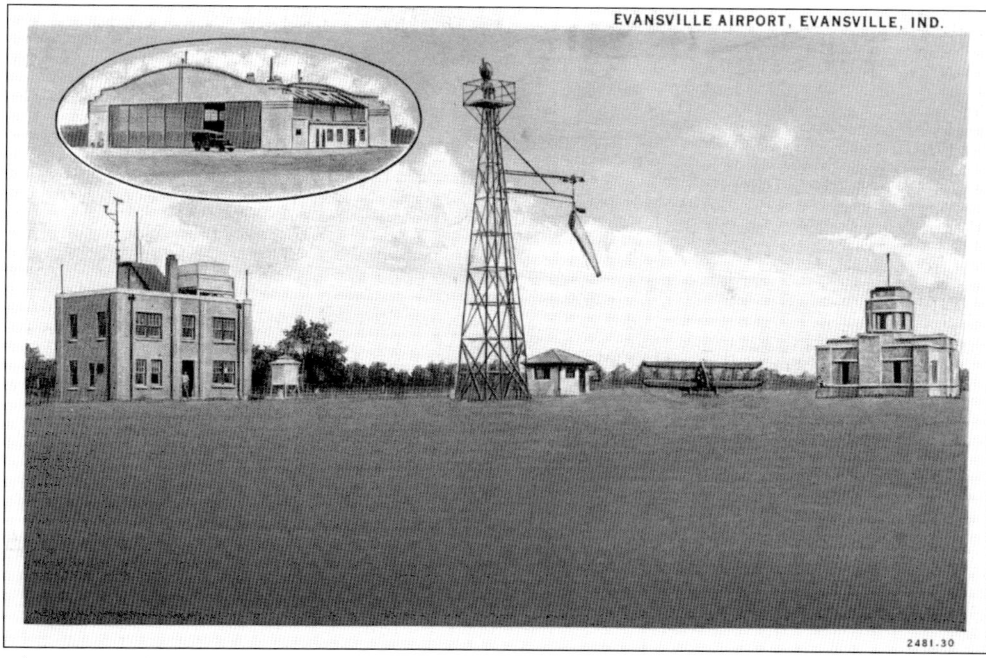

The Evansville Airport dates back to 1928, when the city pushed for its development. A new terminal was built in 1950, and the airport was named Dress Regional Airport after former Evansville mayor William Dress. When the airport moved just north of the old site in the 1980s, the old buildings, including the hangar (inset), became a private airport. (EVPL and the Topper family.)

Seven

No Place Like Home

While things like businesses, civic buildings, and churches are vital to a city, its citizens will always need places to live. Personal residences were originally situated downtown, close to the action. Many of these early homes were demolished as downtown Evansville became more commercial. Newer houses popped up around the outskirts of town, and suburban sprawl saw them move farther and farther away. Some neighborhoods that arose solely around a plant or industry were engulfed by the growing city. Still, many of the city's neighborhoods, especially those listed in the National Register of Historic Places, retain their vitality and sense of identity.

Apartment living was another choice for accommodations and was well suited for those living in the densely populated downtown area. A push in the 1910s for apartments close to the city saw several complexes built—similar to the current trend of condominiums being constructed downtown, sometimes in historic buildings that would otherwise have been demolished.

Institutional housing also played a role in where people lived. Buildings like the orphanage or the Vanderburgh County Poor House offered shelter for those with no other options.

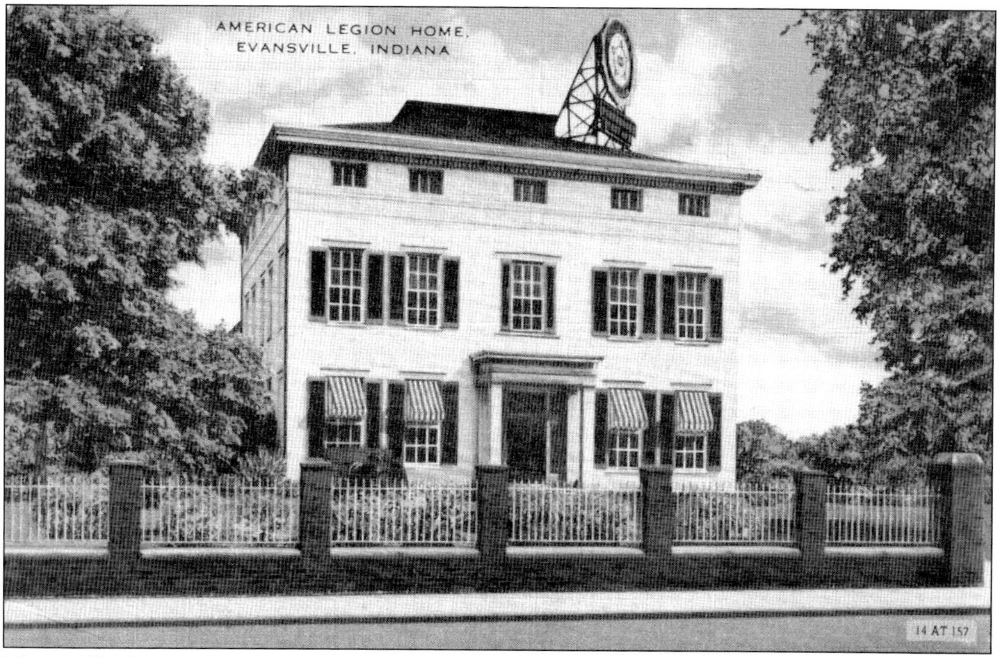

The Willard Carpenter residence was one of the first grand homes in Evansville. Located on Carpenter Street, it was completed in 1849 for the Willard Library namesake. In the 1930s, the house became the headquarters of the American Legion Home, pictured here. It was home to television stations WTVW and WNIN, its current occupant. (Engler family.)

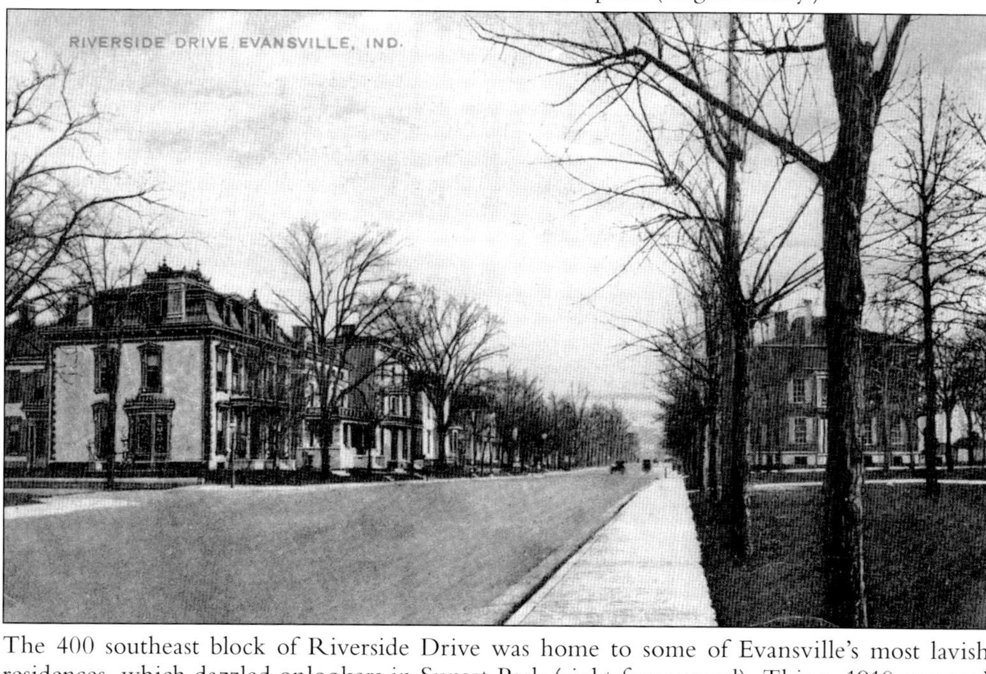

The 400 southeast block of Riverside Drive was home to some of Evansville's most lavish residences, which dazzled onlookers in Sunset Park (right foreground). This c. 1910 postcard shows the Charles Viele residence (left) on the corner of Cherry Street. It was built in 1855 and 1856 and remodeled to this look in 1876. At right is the Robert Barnes mansion, which served as the original Evansville Museum when this picture was taken. (Engler family.)

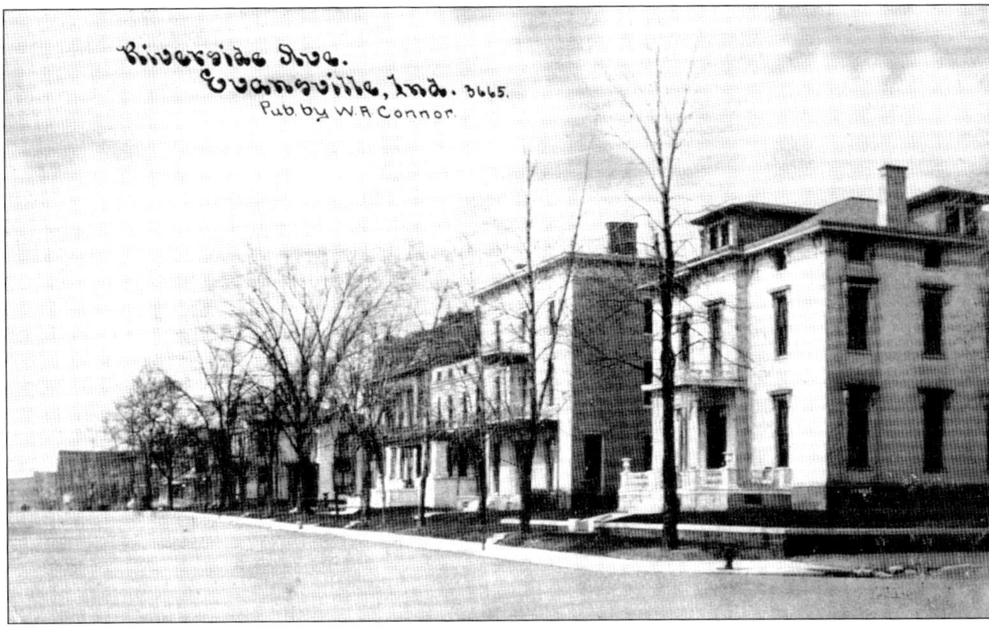

This is the same block of Riverside Drive (400 southeast) looking northwest toward downtown. On the corner of Oak Street (far right) is 420 Southeast Riverside Drive. This house, with its unique observation tower, was built in 1870 for wholesale grocer John G. Venneman. Next to it was the Richard Raleigh house at 414 Southeast Riverside Drive. His Italianate residence was built in 1868 and remodeled in 1893 with a wrought-iron veranda. (Engler family.)

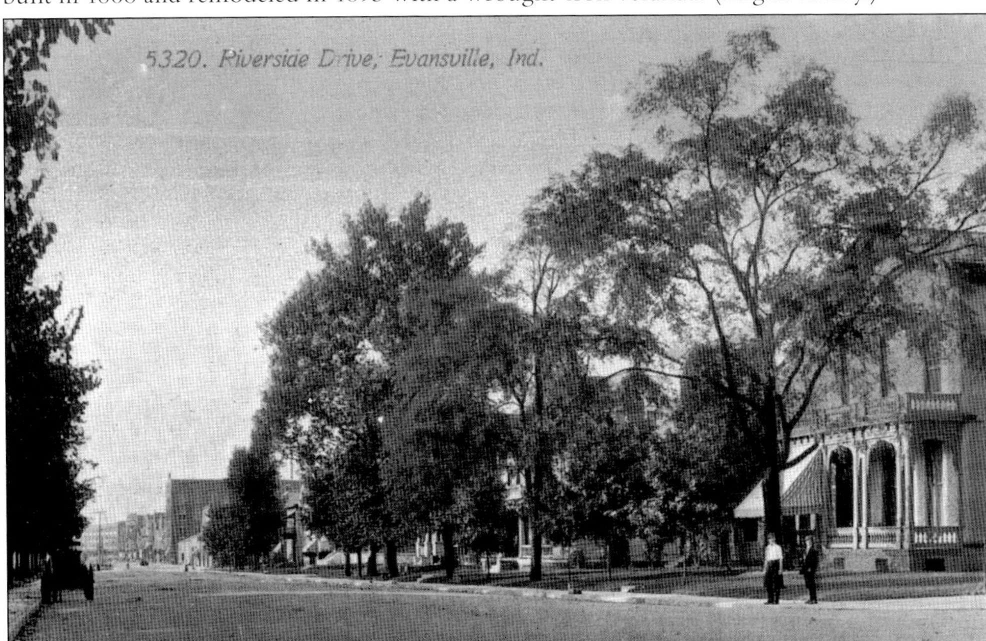

In 1864, Sam Gilbert built his Italianate-style home (far right) on Riverside Drive, opposite the Viele house. The home was altered to its present look in 1911, when it was split up into Reitz Apartments and a two-story front portico was added. The four-story Keller Crescent Building is visible in the background farther down Riverside Drive. (Engler family.)

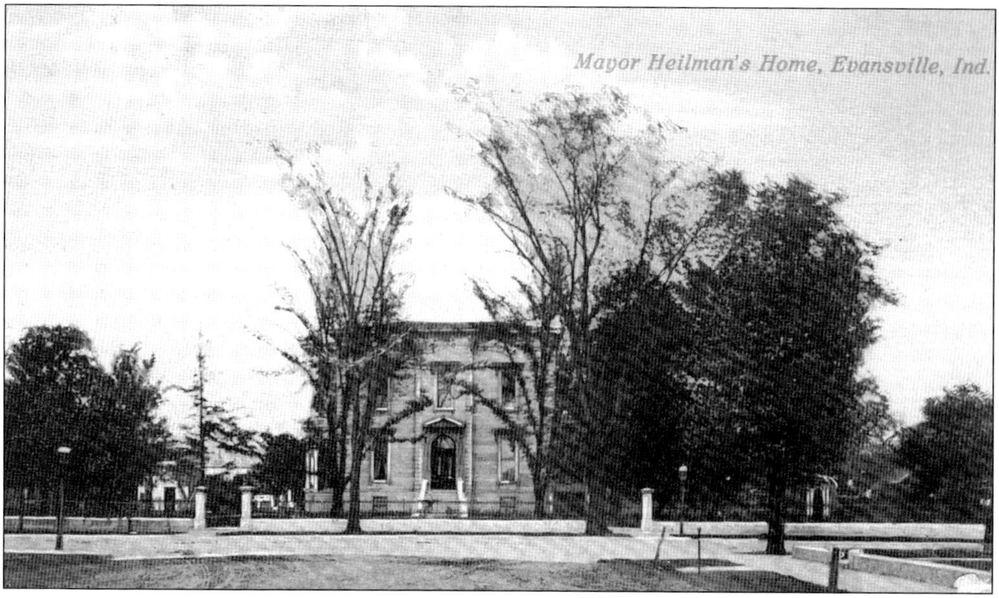

Built in 1869 for Mayor William Heilman, this Italianate structure was one of many stately homes along First Avenue—a handful of which still stand. In 1931, the residence was converted into the St. Vincent Center for Children and Families. The center, which caters to low-income families, has since built additions behind the old house. (Engler family.)

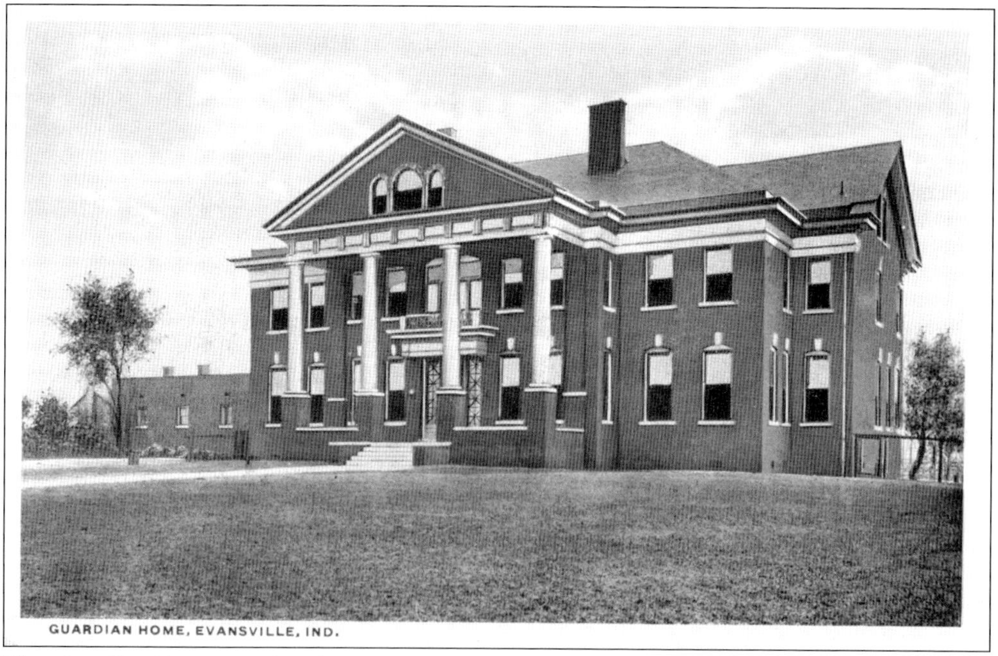

The Guardian Home on Lincoln Avenue was built in the 1850s as a county orphanage. It closed during the Depression, and children were transferred to the Orphans' Home on the West Side (pictured on the following page). The building was later the Carver Center, a community center for African Americans, named after noted scientist George Washington Carver. When the center relocated around 1970, the Guardian Home sat vacant until a fire burned it down in 1972. (EVPL and the Topper family.)

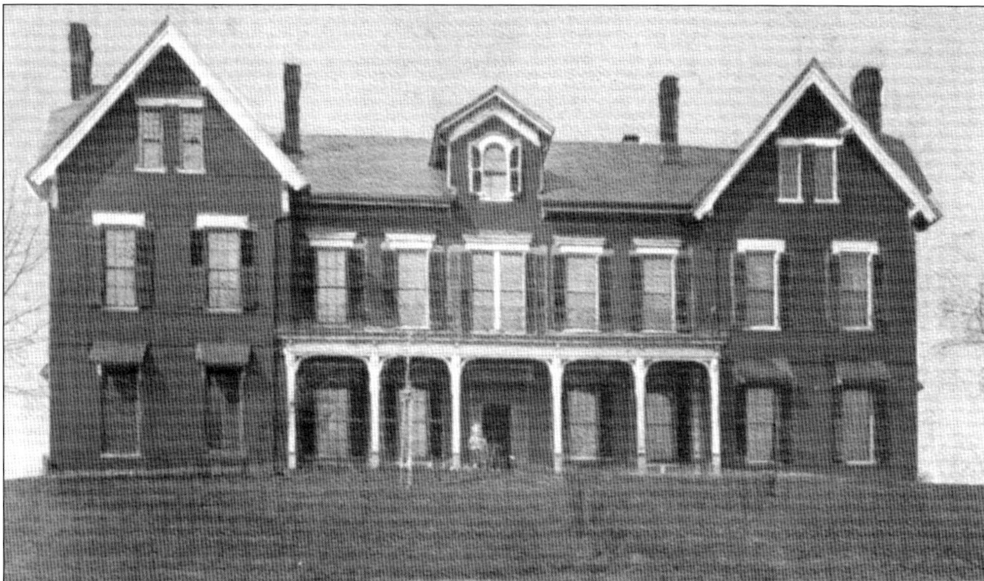

Orphans Home, Evansville, Ind.

Originally built as the home of Dr. John Laval, this building, situated on the West Side at the end of Indiana Street, became the Orphans' Home in 1872. Pictured here is the orphanage after a left wing was added years later. The old orphanage was torn down in the early 1950s, and the Hillcrest Washington Youth Home was constructed on the site in 1952. (Engler family.)

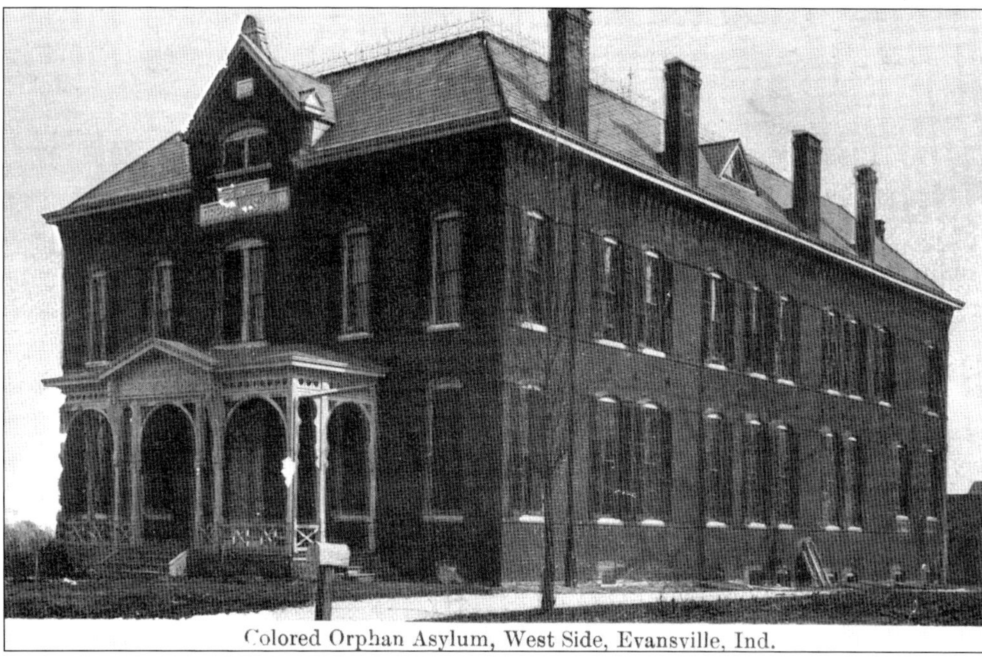

Colored Orphan Asylum, West Side, Evansville, Ind.

When the Orphans' Home segregated in 1883, black orphans moved into this building just behind the old orphanage. The Colored Orphan Asylum, located at the northeast corner of Barker Avenue and Pennsylvania Street, later became known as the Booker T. Washington home. It was torn down at the same time as the Orphans' Home, and the two were rejoined in the Hillcrest Washington Youth Home. (EVPL and the Topper family.)

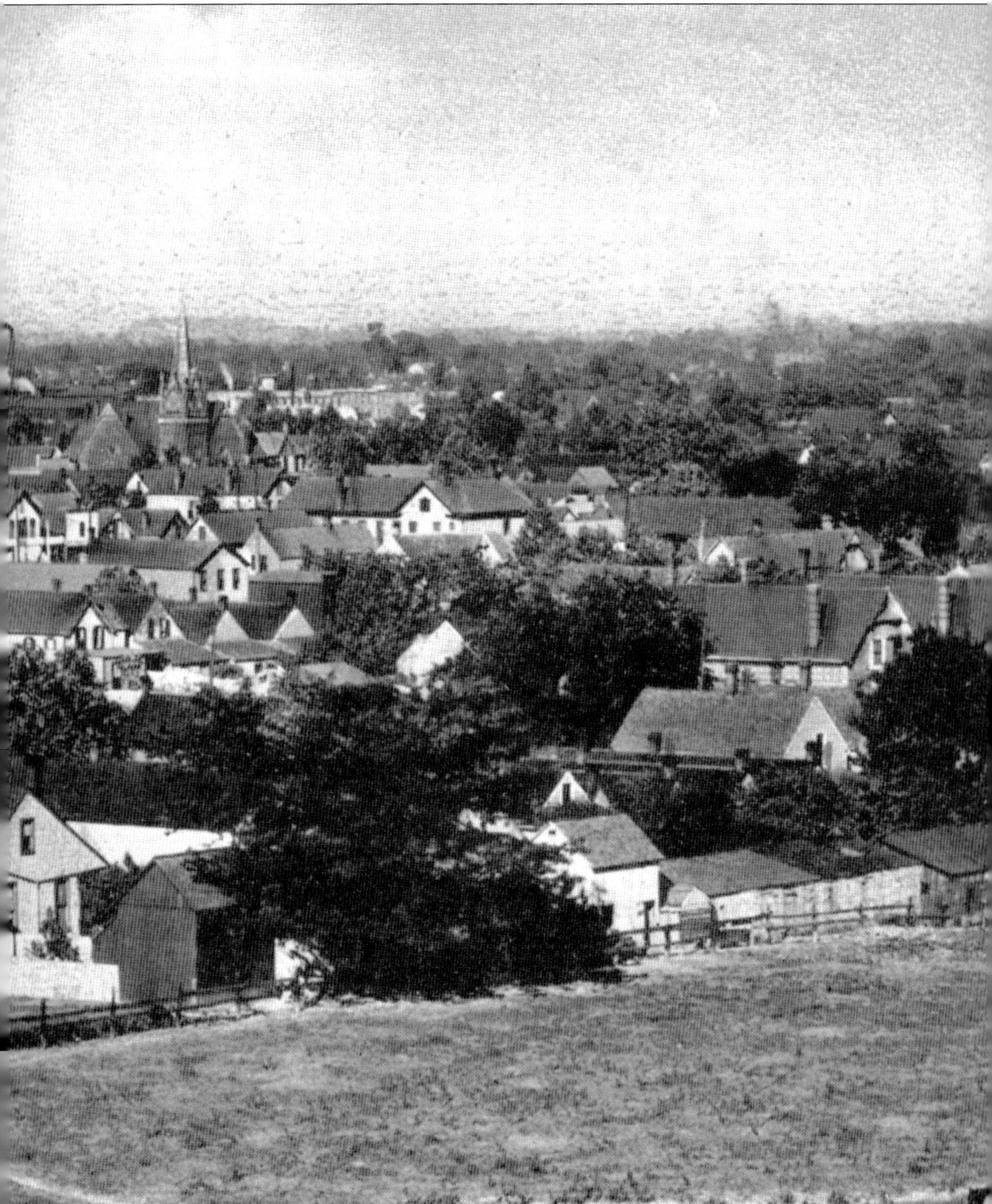

This postcard shows the western edge of Evansville as seen from Coal Mine Hill (now Reitz Hill). The bell tower of the old Centennial School (right) and the spires of St. Boniface Catholic Church (center) and St. Paul Evangelical (left) dominate the skyline. An influx of German immigrants in the late 19th century created a demand for housing. In just a few

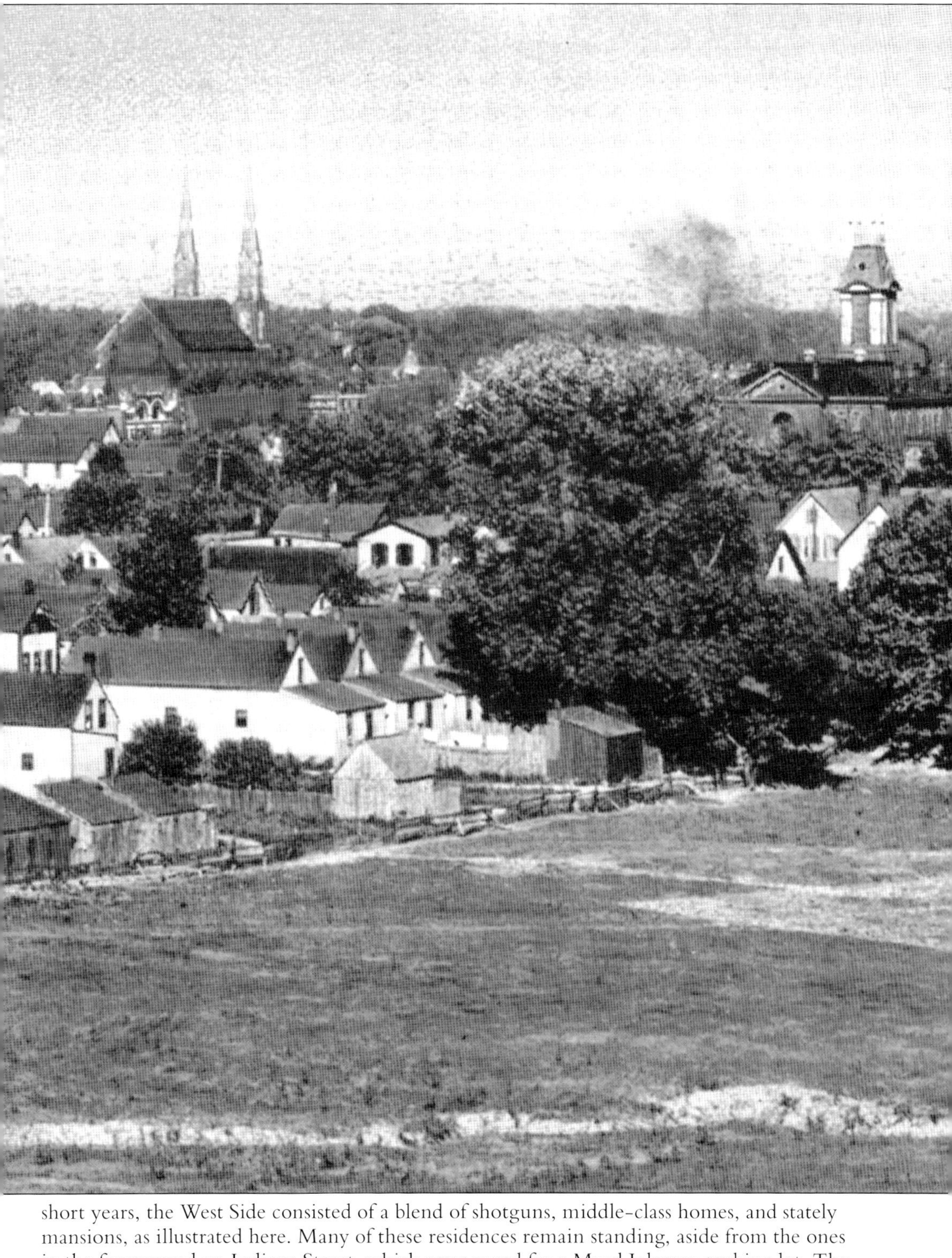

short years, the West Side consisted of a blend of shotguns, middle-class homes, and stately mansions, as illustrated here. Many of these residences remain standing, aside from the ones in the foreground on Indiana Street, which were razed for a Mead Johnson parking lot. The Lloyd Expressway now cuts through the field at the bottom of the image. (Engler family.)

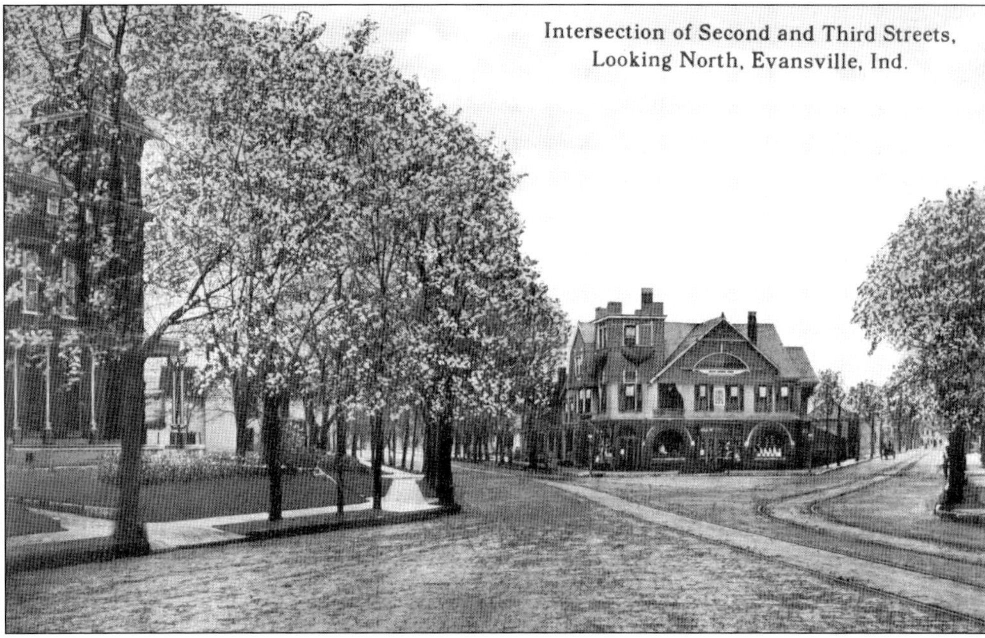

The Goosetown area was another residential neighborhood that experienced a boom in the late 1800s. At the corner of Second and present-day Parrett Streets (center) is Haynie's Drug, built around 1890 and destroyed by fire in 1940. Small businesses like this served the suburban areas. The house partially visible at left was built for Charles Kellogg of Boetticher & Kellogg Company; since 1992, it has been home to Kirby's Private Dining. (EVPL and the Topper family.)

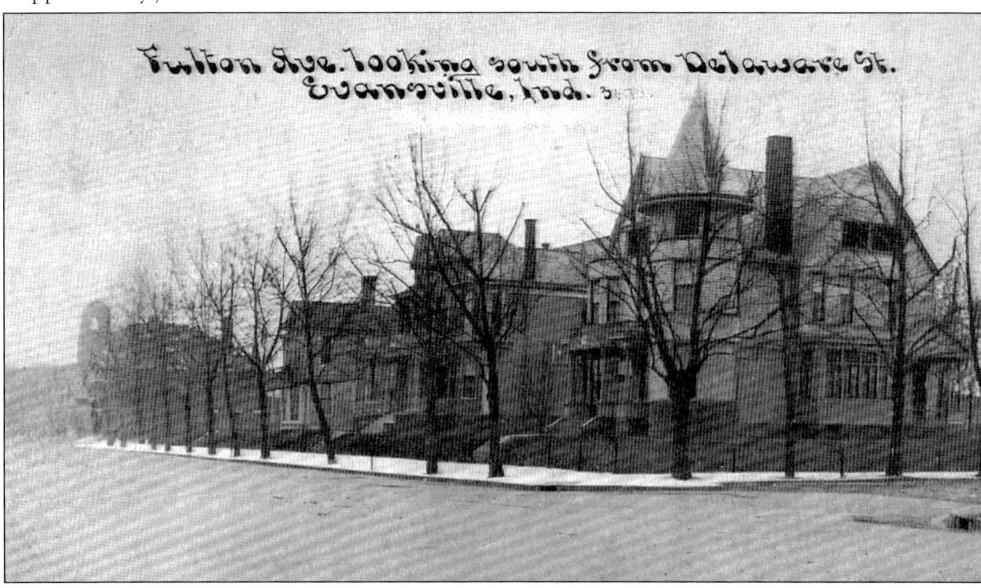

This postcard shows the Cook mansions on Fulton Avenue between Delaware and Iowa Streets, which were home to Frederick W. Cook, of the F.W. Cook Brewing Company, and his two sons, Charles and Henry. Of the three, only Henry's (middle) remains standing, though it is in poor condition. The bell tower of the old Fulton School is visible in the distance at left. (Engler family.)

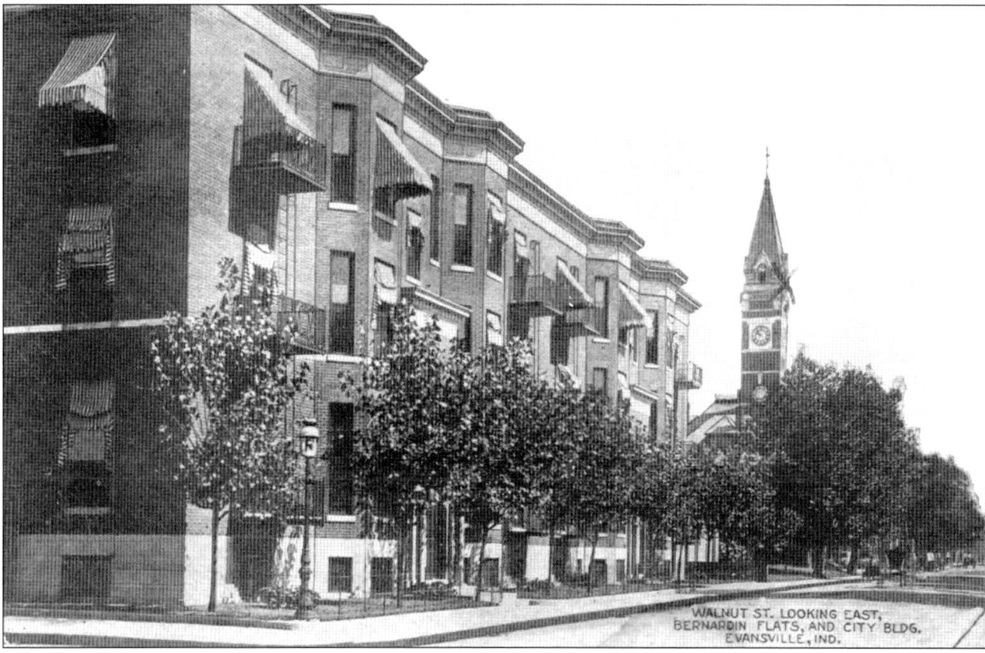

Bernardin Flats, one of a number of apartment complexes built during a boom for downtown housing, were erected around the end of the 19th century at the corner of Second and Walnut Streets. The old city hall building (see page 11) is visible in the background. This apartment building was demolished around 2000 for parking. (EVPL and the Topper family.)

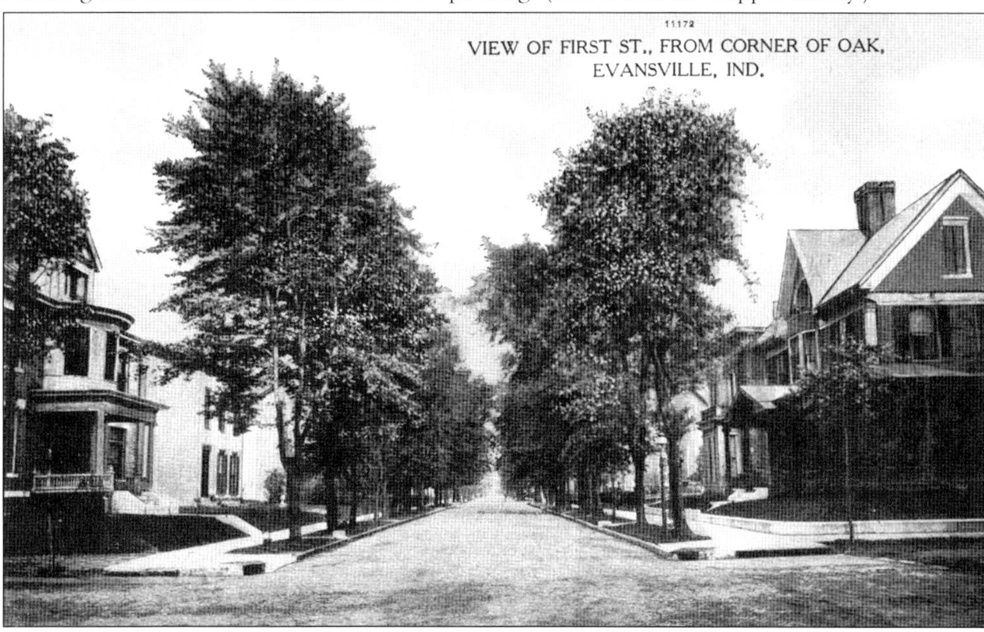

The Riverside district continued to be a desirable neighborhood to live. New residences were built on empty lots or side yards of larger homes. Extremely old houses were either renovated or replaced. This postcard offers a view of Upper First Street at Oak Street. On both corners, a house from the mid-1800s sits next to one from the end of the 19th century, illustrating the blend of old and new. (Engler family.)

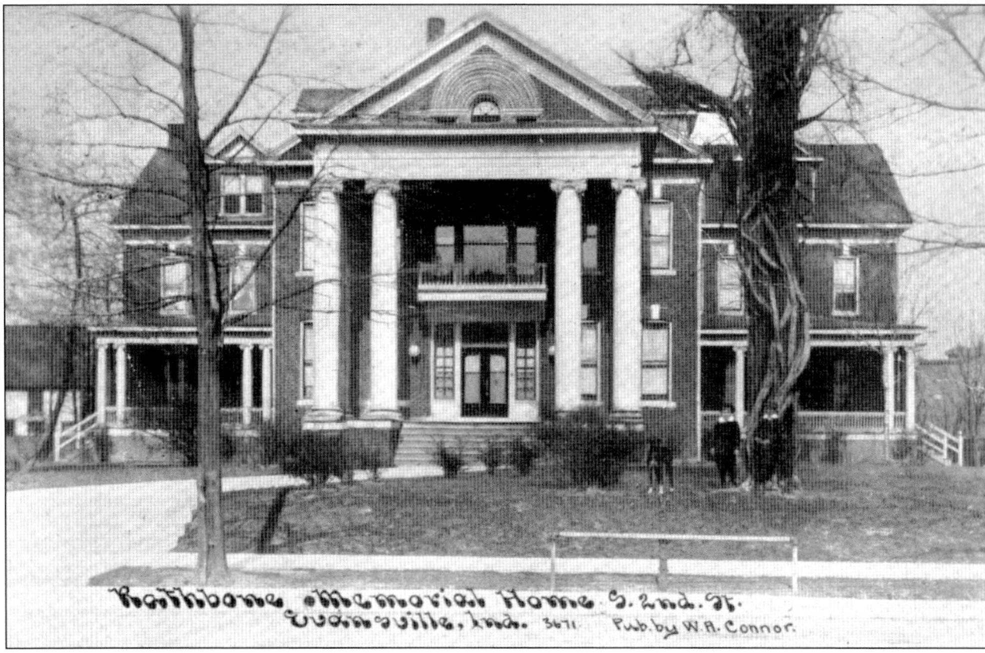

The Rathbone Memorial Home on Second Street was built in 1905 as a retirement center for the well-to-do. Named after Evansville banker George W. Rathbone, it was built in the Classical Revival style by architects Harris & Shopbell. It was operated by Welborn Baptist Hospital from 1967 until 1983, when it closed. After an attempt to convert it into apartments, the Rathbone is again serving as a retirement home. (EVPL and the Topper family.)

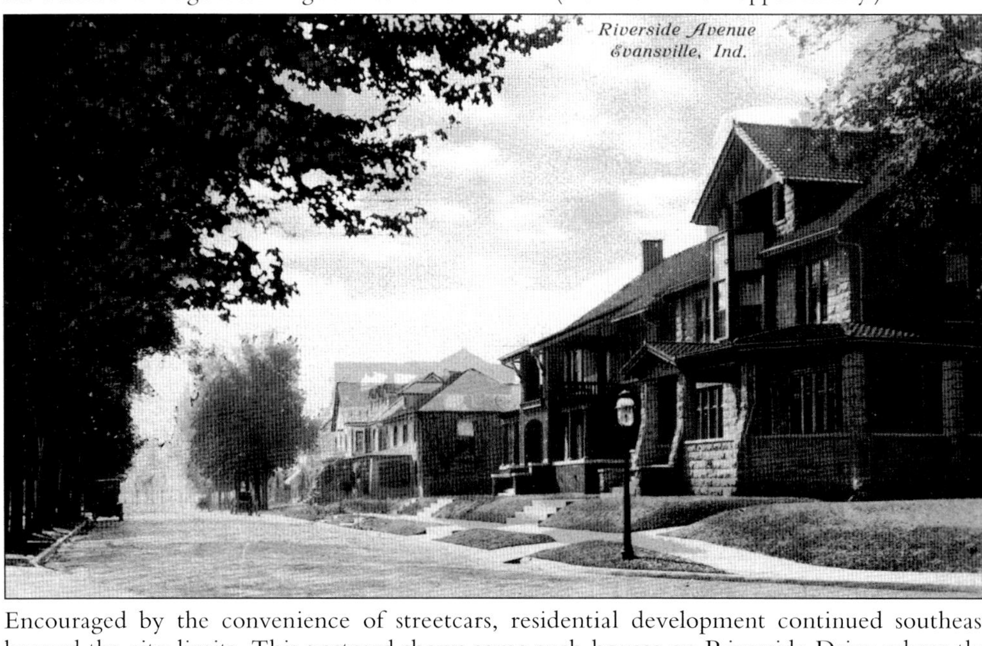

Encouraged by the convenience of streetcars, residential development continued southeast beyond the city limits. This postcard shows some such houses on Riverside Drive where the street narrows, an area formerly known as Union Place. The stone, Craftsman-style home at far right is the S.V. Levi residence, which was built in 1905. Next to it is Edward Kiechle's house, designed by Clifford Shopbell and built in 1909. (Engler family.)

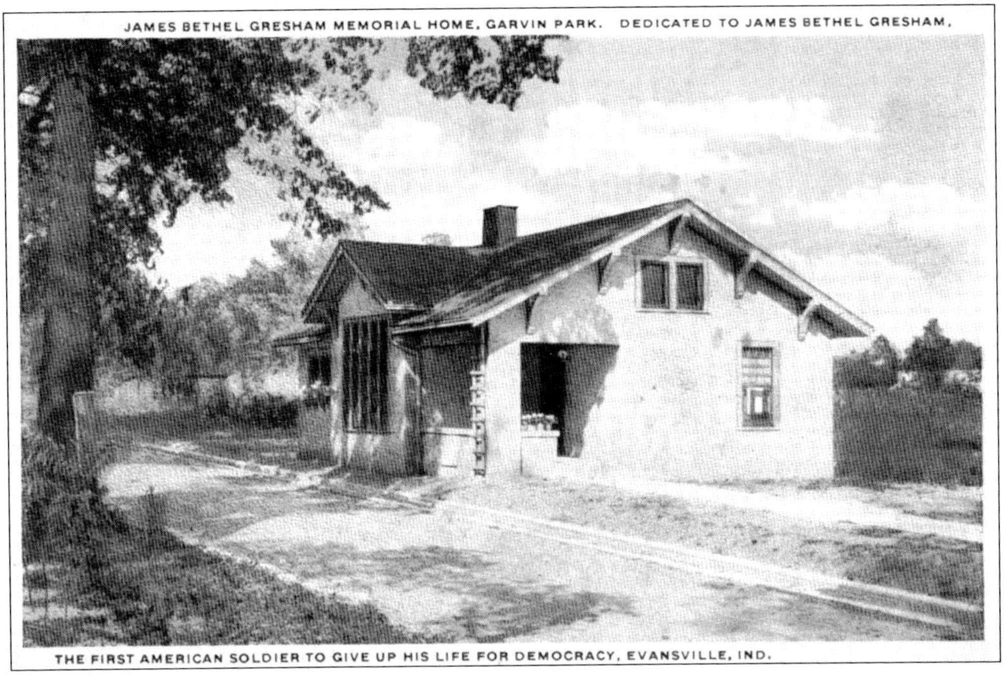

This bungalow is the James Bethel Gresham Memorial Home, built about 1920. It was dedicated to Gresham, the first American soldier killed in World War I, and gifted to his mother. The home, now property of the city, still stands on the edge of Garvin Park at the corner of Herndon Drive and Wedeking Avenue. (Engler family.)

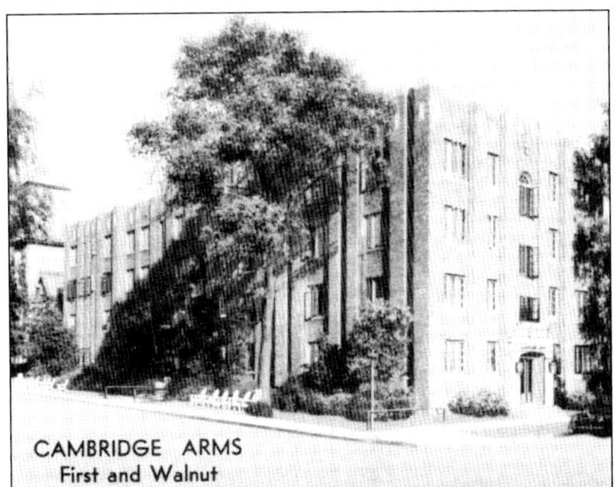

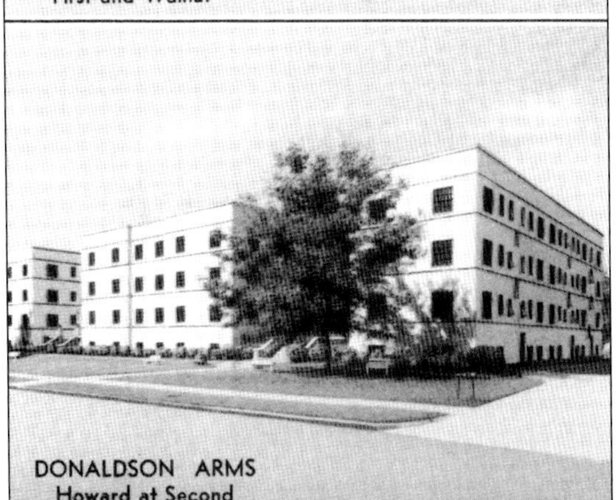

The upper image at right shows the Cambridge Arms at First and Walnut Streets, built in 1929 in the Art Deco style. Behind the trees at left is the old Walnut Street Presbyterian Church (see page 19). The apartment complex in the lower image is the Donaldson Arms, located on Howard Street in the Culver neighborhood. It was built in 1923 and remodeled sometime around 1950. Both of these buildings are still standing. (EVPL and the Geiss family.)

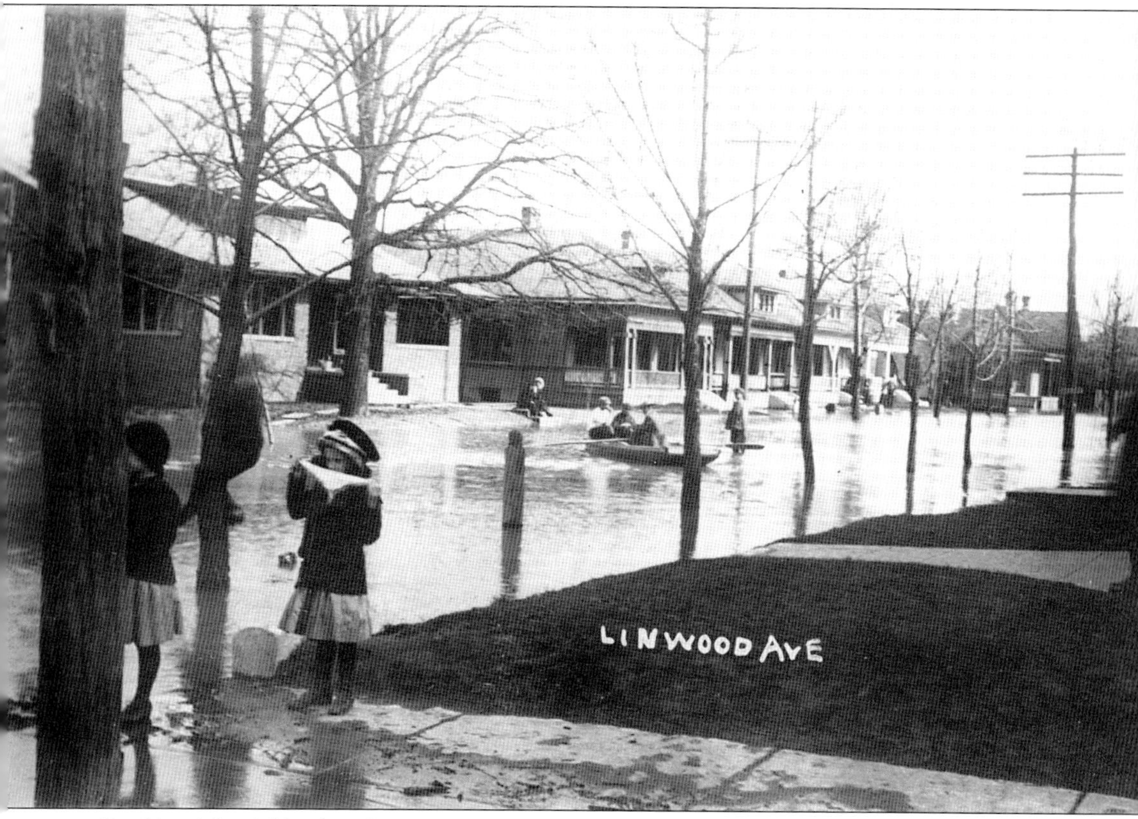

Residential neighborhoods were not immune to the major Ohio River flood of 1937, especially those on the southeast side. Like commercial buildings along the riverfront, homes—like these on Linwood Avenue—were affected by high water. The *Evansville Courier* mentioned that if several of these houses had not had basements (which flooded), the water level would have risen even higher. (EVPL and the Topper family.)

Eight

Leisure Time

Without the luxuries of television and Internet, the citizens of a century ago had to find diversions wherever they could, and people found all sorts of ways to pass the time.

The outdoors provided entertainment that is often lost on today's culture. Pleasure parks, small-scale versions of today's amusement parks, were just a trolley ride away and provided an escape from the routine. A push to improve recreational facilities during Mayor Benjamin Bosse's administration saw several Evansville city parks created or improved—some even included pools and golf courses.

Social clubs and benevolent societies were other recreational outlets, as members donated time and talents to various endeavors. Many of these fraternal organizations, like the Masons and the Eagles, continue to flourish today. Other clubs, such as the YMCA, fostered an environment in which members could develop skills and friendships.

Theaters and opera houses offered another way to pass the time. Many of these establishments, which originally showed live performances and later became nickelodeons, were built on a grander scale than today's multiscreen cinemas.

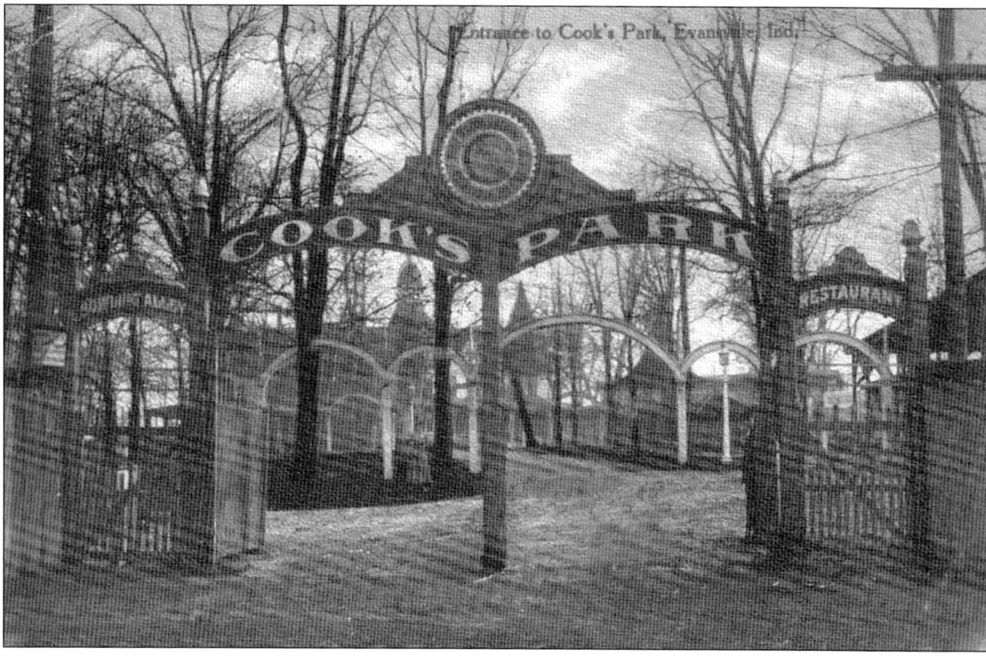

Situated on an old salt well near Pigeon Creek, Cook's Park is the oldest park in Evansville. The production of salt never materialized, so in the 1840s, the land was turned into Pigeon Springs, a health resort where guests could rest and enjoy the mineral water's medicinal properties. The property was later bought by Frederick W. Cook, president of the F.W. Cook Brewing Company, who improved the park by putting up a clubhouse and building a lake (below). By the late 1800s, Cook's Park was just a streetcar ride away for the residents of Evansville. The main entrance, south off Maryland Street, is shown above. (Both, Engler family.)

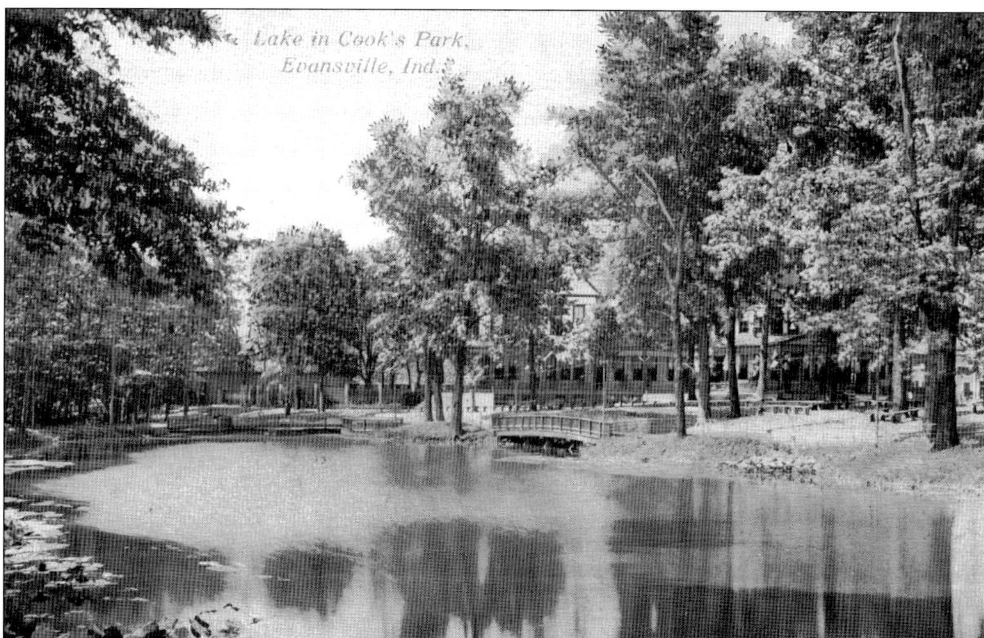

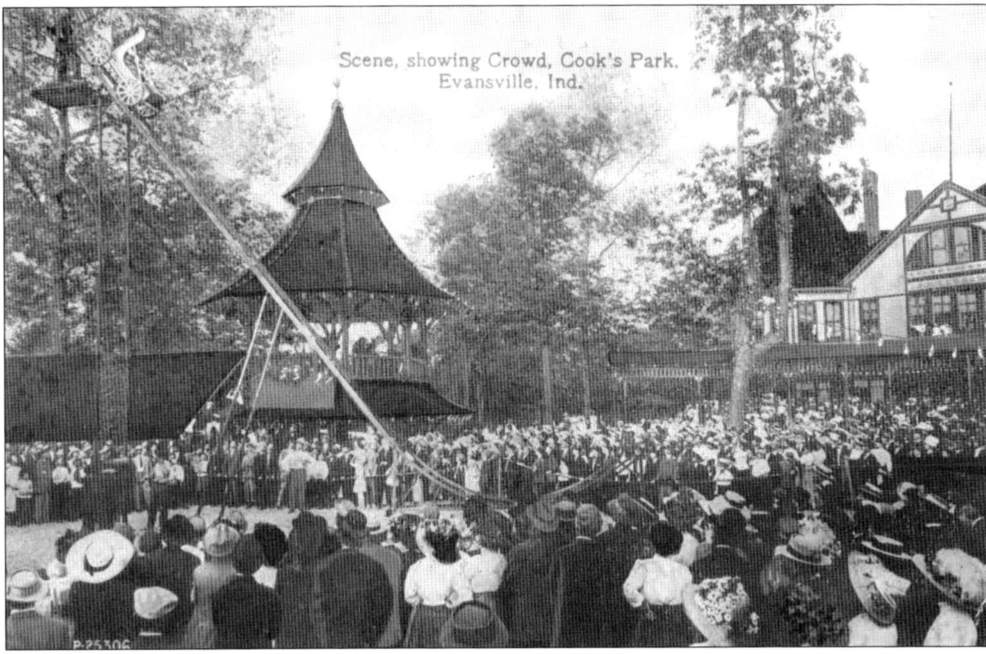

Cook's Park, which encompassed 17 acres, had something for everyone, including a roller coaster, a merry-go-round, a swimming pool, a dance hall, and even a casino. The scene above was common, as crowds would gather to see performers on the Aeroplane swing or to watch fireworks or to check out the electric fountain. An open-air café and beer garden (below) served refreshments—most likely Cook's beer. Around the 1920s, the park became known as Exposition Park and later still as Pleasure Park. It met its downfall when it was forced to close during Prohibition. Part of the park's land was taken by the Columbia-Delaware Bridge, which opened in 1956 and passes over the old entrance. The remainder of the land is the present-day site of the Lamasco Park baseball field and skate park. (Above, EVPL; below, Engler family.)

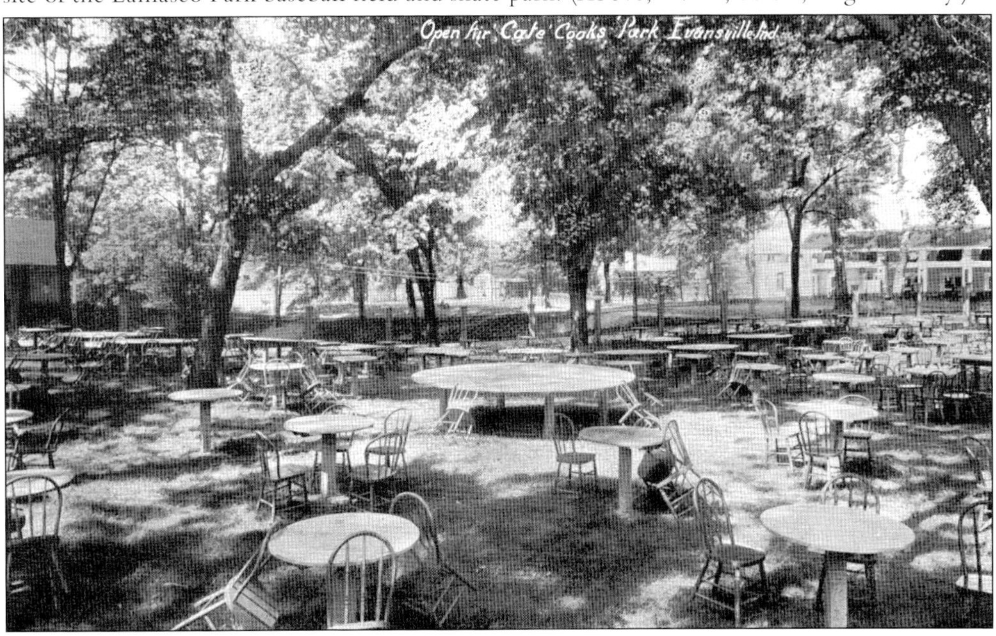

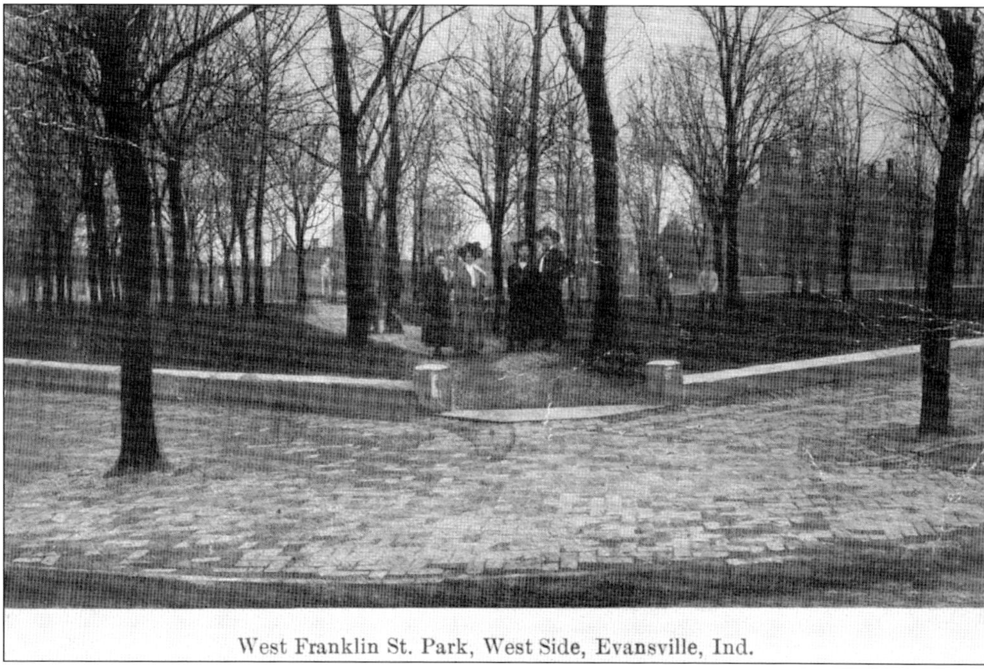

West Franklin Street Park was bounded by Franklin Street, Tenth Avenue, Illinois Street, and Wabash Avenue. The lot was reserved when the city of Lamasco was originally laid out, but stacks of lumber had to be cleared and trees needed to be planted before it was an actual park. The West Branch Library has occupied the park since 1912, and the park also hosts the rides for the annual West Side Nut Club Fall Festival. (Engler family.)

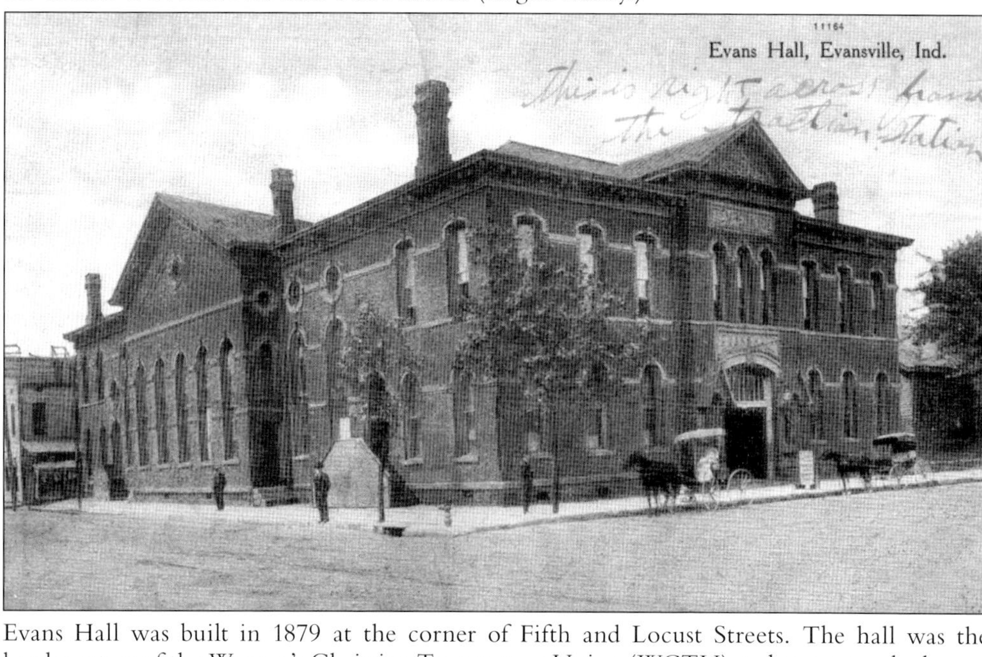

Evans Hall was built in 1879 at the corner of Fifth and Locust Streets. The hall was the headquarters of the Woman's Christian Temperance Union (WCTU) and was once the largest public gathering place in Evansville. It was razed around 1930, and the old Central Library (see page 50) was built on the site. (Engler family.)

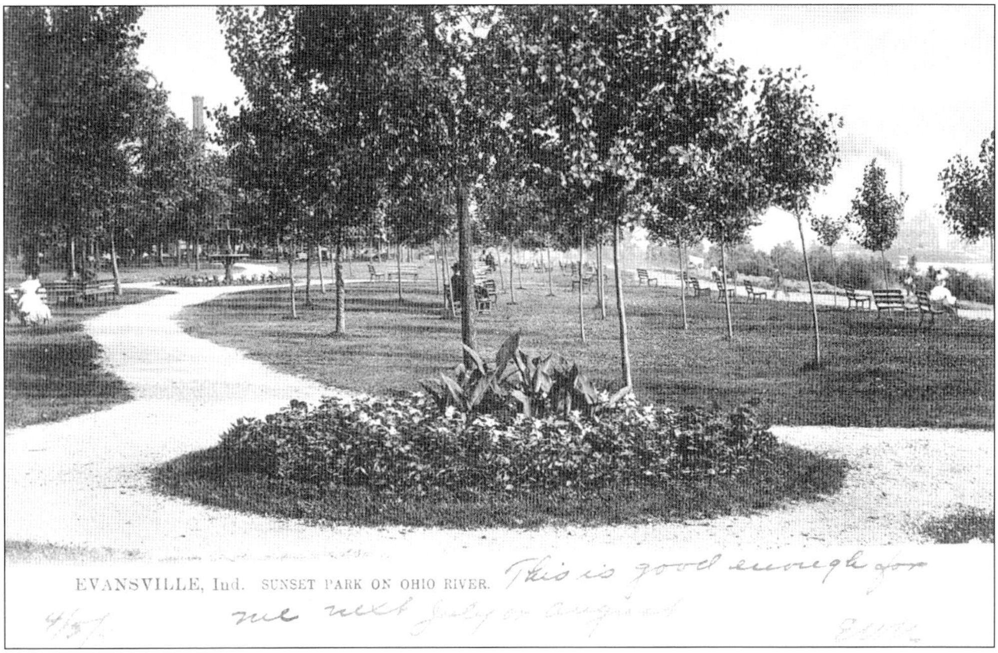

The riverfront was once the hub of the Evansville's commercial activity, but residents soon recognized its potential as a park. By the 1880s, Sunset Park became a popular gathering spot. Its location on the Ohio River offered a magnificent view of the setting sun—hence the name. The scene above shows flower beds and trails in the park. Playground equipment and tennis courts were added later. Upper Water Street (later renamed Riverside Drive), located near the park, became the premier neighborhood for Evansville's elite. To handle increasing demand, an additional street—Sunset Avenue—was laid out; several houses (with spectacular views of the park and river) were constructed there in the early 1900s. (Both, Engler family.)

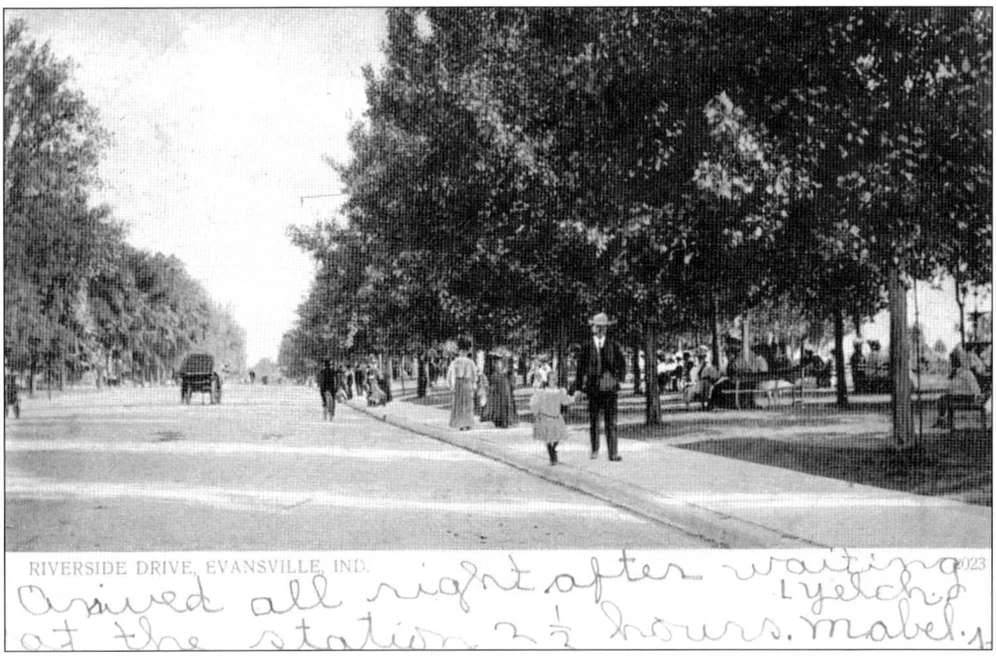

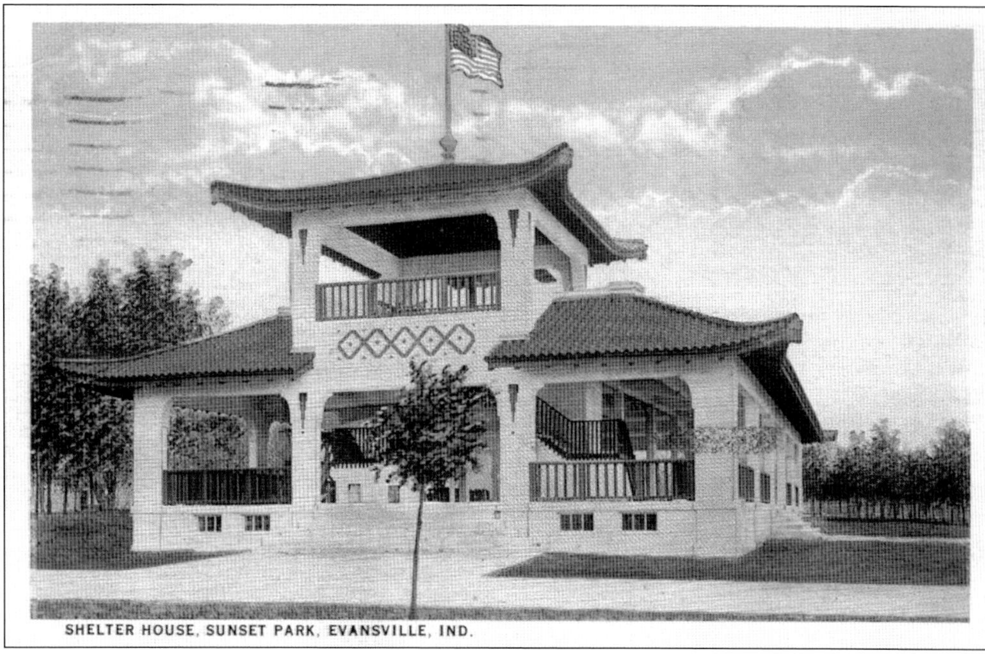

The Japanese-style shelter house above, commonly known as the Pagoda, was constructed in Sunset Park in 1912. Park visitors could enjoy its roof garden, cupola, bandstand, and public restrooms. After surviving the flood of 1937, the Pagoda sat neglected until it was restored in 1995 as a visitors' center. Before the park was divided by the Evansville Museum and, later, by Southlane Drive, it was immense. Now enhanced by the Pigeon Creek Greenway Passage, Sunset Park's natural splendor and commanding view of the river still draw visitors. Below is a view from the park toward downtown, with the Keller Crescent Building in the background. (Both, Engler family.)

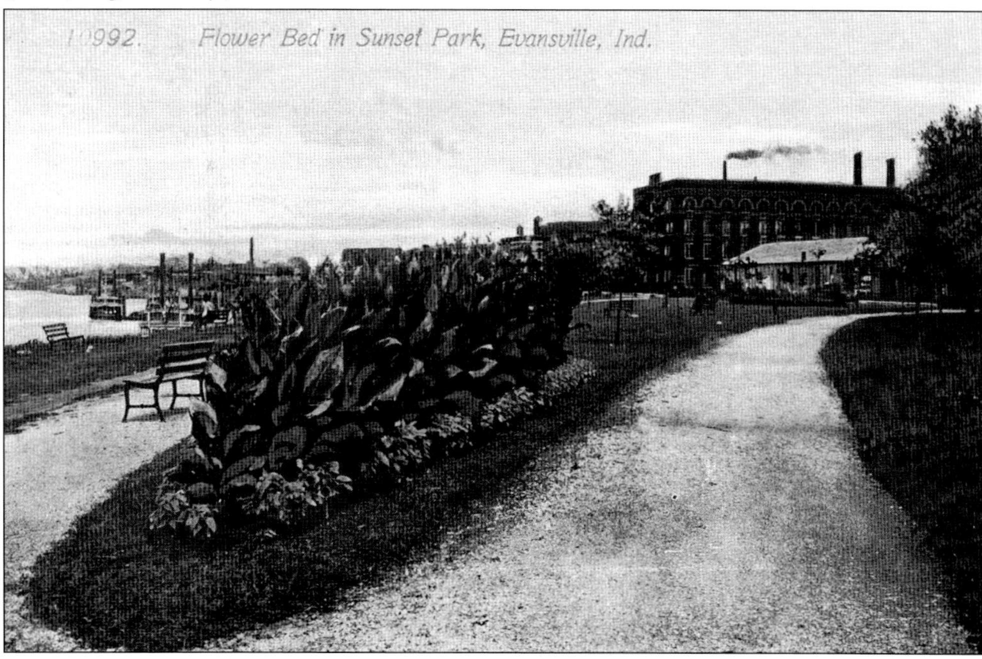

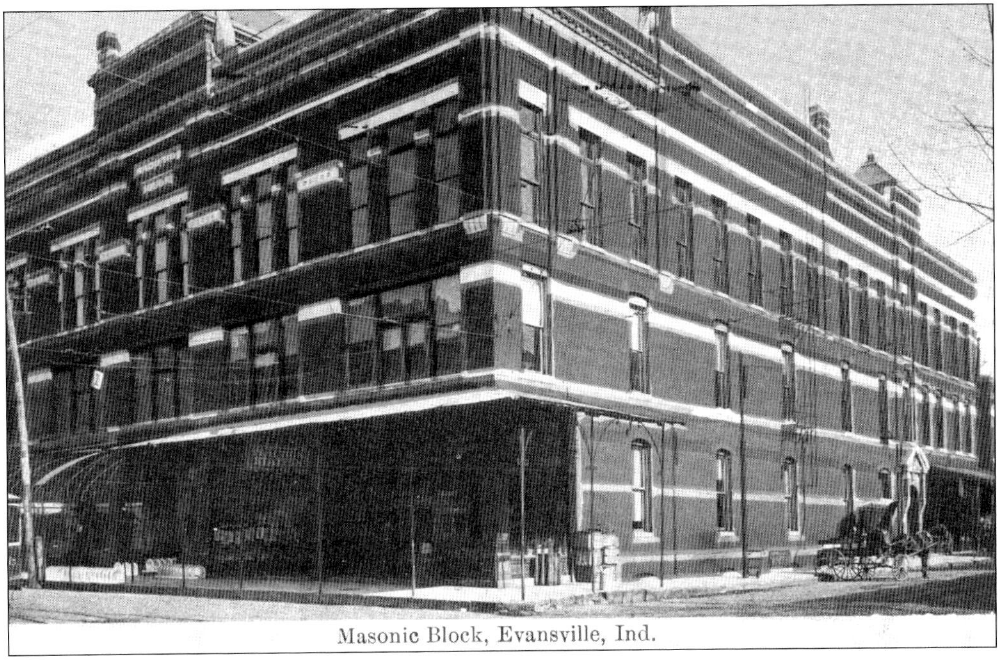

The Orr Block was built in 1887 at the corner of Second and Locust Streets. It was often called the Masonic Block because several Masonic lodges held meetings in the upstairs rooms. Sometime around 1970, the top story was removed, and the building was modernized. It was torn down in 1995, and the site is now a parking lot. (EVPL and the Topper family.)

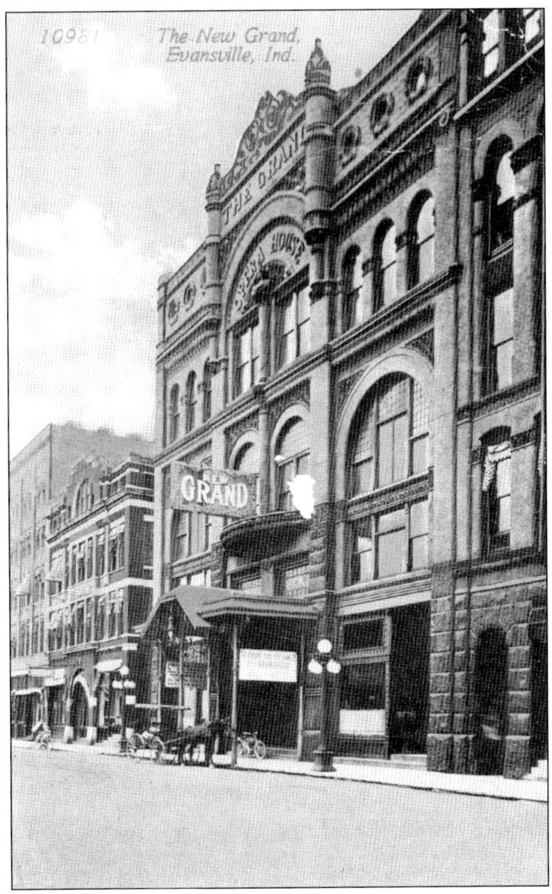

The Grand Opera House, built in 1889, was sandwiched between the Business Men's Association Building and the Vendome. In 1909, it was reopened as the New Grand, and by the 1930s, it was converted to show motion pictures. The Grand closed in 1962, and the theater was razed soon after. The Fifth Third Bank Building now occupies this site. (EVPL and the Topper family.)

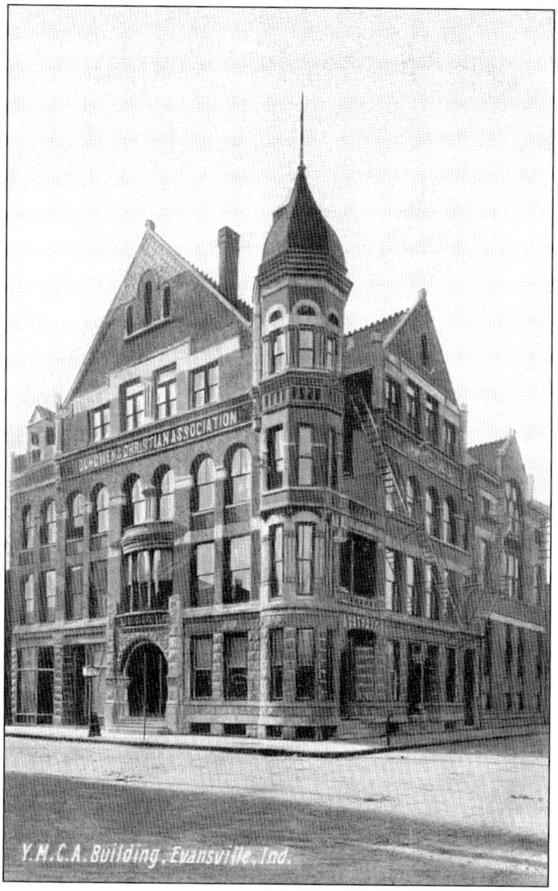

The original YMCA Building was erected in 1891 at the corner of Fourth and Sycamore Streets. Its membership swelled so much during the first several years of operation that a larger building was needed. A new YMCA (see page 121) was built just a few blocks away, and the organization vacated this building in 1914. It later became a business college and was torn down in 1928. (Engler family.)

A salt pool opened in 1894 and was managed by Dr. Edward C. Cluthe. It was located just west of Pigeon Creek on present-day Buchanan Road. By 1922, it was under new ownership as Fritzlar Mineral Springs. The pool closed in 1937 and was eventually torn down. The Vanderburgh County Humane Society building later occupied this site, but that was razed around 2010. (Engler family.)

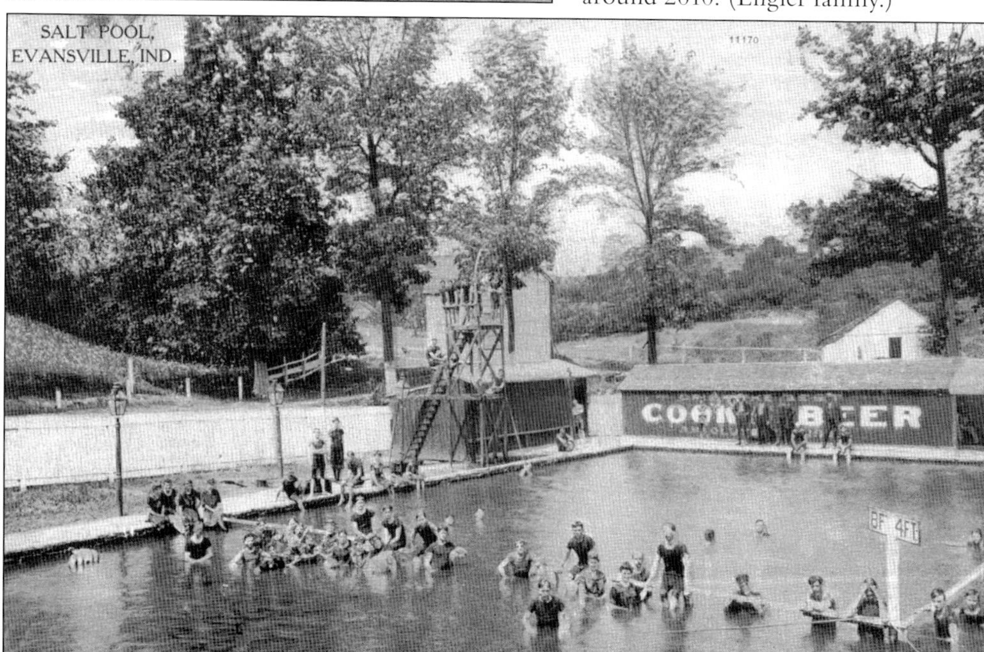

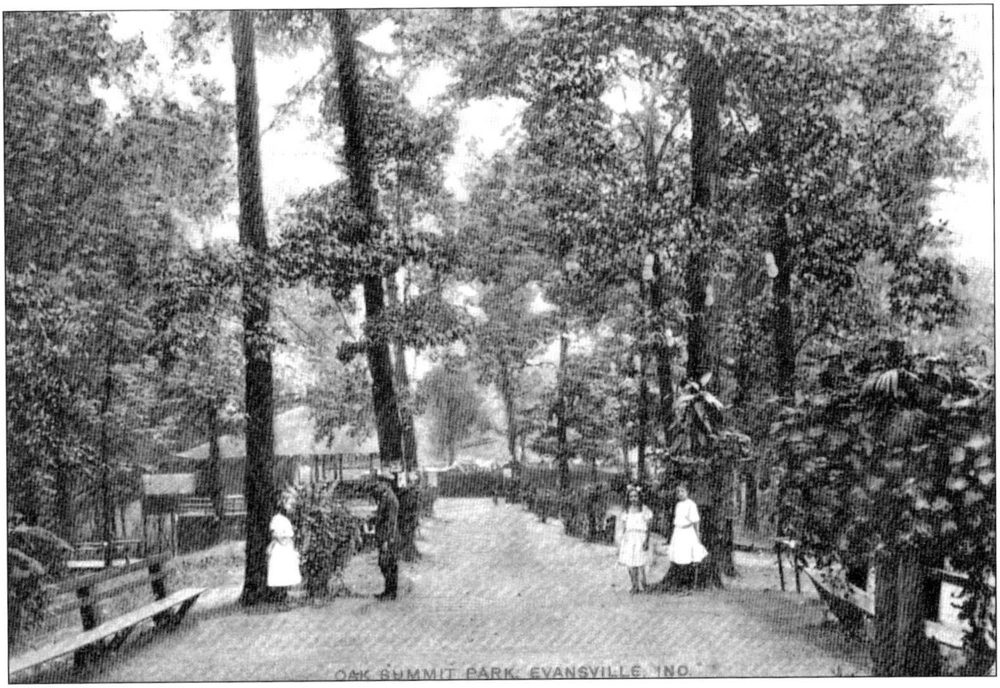

Oak Summit Park dates back to the end of the 19th century, when the Evansville Street Railway Company laid out a pleasure park at the end of its route on Little Cynthiana Road (now Mesker Park Drive). Nestled among the rolling hills of the West Side, the park was a suburban attraction for those trying to escape the city. Oak Summit Park hosted concerts and other social events and had picnic grounds and rides, such as the School of Mines ride (pictured below next to the park's entrance). (Both, Engler family.)

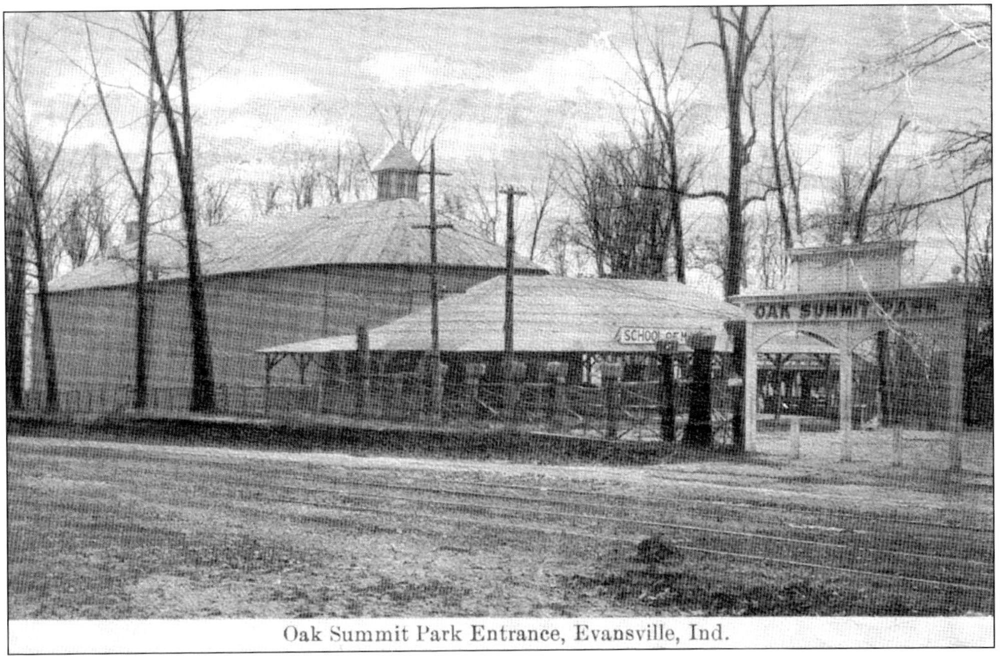

Oak Summit Park Entrance, Evansville, Ind.

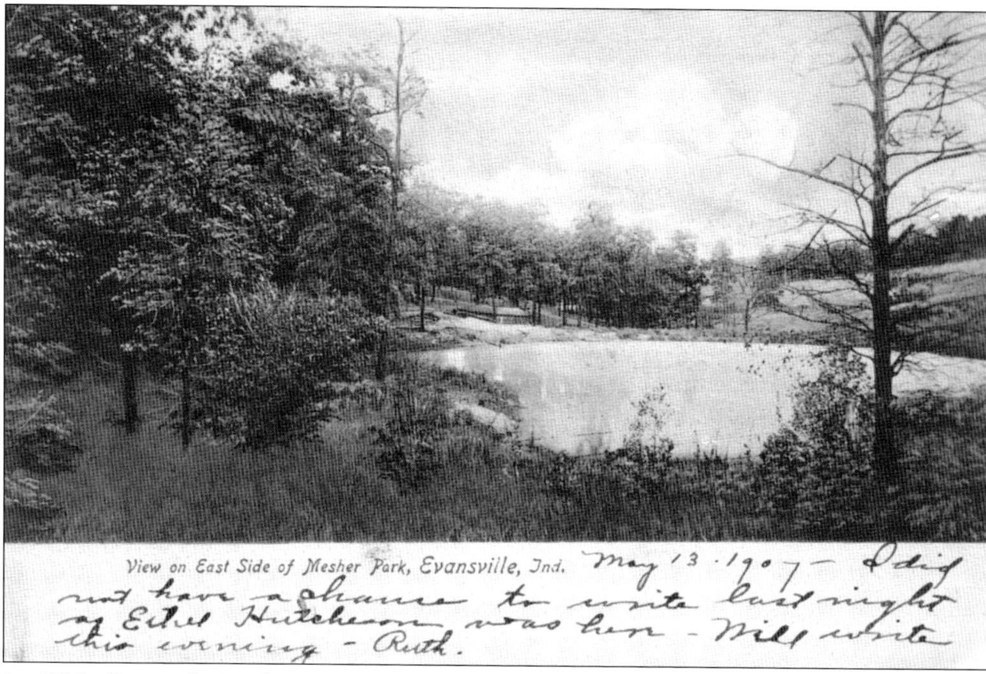

In 1900, George L. Mesker, owner of the Mesker Iron Company, donated 40 acres of land situated across the street from Oak Summit Park, creating Mesker Park. In 1915, Mesker donated $25,000 to acquire more land and improve the park. Playground equipment was installed in 1915, and the shelter house was completed in 1917; around this time, the two parks merged. In its early days, the park had a few animals on exhibit, but the Mesker Park Zoo, established in 1928, experienced substantial growth in the 1930s, including the construction of the Monkey Ship (pictured below). The General Animal House, the first major building to open on the zoo grounds, is in the background below. It was later called the Knecht Building, which was torn down and replaced with the Discovery Center in 1992. (Both, Engler family.)

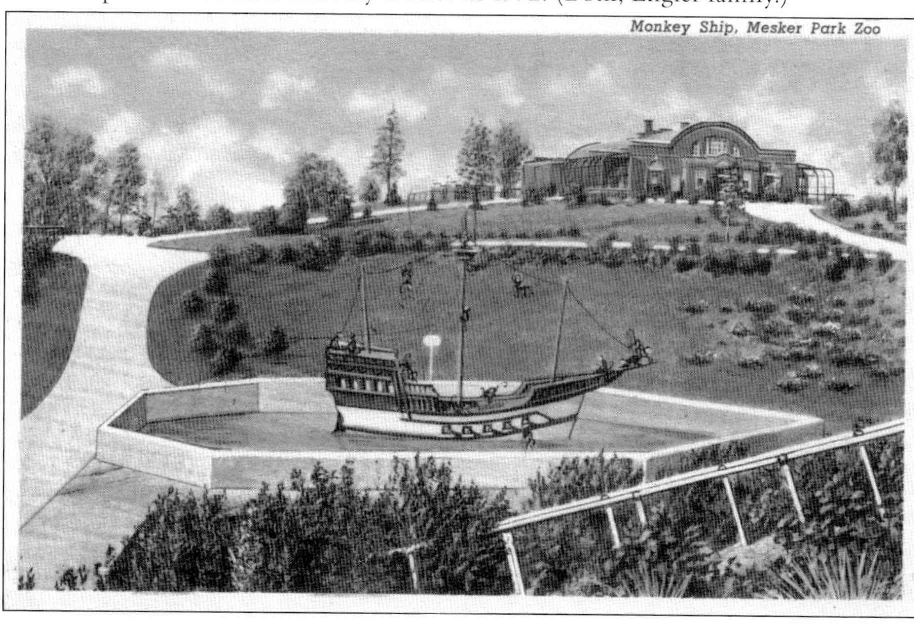

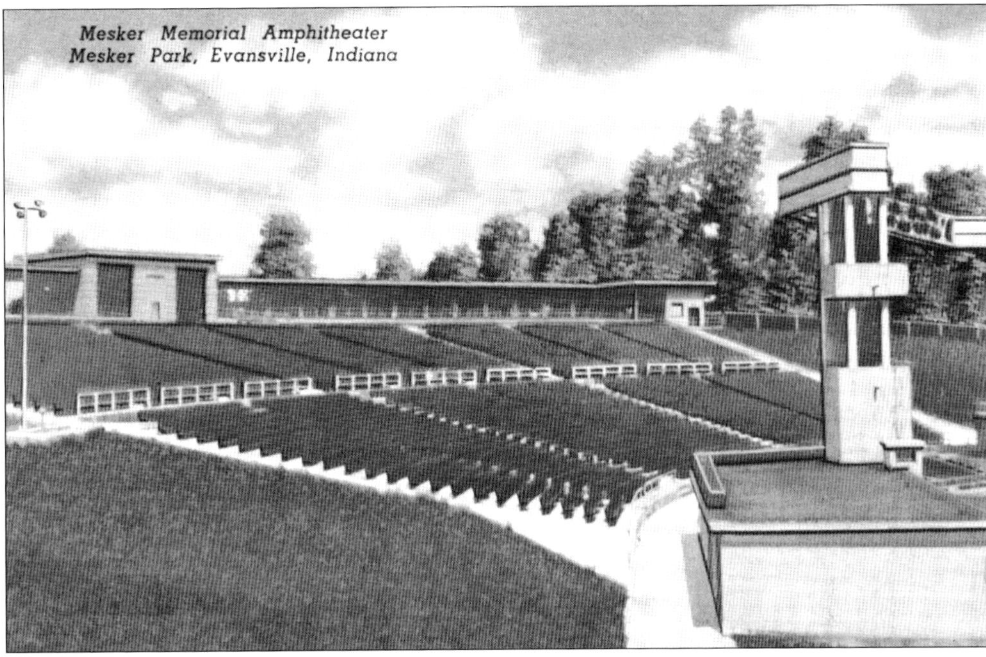

The creation of Mesker Memorial Amphitheater was the final wish of George Mesker, who donated another large sum of money upon his death in 1936. The trust would improve park facilities and support music programs, though construction was delayed by World War II. The amphitheater opened on June 15, 1952, and was a popular outdoor venue for years. The city recently closed the amphitheater, citing a need for serious repairs, and its fate is uncertain. (EVPL and the Geiss family.)

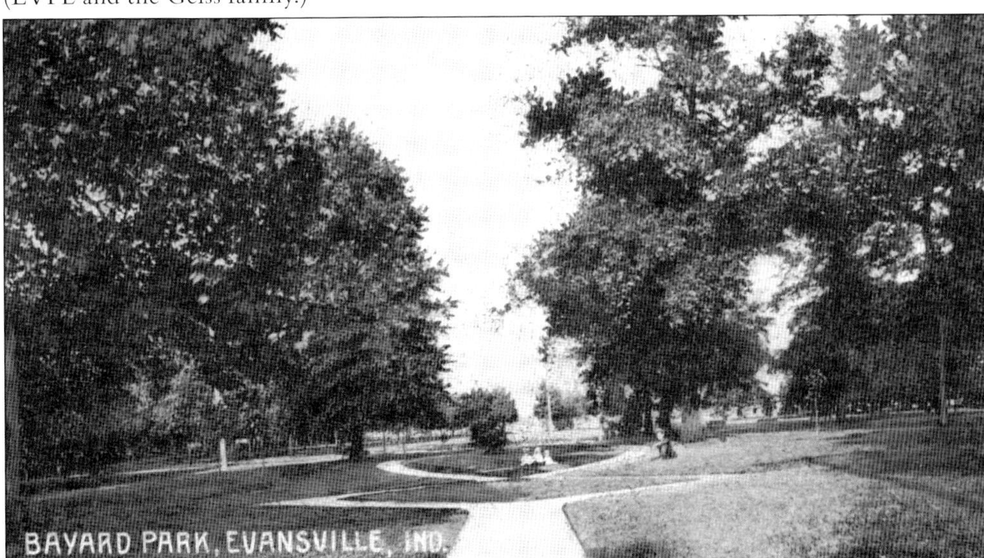

When part of the East Side was annexed in the late 1890s, a middle-class residential development was planned around Bayard Woods. Bayard Park, which was named after prominent Evansville banker Samuel Bayard, was established in 1901 when his widow donated 10 acres to the city. In 1912, the East Branch Library was built adjacent to the park. Today, the park is the centerpiece of the Bayard Park Historic District. (EVPL.)

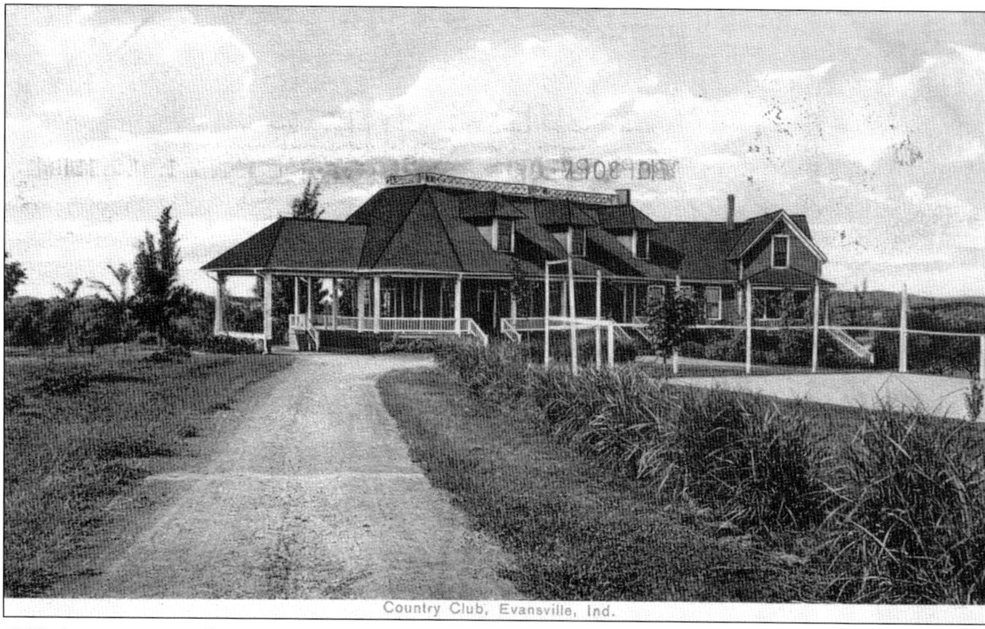

Offering a retreat from everyday life, the Evansville Country Club built this clubhouse on Stringtown Road around 1902. Sometime around 1908, it became the first in the city to have a nine-hole golf course. In the 1970s, a push to relocate the country club stalled, and the original clubhouse was expanded instead. (Engler family.)

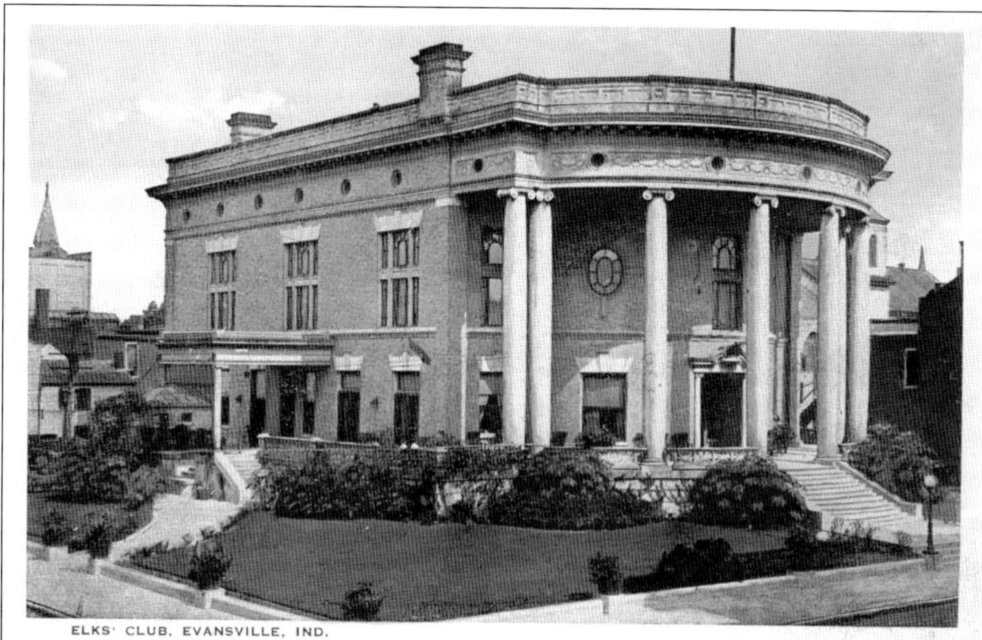

The Elks' Club, built from 1904 to 1906, occupied the corner of First and Locust Streets. The massive yellow brick building was dubbed one of the state's finest. By 1974, dwindling membership and increasing maintenance costs forced the club to sell, and the building was converted into the Upstage Dinner Theater. Sadly, it burned down in the winter of 1977—a spectacle, with icicles dangling from the fire-damaged building. (EVPL.)

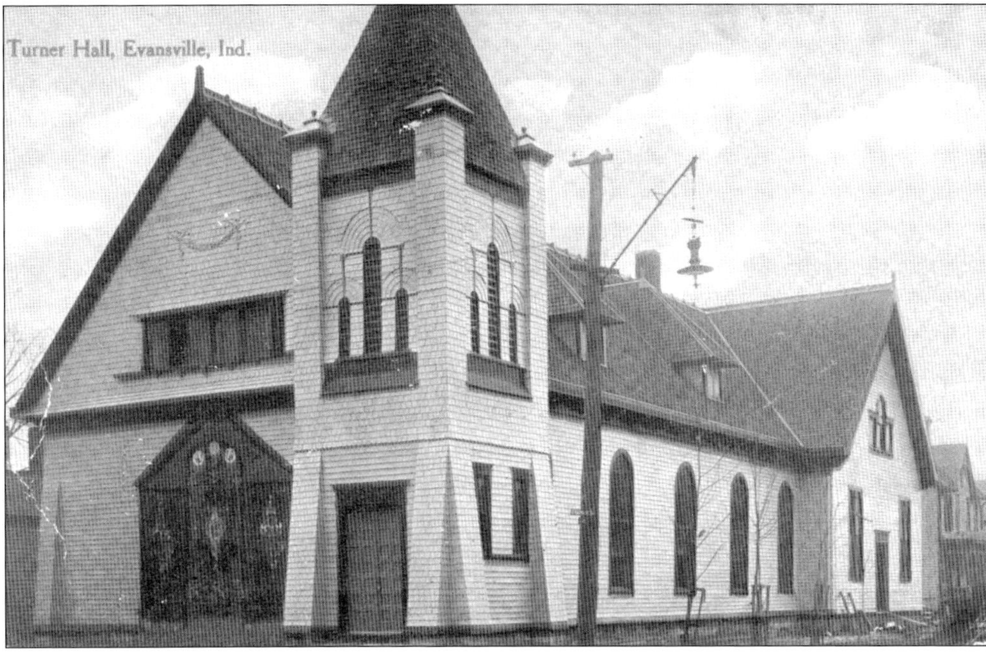

The Central Turners took over the old Kingsley Methodist Church in 1908. This church building at the corner of Eighth and Gum Streets was built around 1870. It served as Turner Hall until the club erected a new building on the same site in 1913. The newer Turner Hall is still standing, though the front has been modified. (EVPL and the Topper family.)

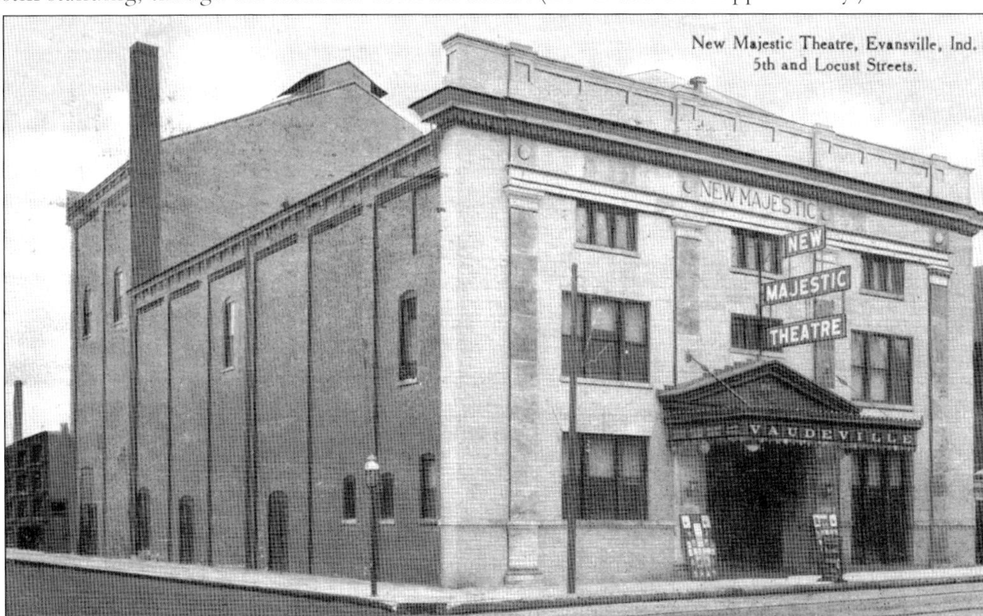

The New Majestic Theater was converted from the Igleheart Mill at Fifth and Locust Streets. In 1909, part of the old mill was torn down, and the New Majestic was built on the corner. The theater later became part of the Loew's chain and remained in business until 1973. It was torn down the following year and made into a parking garage. (Engler family.)

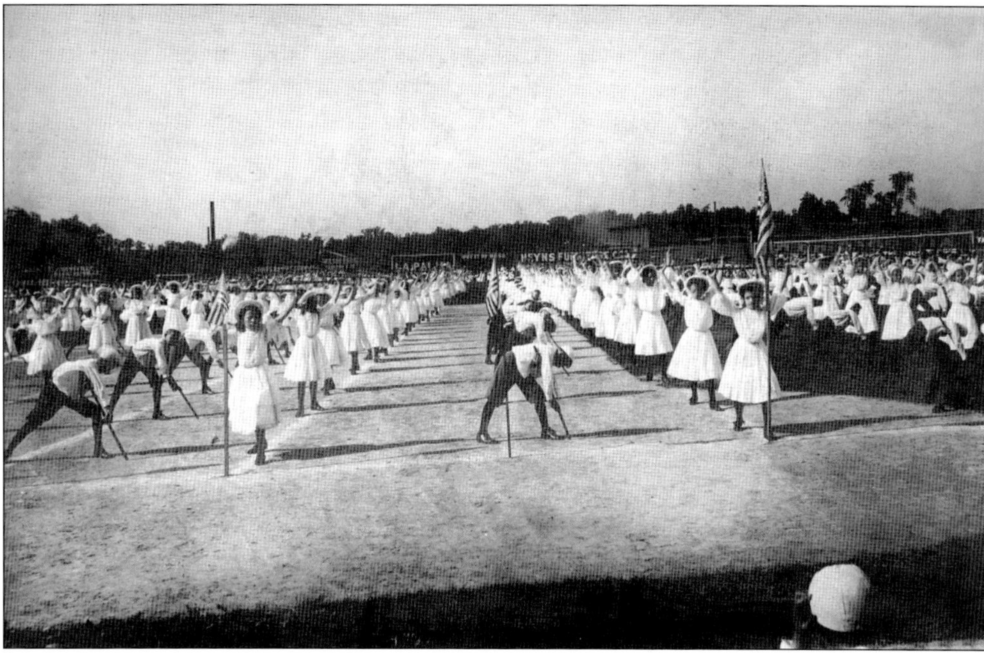

In the early 1900s, schoolchildren would participate in Field Day exercises each May. Field Day was first held at the old baseball park at Read and Louisiana Streets, pictured here in 1912, and later at Bosse Field. (EVPL.)

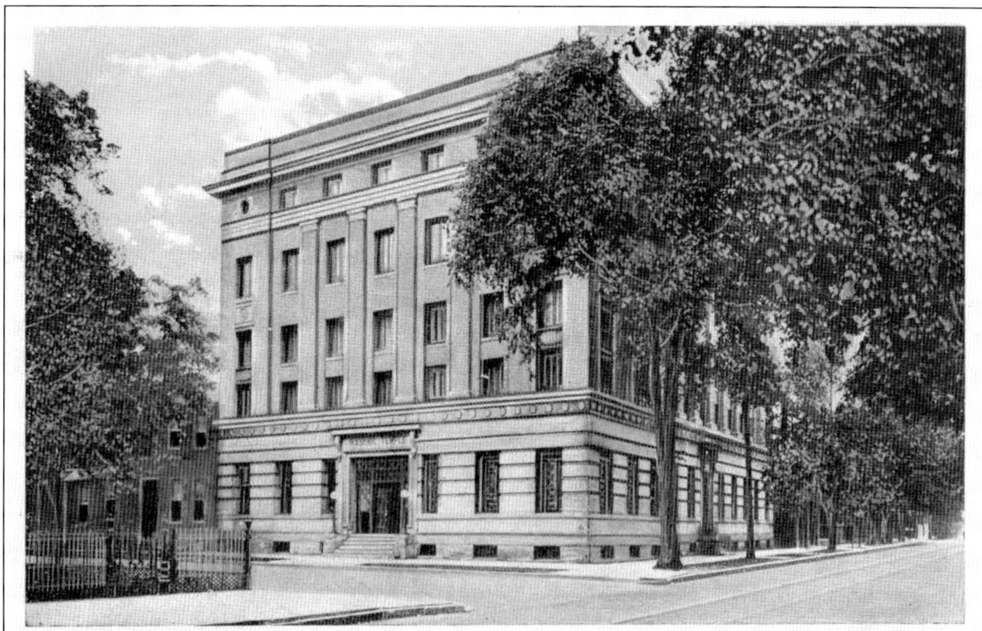

MASONIC TEMPLE, EVANSVILLE, IND.

This building was erected from 1912 to 1913 by the York Rite branch of the Masonic Order. Located at the corner of Chestnut and Third Streets, it was made of stone and decorative brick and was a collaboration of architects Clifford Shopbell and Frank Schlotter. The building, simply called the Masonic Temple (because it was used for various lodges), is still used by the Masons. (EVPL.)

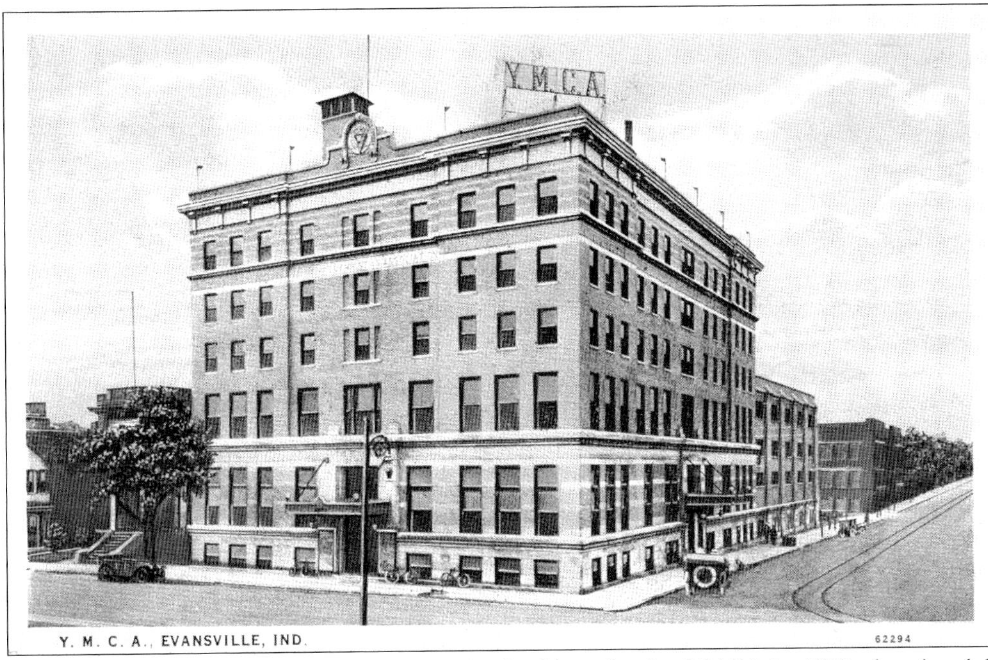

Clifford Shopbell and Company designed this building for the YMCA in 1913 after the club outgrew its old facility, located a few blocks away (see page 114). The six-story, yellow brick and stone structure was situated on the corner of Fifth and Vine Streets. Sometime after Old Central (High School) was demolished, the YMCA constructed its current entrance behind this building and took over the school's old gymnasium. (Engler family.)

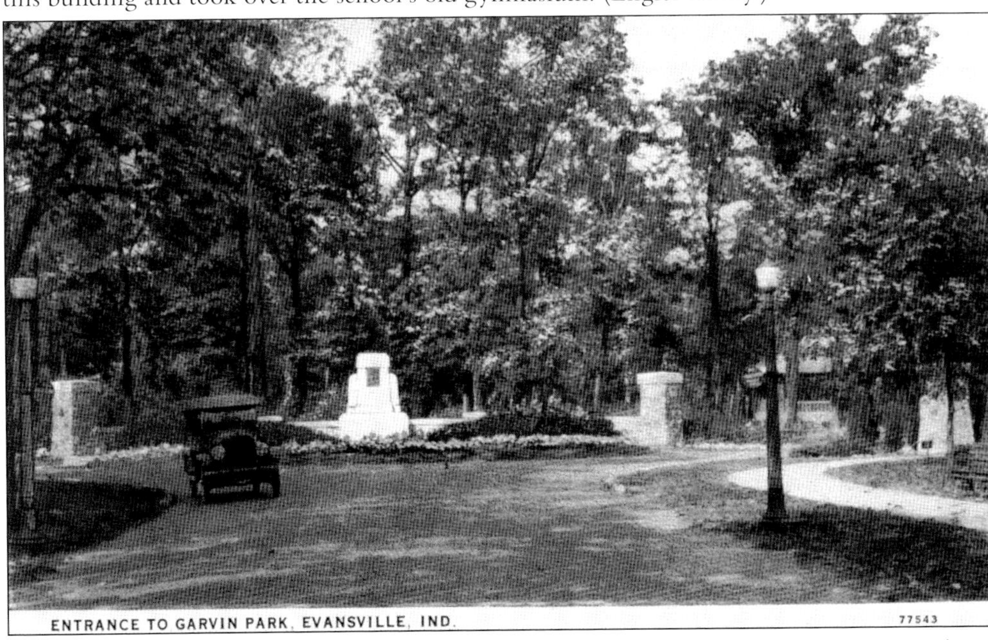

At the north end of Main Street was a wooded area owned by Thomas E. Garvin, a prominent Evansville attorney. First known as Garvin's Grove, it was open to the public and served as a retreat away from the city. In 1915, the land was given to the park system, thereby establishing Garvin Park. (Engler family.)

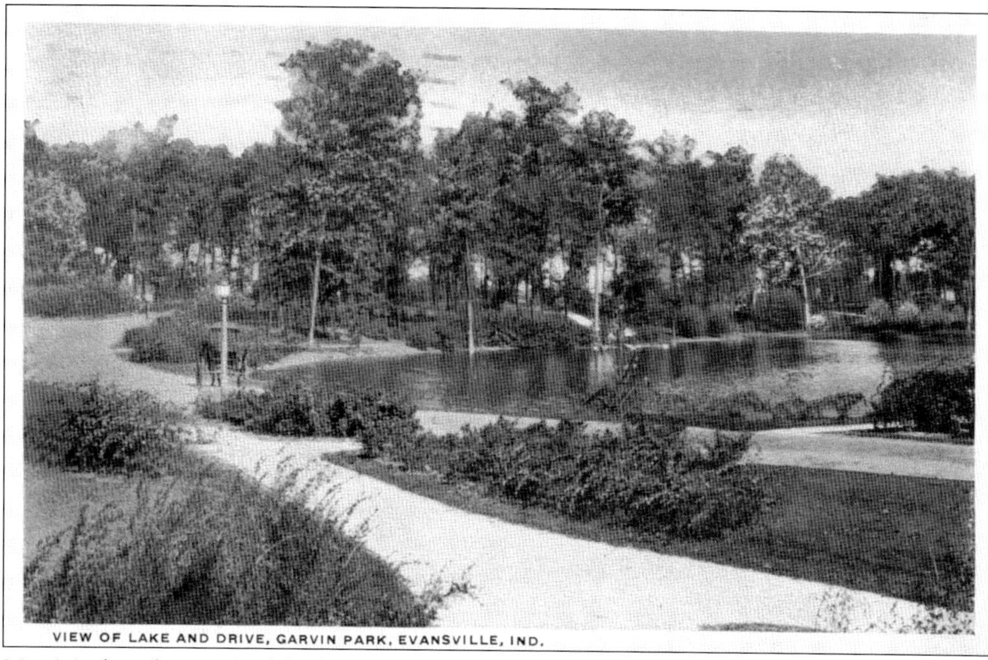

VIEW OF LAKE AND DRIVE, GARVIN PARK, EVANSVILLE, IND.

Municipal parks received high priority under Mayor Benjamin Bosse, and probably none more than Garvin Park. The park was laid out by a former student of Frederick Law Olmsted (who designed Central Park in New York City). The lake was built to remedy flooding from nearby Pigeon Creek. An entry gate and the electric fountain (shown below), were added shortly after the park opened. In the 1930s, architect Harry E. Boyle designed a bandstand and picnic shelter for the park. Amenities such as a pool, tennis courts, and playground equipment were added later. The recently refinished trail around the lake is still a popular destination for visitors looking to go for a stroll. Garvin Park hosts Ritzy's Fantasy of Lights each year around Christmas. (Both, Engler family.)

Electric Fountain in Garvin Park, Evansville, Indiana

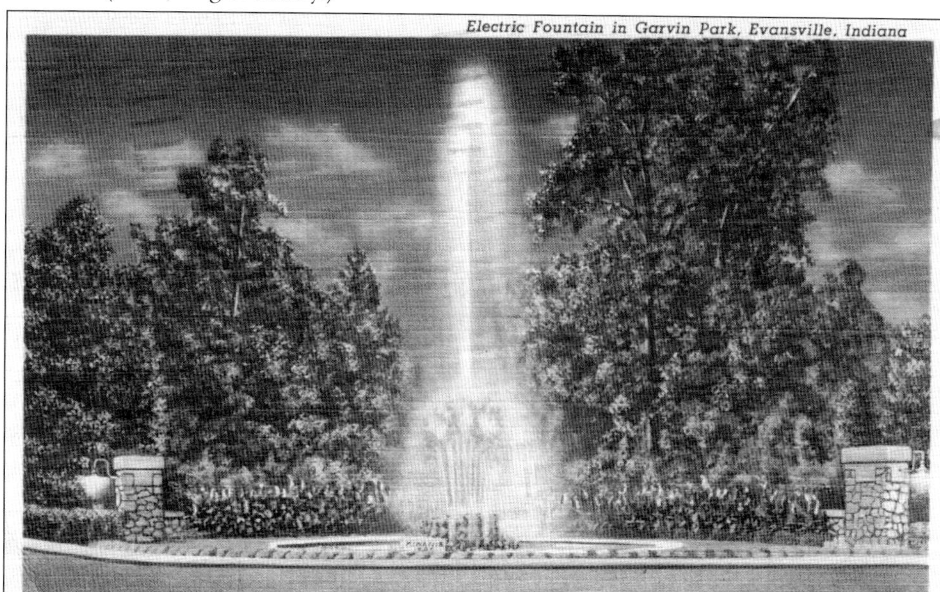

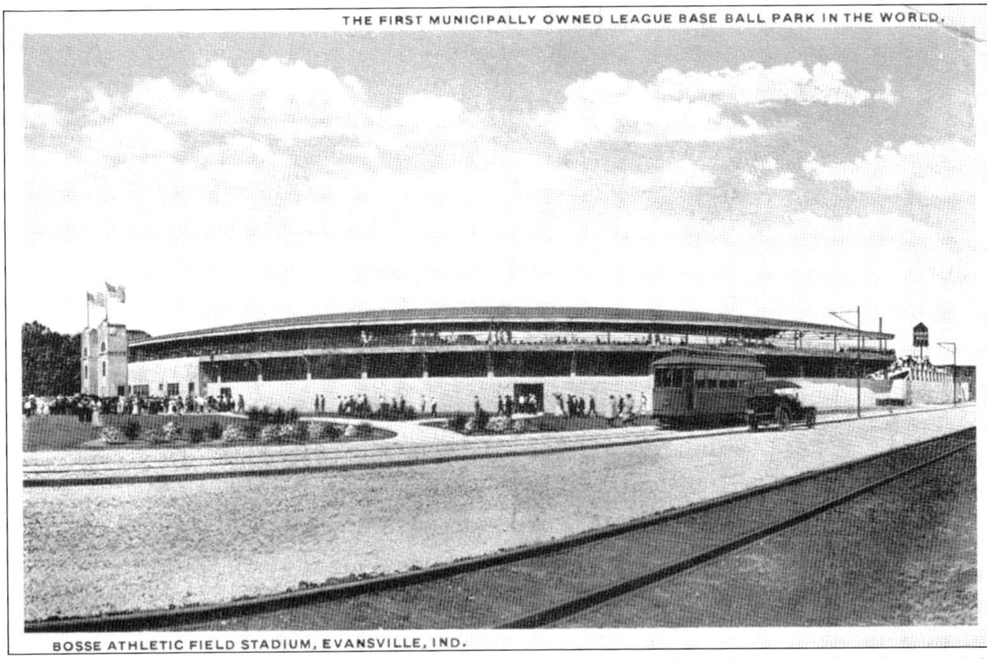

Located near the entrance of Garvin Park, Bosse Athletic Field had its opening day on July 17, 1915. It was named after Mayor Benjamin Bosse, who helped realize the project. Bosse Field was the first municipally owned stadium in the country and the third oldest professional ballpark, after Fenway Park (Boston) and Wrigley Field (Chicago). It has been home to several teams over the years, including the Evansville Triplets in the 1970s and 1980s. Since 1995, Bosse Field has been the home field for the Evansville Otters, who play in the Frontier League. The stadium's historic backdrop landed it a role in the 1992 movie *A League of Their Own*, with several local residents acting as extras. (Both, Engler family.)

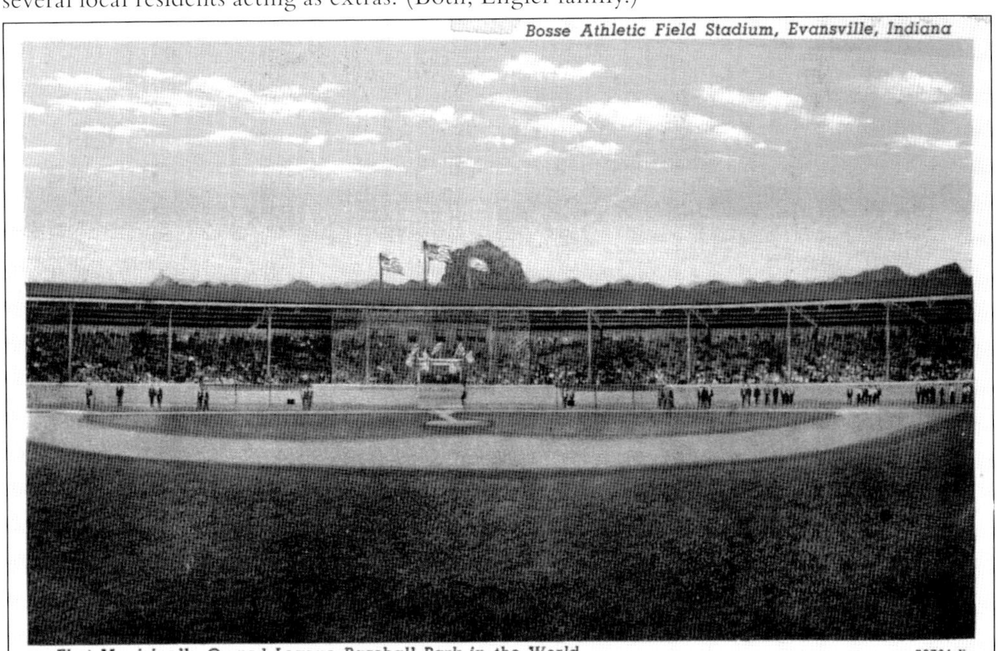

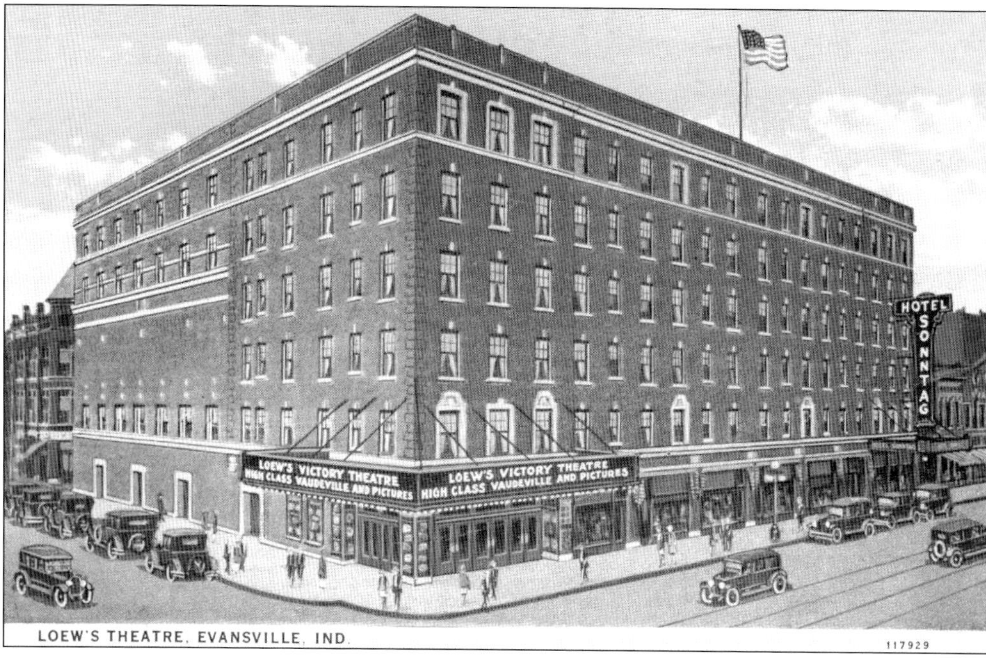

Victory Theater opened in 1921, along with the adjoining Hotel Sonntag. Situated on Main Street at the corner of Sixth Street, the theater became part of the Loew's chain in 1926. With multiplexes replacing downtown theaters, the Victory closed in 1979 and was later used as a nightclub. The Victory Theater reopened in 1998, and the hotel is now part of the Signature School campus. (EVPL and the Geiss family.)

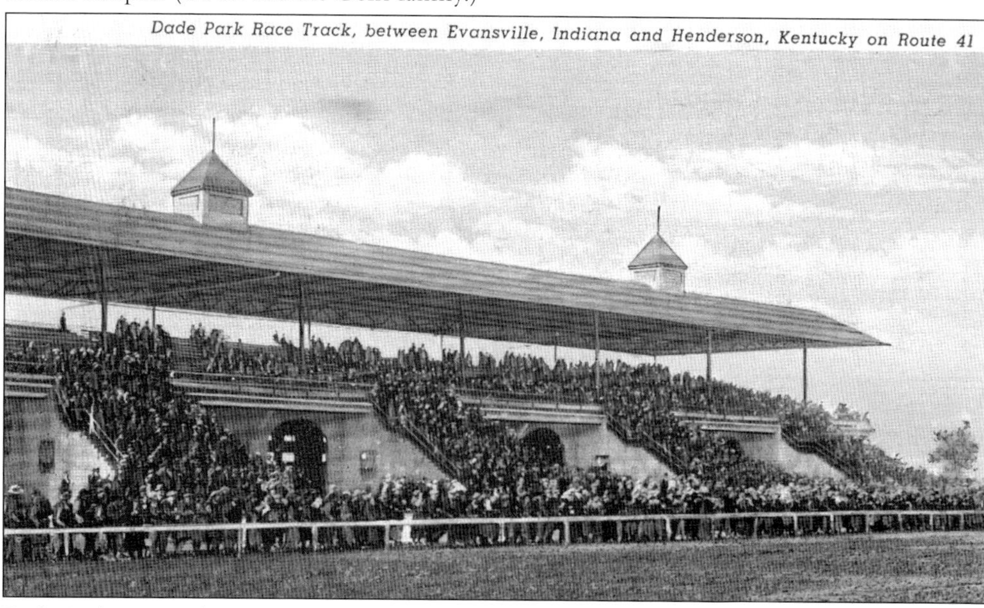

Dade Park racetrack was located just south of Evansville, between the Kentucky state line and the Ohio River. After a track and grandstand were completed in 1922, gambling and other illicit activity ensued; the river bottoms were physically isolated from Kentucky and out of jurisdiction for Indiana police. Ellis Park, renamed in 1954 after longtime owner James C. Ellis, still hosts live horse racing every season. (Engler family.)

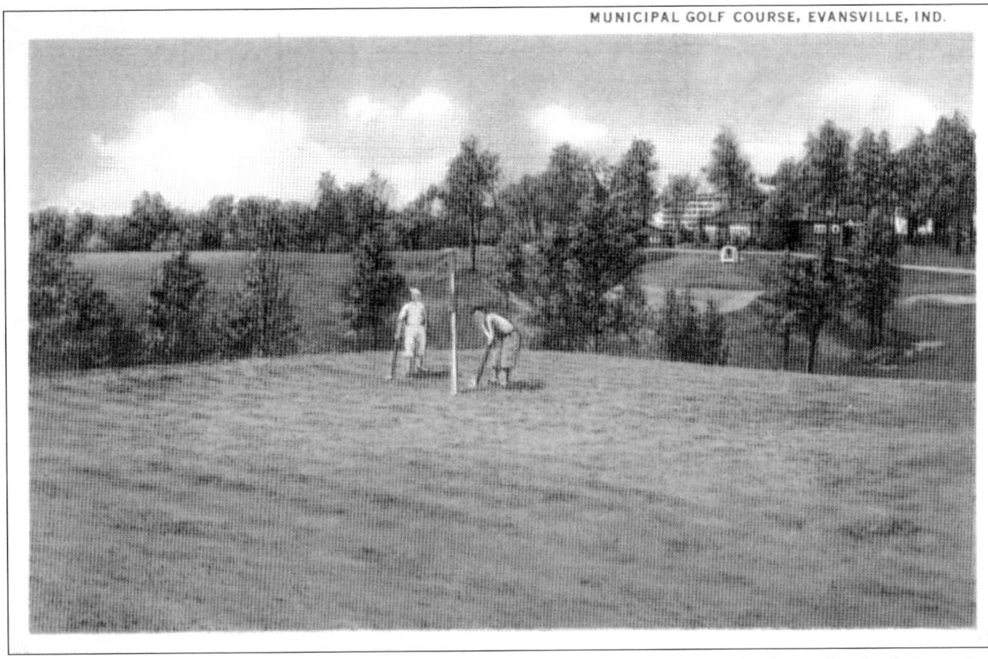

Helfrich Park was another city park established during Mayor Benjamin Bosse's administration in the 1920s. The municipal golf course and clubhouse were added around 1923, and the front gate at the corner of St. Joseph Avenue and Maryland Street was laid out around the same time. The pool and shelter house were constructed later in the 1930s as a public works project. (EVPL and the Geiss family.)

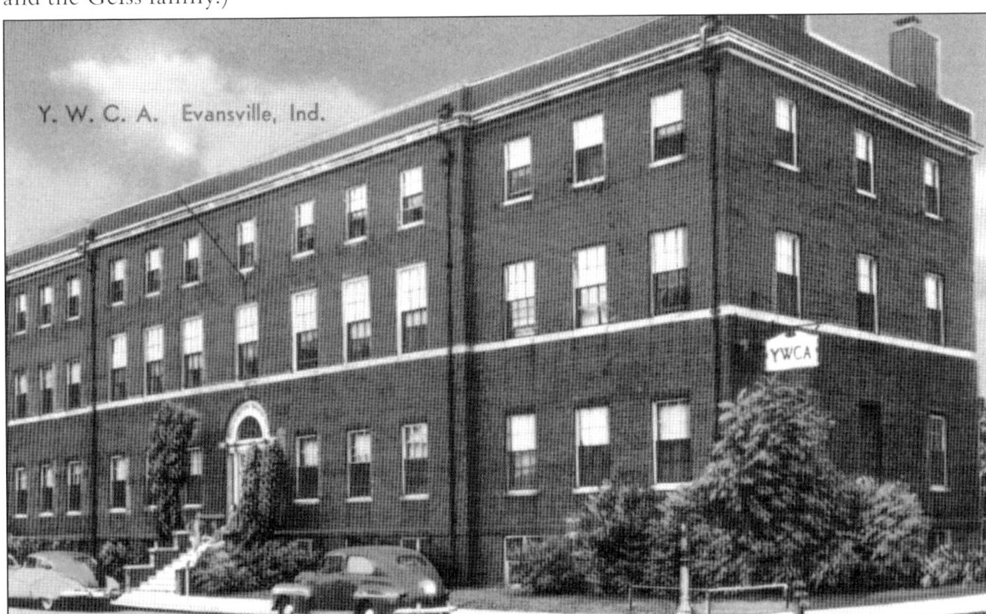

In 1911, the local chapter of the YWCA was founded. The organization erected this facility at the corner of Vine and Second Streets (next to its old location) in 1924. After over a century of serving Evansville's women and girls, the three-story brick building is still in use by the YWCA. (EVPL and the Geiss family.)

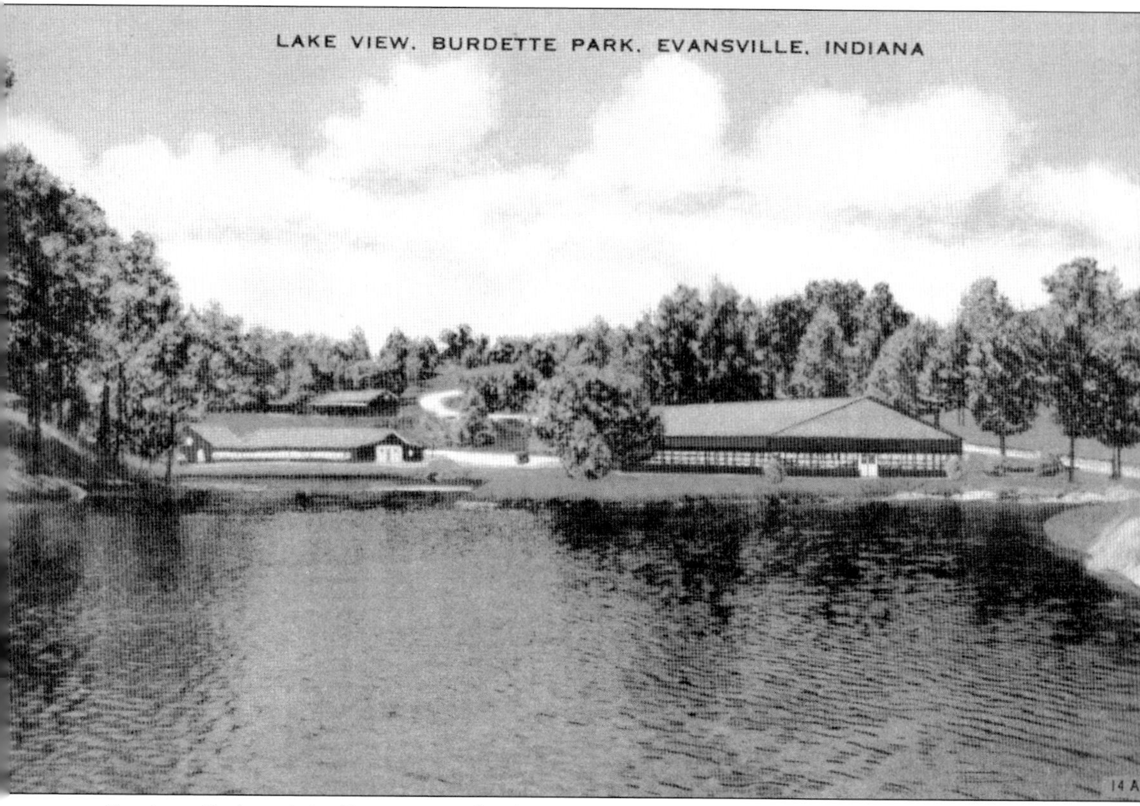

Burdette Park, originally a retreat for the American Legion, was established in the late 1920s on 40-plus acres of land in Perry Township. It opened to the public on July 16, 1936, after the Works Progress Administration improved the park, adding amenities such as cabins, footbridges, and a pool. This postcard shows the fishing lake, which still sits near the park's entrance. (EVPL and the Geiss family.)

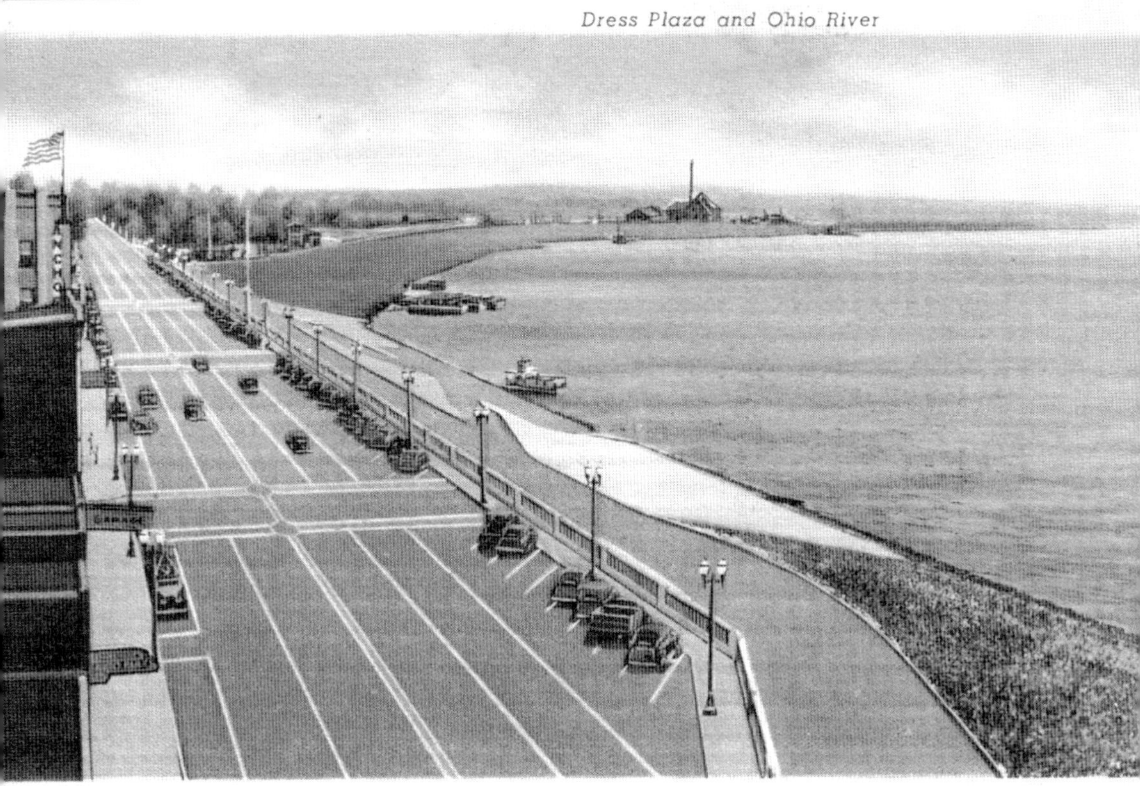

Dress Plaza was constructed in 1936 by the Public Works Administration. It had just been completed when the flood of 1937 inundated downtown, putting the new plaza underwater. Dress Plaza was remodeled around 2000 to include permanent seating and is now part of the Pigeon Creek Greenway Passage, once again making the riverfront a desirable spot for walkers, runners, and bikers. (Engler family.)

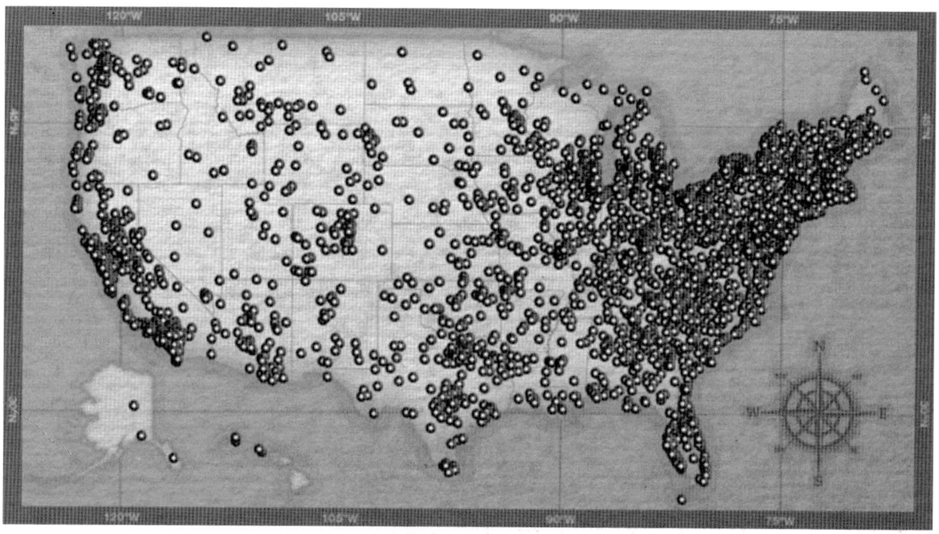

Consistent with our mission to preserve history on a local level, this book was printed in South Carolina on American-made paper and manufactured entirely in the United States. Products carrying the accredited Forest Stewardship Council (FSC) label are printed on 100 percent FSC-certified paper.

MADE IN THE USA